An Expedition Handbook

An Expedition Handbook

with Mountaineering Case Studies

Dave Wynne-Jones

Whittles Publishing

Published by

Whittles Publishing Ltd.,
Dunbeath,
Caithness, KW6 6EG,
Scotland, UK

www.whittlespublishing.com

© 2023 Dave Wynne-Jones

ISBN 978-184995-535-5

Printed in the UK by Severn, Gloucester on responsibly sourced paper

In memory of Pam Caswell, Yvonne Holland, Chris Astill, Martin Scott and Dick Isherwood and with thanks to the expedition teams I have climbed with who made it all possible.

Dave Wynne-Jones has an impressive record of leading expeditions all over the world and has introduced many ski-mountaineers to the challenges and joys of remote and adventurous trips. He is also a natural storyteller and this book hands on some of that hard-won expedition experience especially through the recounting of real events. An entertaining and insightful read.
Declan Phelan, President of the Eagle Ski Club.

This expedition handbook is a perfect place to start planning your first big adventure to the Greater Ranges. Here you will find comprehensive lists to set you on the right path and case studies to help you avoid some of the most painful pitfalls. Read, learn and most of all... enjoy.
Victor Saunders, President of the Alpine Club

They say that a battle is won or lost before it is even fought, and that victory and failure also most often comes down to the small things, not the large. These two ancient insights can easily be translated into another form of high-risk campaign: mountain and wilderness expeditions, where planning and execution, especially in regard to the small things, are key to maximising the privilege of visiting wild places. Just as Sun Tzu provided a text book for future generals, Dave Wynne-Jones has produced a valuable guide for future expeditioners.
Andy Kirkpatrick, author of Psychovertical and other books

CONTENTS

Foreword

Out of all the expeditions in which I was fortunate to take part, I think that only two could truly be described as having a leader.

One of these was my first, led by an eminent Irish mountaineer whom I'm happy to say would in later life become a great friend. I was just a whippersnapper, by far the youngest of a large team that had specific goals, with various members tasked to achieve them.

The first attempt on 'our mountain' resulted in ignominious failure relatively high on the ascent due to not having scoped the line properly. The four of us retreated to camp with our tails between our legs but with a different plan. Whilst climbing, my attention had been captured by an elegant rock ridge on the mountain opposite. This peak had received one previous ascent from the opposite side and therefore wasn't part of 'The Plan', but the towered arête that held my vision had far greater appeal than our designated objective. When we left camp again our two friends returned to the previous objective, wisely to investigate a better route: we, less wisely, went straight for the ridge.

The climb proved hard; probably too hard for me at that time given the remote location. We bivouacked a little below the top and during the night were hit by a ferocious storm, which continued next day as we inched over the summit and down the broken rock of the south ridge. Shortly, according to our relatively scant information, we'd find the top of an east-facing chimney. A couple or three pitches down this, followed by easy ground, would lead to a high glacier plateau and a quick romp back to the tents. This was just as well. We were in pre-Goretex days, or in fact pre-anything-that-worked days. Soaked to the skin, our chattering teeth were already beginning to make communication troublesome.

Fortunately, the chimney was obvious and proved amenable at first – I think we down-climbed a couple of pitches – but then it steepened significantly. Despite almost zero visibility we assured ourselves we must be in the correct place, set up an anchor and threw the ropes over a large overhang. A couple of airy and committing rappels later we had completely burnt our bridges. We had also run out of chimney.

It was at this moment that a large gust of wind rent the mist, revealing, to our disbelief, that we were perched on a small ledge atop a vast granite wall. When crossing the summit, blind, we had inadvertently strayed onto a spur that bent to the west and were now rappelling the big wall of the southwest face.

I'd rather not revisit the rest of that day. Many anchors were single point, several were decidedly sketchy, and one completely broke as we pulled the ropes. When we finally reached the glacier, I don't believe we knelt and kissed it, although that would have been entirely appropriate. Two days later we crept into base camp to be rightly castigated by our leader for violating The Plan.

This was 50 years ago, when the 'Information Highway' was a minor B-road, or more often unpaved single-track. When leaving the Alps for unknown terrain in the Greater Ranges we had no knowledge of WH Tilman's sound axiom, "time spent in reconnaissance is never wasted". We came from an era where rappelling fatalities were numerous and embarking on a big multi-rappel descent was the last thing you'd ever want to do. Yet, we had just learnt the hard way that when in doubt about the escape, rappelling known ground, such as your ascent route, may not be such a bad idea.

Had we been exposed to works such as this *Expedition Handbook* by Dave Wynne-Jones, or the various symposia that would become common in the following decades, we may have learnt some lessons the soft way.

We might, for instance, on a subsequent expedition and my first to India, have carried out more research into the approach. We might then have realized the stupidity of coinciding our arrival with peak harvest time, when all possible porters for the final stage to base camp up a long uninhabited valley were fully committed to the fields.

Prior to taking early retirement from the teaching profession in the 1990s, Dave had concentrated his efforts mostly on the Alps, where he gained a wealth of experience, notably on the 4,000m summits. Subsequently, he has taken part in almost 30 expeditions, for the majority as group leader. Since 2003 many of these have been adventurous tours with the Eagle Ski Club. These can be quite different from going into a remote area with a group of mates, whose reliability, proficiency, and idiosyncrasies are known. The ESC, for example, will often require a selection process with a standardized application form followed by less formal assessment. The final team members may have little or no prior knowledge of each other, and this can lead to unusual and challenging situations for the leader. Dave has experienced no shortage of these and has used around ten as the basis for the second part of the book, entitled Case Studies: relatively comprehensive expedition reportage providing a clear message. Here you will not only read of the joy of climbing and skiing in remote ranges, but also the problems caused by communication issues within the team, political and local unrest, incident creep, and potentially fatal consequences of using stoves with heat exchangers – and how best to deal with them.

The year 2019 marked the end of the warmest decade recorded. Climate change is affecting every country. With increasingly widespread awareness of the potentially catastrophic effects of global warming and, for many, the feeling of inadequate government response, there is an emerging sense of personal responsibility. Guardian columnist and environmental campaigner George Monbiot has stated simply that long distance travel and the curtailment of climate change are not compatible. At first sight this makes a new book on expedition management in far-away places seemingly a hard sell. For many mountaineers the expedition is their raison d'être. We will need to adapt our behaviour and Dave has already limited his long-haul flights and off-set his energy use. He hopes that if this book helps readers to achieve more successful and safer expeditions, they may be content to make fewer flights.

Lindsay Griffin

Senior Editor - American Alpine Journal
Denbigh, North Wales, UK

Preface

I should say from the outset that though this book is concerned primarily with mountaineering expeditions there is no reason why it should not be useful to others planning cycling or kayaking expeditions for example; the organisational stages and equipment notes are obvious areas of overlap. Some of the seasoned expeditioners who have commented on drafts of the work have also held senior management posts and noted the usefulness of the principles and case studies with regard to the whole issue of successfully leading teams engaging with challenging projects.

People who sign up for an expedition are fundamentally volunteers and in management terms, volunteers are the most difficult people to manage; they can so easily just walk away. Whilst walking away is possible with regard to expeditions in the preparatory stages, in the field it's a less easy option, although with a fixed base camp I have seen one person just refuse to leave it and with regular flights out of a remote base camp, leaving an expedition can remain a possibility. Travelling through a remote landscape without those options means members of a team have an imperative to get along but that can be stress-tested by a potentially hostile environment and the tensions generated when there is so little respite from the company of the team. Adopting an hierarchical approach can be counter-productive, as Eric Shipton pointed out, because a team is usually most effective when it plays to the strengths of every member. Managing teams of volunteers and expeditioners both as a leader and as a team player can be a valuable learning experience!

I've been very lucky that for a period of about 20 years I was able to organise and participate in expeditions from East Africa to Antarctica, making a number of first ascents in the process. In some ways it was a logical extension of 15 years of Alpine climbing but I began cautiously in 1994 with a self-organised ascent of Kilimanjaro and an unsuccessful attempt on the main summit of Mt. Kenya. Through the 1990s, I tried to visit expeditionary places on ski as well as signing up for a climbing expedition every year, often to South America. Success was mixed. As Paul Ramsden said to me after winning his second piolet d'or; "Success is built on a fair few failures." For example, in 1999 I climbed Denali then failed to get higher than 5500m on an expedition attempting a 7000m peak in the Hindu Kush.

During the first decade of the 21st century I continued to manage an expedition per year with two or three some years and in 2010 there were five, to Chile (twice), Georgia,

India and Antarctica. Carbon off-setting is essential to compensate for that number of flights! One of the best years was 2007 when, in addition to completing my mission to climb all 52 of the 4000m independent mountains of the Alps, I made eight first ascents in Kyrgyzstan, India and China. The last decade has included expeditions to Mongolia, Canada, Greenland, the Caucasus and Oman together with an extended trip to Argentina and Chile for andinismo on ski. An attempt to organise a trip to Kamchatka failed when the mountain obstinately refused to stop erupting but health issues have also curtailed my ambitions together with my feeling that it is now so much less justifiable to base expedition climbing on long-haul flights. I'm writing this during lockdown related to the corona virus pandemic and it is thought likely that global warming has contributed to that crisis, not least by the ease of transmission via international flights.

With a growing awareness of the effects of long-haul flights on the problem of climate change in an economy that seems to be addicted to fossil fuels there is also a growing sense of responsibility that has moderated the drive to seek adventure in far flung places. The British mountain guide, Rob Collister, has described in *Days to Remember*, what amounted to a conversion experience for him on reading George Monbiot's book, *Heat*, while delayed for his flight out of Antarctica. It's not that he had been unaware of the ongoing problem with climate change, but that he hadn't realised its full enormity. He quotes Monbiot, "Long distance travel, high speed and the curtailment of climate change are not compatible," and the French alpinist, Jaques Lagarde, "Ever since man has been drawn to the mountains by a love of wild nature, rigour, solitude and the unknown, all of which he found in that final refuge, he has done everything to eliminate precisely what he sought."

From my point of view, it has been a case of "boiling a frog." Because the effects happened slowly, year by year we became accustomed to them only to realise, perhaps too late, that they will destroy us unless we do something about it. For a long time, I couldn't afford to fly and drove to the Alps in a car packed with passengers. Little wonder that I welcomed the opportunities to travel when I found myself with time to do so. But no reasonable person can persist with such folly. Personally, I have tried to limit long-haul flights to a maximum of one destination per year, to use train, boat and shared car transport to avoid short-haul flights, and to offset the carbon debt with carbon credit schemes like the one offered by the Eagle Ski Club, of which I am the President at the time of writing.

Skiers cannot practise their sport with any confidence in the UK but there's no reason why they can't behave responsibly with regard to their travel arrangements. In the same way, expeditionary climbing and skiing can still be achieved without compounding the existential threat to our species represented by global warming if we look to explore areas closer to home and offset our energy use in doing so. Of all flights in Great Britain 70% were taken by 15% of adults according to a 2014 government survey. The government could counteract this by introducing a frequent flyer levy but we can all make a difference by modifying our behaviour.

Over the years, I've been asked for advice about expeditions on a number of occasions and this was formalised when I ran seminars on expedition planning at

Symposia at the National Mountaineering Centre, Plas y Brenin. On every occasion I was left thinking that there was so much more to be said and I gradually came to the conclusion that the subject would best be treated in book form.

This book is organised into two sections. The first sets out an organisational framework with detailed notes. The second section provides some case studies which provide examples of the principles in action, or not. We can learn from negative experiences as well as positive ones or at least we should do if we want to survive. "Near miss" recording and discussion plays a valuable part in reviewing the ski season within the Eagle Ski Club, helping to raise the safety levels of our programme of tours as it has in the aviation industry.

Finally, if it means that readers achieve more successful and safer expeditions after reading this book, I hope that they will have the confidence to be contented with fewer expeditions and fewer flights as a result.

Acknowledgements

I should like to thank the various editors of journals and magazines in which original reports of many of my expeditions were published over the years, including Steve Goodwin (*Alpine Journal*), John Harlin III, Kelly Cordes and Lindsay Griffin (*American Alpine Journal*), David Seddon, Mike and Jenny Spencer, Mike Hendry (*Eagle Ski Club Yearbook*), Geoff Birtles and Ian Smith (*High* magazine) Cameron McNeish (*The Great Outdoors.*)

Many of the expeditions were supported by grants from the Mount Everest Foundation, Alpine Club and Eagle Ski Club.

Thanks are due to Mike Sharp of Antarctic Logistics and Expeditions, Derek Buckle former vice-president of the Alpine Club and Cathy O'Dowd who read the first draft of the book, whilst Dr Declan Phelan, current president of the Eagle Ski Club, provided invaluable advice on medical matters.

Keith Whittles had faith in the book, despite the effects of Covid-19. Liz Lemal deserves thanks for her editorial work as does Lindsay Griffin for kindly providing a Foreword.

Part One: An Approach

Chapter 1: What is an Expedition?

Strange question since you wouldn't be reading this book unless you already have some ideas about that. But it's worth thinking through. I have been involved in awarding grants to people who have applied for support for their expeditions and have seen some odd claims put forward to lend credibility to applications. Sometimes such claims actually detract from any credibility. Is it possible to have been on an "expedition" to Scotland or the Alps? Not in my view, but why?

Two factors are required for a genuine expedition:

1. Remoteness

The area targeted should be remote enough to justify a more sustained level of commitment than is found in places where an infrastructure has been developed sufficient to provide something like what would be available at home. Rapid support or evacuation in the event of an accident or emergency is possibly one of the indices by which that could be judged.

In Scotland it's generally possible to walk out to a road, even a pub, within a few hours, and mountain rescue services are available. Even the notorious weather is rarely severe enough to absolutely prevent climbing; a feature commented upon by foreign visitors to the British Mountaineering Council (BMC) international meets at Glenmore Lodge. In the Alps, while conditions can be more extreme and walking out less feasible, huts provide relatively luxurious refuge and helicopter rescue can usually be called in quickly by mobile phone.

Remoteness is implicit in the Mount Everest Foundation guidelines for applicants which emphasise the exploratory element of expeditions. How could an expedition be exploratory in areas so thoroughly explored as Scotland or the Alps?

But not all expeditions are exploratory. Climbing Denali by the West Buttress route or repeating Shackleton's traverse of South Georgia would not qualify as exploratory but earn their right to be considered as expeditions because they are very definitely remote and demand a high level of commitment. Statistically, fewer than fifty per cent of climbers setting out on Denali reach the summit.

Of course, if such expeditions attain a level of popularity whereby a sophisticated infrastructure develops to support those endeavours then the level of commitment is reduced, perhaps to a point where they can no longer be considered as expeditions

So much choice! The Canadian Rockies.

any more. In Nepal for example, it's a fair question to ask whether repeating "Snotty's Gully" from a tea house in Gokyo be considered an expedition or not.

2. Challenge

Put simply an expedition has to be challenging both in an organisational sense and in the nature of the objective. Underlying that is the assumption that the mountain should be worth climbing or skiing; walking up some insignificant bump, no matter how remote, does not qualify as mountaineering. We should not adopt a *Guinness Book of Records* or "extreme ironing" approach either, where the outlandishness of the terms of the challenge are often the only reason for it. It may not have been done before but there may be a very good reason for that; you don't want the challenge to be mainly testing the expedition members' tolerance of boredom! Again, the level of commitment is a useful guide.

It may seem unnecessary to make this point but a mountaineering expedition should involve climbing mountains and a ski-mountaineering one should include skiing, but I have seen proposals that have ignored these basics.

I'm wary of trips tending to emphasise the benefits of the "cultural experience", often a euphemistic description of the touristy stuff. It's not that the experience of different cultures cannot be worthwhile, but it has to be said that when you've seen one Buddhist temple you've pretty much seen them all. A misguided flying visit to the Taj Mahal on a spare day at the end of an Indian expedition turned out to be more of an appreciation of local refinements of the rip-off than India's architectural gem. It actually detracted from the overall impression of India gathered during the course of the expedition. Moreover, concern for the cultural experience can lead to a lack of focus on the main purpose of the expedition which should be the climbing, skiing or exploring that are its *raison d'être*. Bill Tilman summed it up succinctly: 'Singleness of purpose is a sound principle. The killing of two birds with one stone, however desirable, is seldom achieved intentionally and never by aiming consciously at both.'

There is usually some expectation that one of the results of an expedition will be some addition to the sum of human knowledge about the mountains or area or people encountered, although in point of fact it may only be about oneself or one's comrades in the final analysis.

Everyone considering an expedition for the first time should be aware of the marked distinction between Alpine climbing and expedition climbing that has been noted by some of our expedition pioneers.

It is a step change that Frank Smythe describes in *The Kangchenjunga Adventure*, warning:

ABC on Pokharkan, Nepal.

Himalayan mountaineering only resembles alpine mountaineering so far as the actual technique of climbing is concerned. In scale, snow and weather conditions, route finding, and general organisation, it is so different that only by experience can the alpine-trained mountaineer learn safely to tackle its manifold problems – this experience is gained too frequently at the cost of valuable lives.

And more grimly:

Himalayan peaks are cruel. The Alps are the "Playground of Europe", the Himalayas the Playground of the Gods. The Alps provide physical and aesthetic enjoyment, the Himalayas the fiercer joys of achievement. In the Alps, when you have climbed a mountain you want to climb it by other routes, explore every ridge, tramp every glacier to make a friend of it. You get to know its moods learn to appreciate its weather vagaries. There is nothing friendly about a Himalayan peak. You feel that it is coldly hostile, that it resents intrusion. It allows no latitude and seizes upon the slightest mistake. It will kill you if it can. And so, if you climb it, you climb it only to conquer it for the sake of achievement. To do so you may have to mortify the flesh, steeling yourself to overcome bodily and mental weariness. When you have reached its summit, you have finished with it. There is no desire to renew acquaintances, or make a friend of Himalayan peaks, they resent familiarity. And always they will kill you – if they can.

There's no doubt that a thorough grounding in Alpine climbing is an essential foundation for climbing in the greater ranges but anyone who expects the equivalent of an Alpine season at greater altitude will be disappointed. In *The Mountains of Tartary* Eric Shipton goes into more detail with a good deal less foreboding than Smythe:

I have always been of the opinion that the art of mountaineering, in the perhaps limited sense of climbing difficult mountainsides, can be learnt only in the Alps or some similar comparatively small and much-frequented range. In the first place, in the Alps the length of the climbs is such that they can mostly be done in a day, while huts and other facilities enable a man to spend a very long proportion of his time actually climbing difficult snow, ice and rock. Given fine weather, there is no reason why, in say, a month, he should not do some twenty climbs, each twelve or fifteen hours in length, so that by the end of that time he has acquired an immense amount of technical practice and experience. Secondly, the great number of mountaineers who visit the Alps, the fact that a number of experts can, year after year, specialise on one mountain face or group of peaks, and also the easy accessibility of the mountains – all these factors have naturally resulted in an exceedingly high standard of performance. And however modest a climber's ambitions, his standards are almost bound to be improved by the raising of the general level: climbs that twenty years ago were tackled only by the most daring experts are today undertaken by very mediocre performers. Thirdly, the fact that the climbs are so well known, documented and classified, deprives the mountain of one of its most formidable defences, the unknown; so that, apart from the factors of changing weather and snow conditions, a climber can concentrate almost entirely on the purely technical difficulties. This again, of course, provides him with greatly increased facilities for improving his technique and, even more important, of measuring his skill against an accepted standard of excellence.

In the greater and comparatively unknown ranges, the case is just the reverse. The greater distances involved, the long glacier approaches, the slow, laborious business of establishing camps and of reconnoitring, result in only a tiny proportion of the time being spent actually climbing in the Alpine sense. The fact that heavy loads have to be carried a long way up the mountain, the physical disabilities resulting from altitude, the disastrous consequences that threaten from bad weather, these so often make it impossible to accept the challenge of a difficult ridge or face. The emphasis therefore is always on the avoidance of difficulty, and one very rarely allows oneself to be committed to a spell of many hours of really hard climbing, which is commonplace in an Alpine season. With so many new mountains to tackle, climbs are hardly ever repeated, so that a comparison of standards is almost impossible. Lastly, perhaps the most important element of all, the fact that each upward step is on new ground, each ridge of unmeasured length, each slope of unknown steepness, absorbs so much of the climber's attention and his nerve that he cannot give the whole of himself to grapple with sheer technical difficulty.

Thus a man might spend a whole lifetime climbing in the Himalaya and never acquire the skill, the experience or the judgement needed to tackle a really difficult mountains (in the Alpine sense of the word 'difficult'), which a few good seasons in the Alps would give him. I have always said that if I had to choose, for an Everest expedition, between a man who had a thorough training in the Alps and one who had only climbed in the Himalaya, even though his experience there had been great, I should, other things being equal of course, unhesitatingly choose the former.

Unfortunately, all skills need practice if they are to be retained. Just as the athlete will lose his speed, dexterity and strength without practising his sport, so the Alpine mountaineer may lose, not only his gymnastic agility on difficult rock, but that instinctive power to distinguish between danger and difficulty, that confident poise on a knife-edged arête, the acute judgement of difficulties ahead of him, that automatic adroitness in handling the rope and axe, that toughness of nerve that can withstand long hours of delicate movement over, say, precipitous, ice-covered rock, which in some degree must form part of his stock-in-trade. Thus, as it is almost impossible to learn the art of mountaineering in the Himalaya, so, by climbing exclusively in the Himalaya for a long period, one tends to lose the art one may have learned. I do not deny that there is a vast amount that one learns in the Himalaya that one cannot possibly learn in the Alps, but here I am discussing mountaineering in the strictly limited alpine sense of climbing difficult ice, rock and snow.

Hard climbs are now done "Alpine-style" in the greater ranges more often than in Shipton's time, although it's been argued that a generation of British climbers almost climbed themselves into extinction in establishing that approach. However, it's still the case that in the time devoted to each climb of that nature in the greater ranges, it would have been possible to complete many more routes of comparable difficulty in the Alps. The Alps or similar ranges remain the essential training ground for expedition climbers, but an expedition is much more likely to be a journey of exploration than an opportunity for hard climbing.

In *Nepal Himalaya*, Tilman offers another, not exactly serious, perspective on expedition climbing:

> I should not wish anyone to believe that because such arduous day-to-day exertions are passed over more or less in silence the Himalayan climber is therefore a man of ape-like strength and agility, with an immense capacity for breathing rarefied air, drinking melted snow or raw spirit, and eating fungi and bamboo shoots. True, on occasions he must live hard or exert himself to the point of exhaustion, necessarily when at grips with a big peak; but for the most part his condition is one of ease bordering upon comfort; he suffers from heat rather than cold, from muscular atrophy rather than nervous exhaustion; and for a variety of reasons – the weather, the worsening snow, the porters' fatigue – his days are usually short. Thus he spends more time on his back than on his feet. His occupational disease is bedsores, and a box of books his most cherished load.

In conclusion, it should be noted that all the above remarks do not necessarily apply to scientific expeditions where the remoteness and challenge involved will be subject to overriding research objectives which will hopefully add to the sum of human knowledge.

Chapter 2: Where, when and what to do

Much of this depends on who will be involved and the time off work that they can manage. Teachers may be able to get a month off in the summer but that limits them to areas like South America or the Garhwal, too late for Alaska, and smack in the middle of the monsoon so much of the Himalaya is out. Those not shackled to school holiday periods may have more choice, but on the other hand they may only be able to arrange a couple of weeks leave. That rules out any areas with a lengthy approach trek or with a reputation for bad weather; who wants to spend ten days listening to the rain on the flysheet only to discover that that elusive weather window opened on the

People are part of the place; ethnic Tibetan area of China.

day they flew out? Alaska or Greenland may work within short periods of time but the costs can be high and there needs to be some preparation in the workplace just in case exit strategies are frustrated by weather or transport problems. For those who can negotiate a sabbatical year or take early retirement there's a world of choice!

Another factor is cost. The team all have to be able to stump up the required cash to pay for the expedition. Costs vary widely. Permits to climb mountains in India, Pakistan and China can bump up the cost while paying and equipping a liaison officer (LO) to sit in base camp drinking tea has been a perennial cause of complaint. If keeping costs down is important then areas like South America or Kyrgyzstan are a much better bet.

Language can also be an issue. Former British colonies like India often have significant numbers of English-speaking people. Former Spanish colonies make organisation easier for Spanish speakers, but despite the internationalism of the English language, without an agent there are likely to be communication problems in China and the countries of the former Soviet Union.

Expeditions can vary in their approach too. When Martin Scott, Kaji Sherpa and I made the first ascent of the south face of Pokharkan, a 6000m peak in Nepal, it involved trekking in to the area, identifying the mountain, scouting approaches to it, finding a feasible line to climb, putting in subsidiary camps from which a summit bid could be made, then making it and successfully evacuating the mountain. That was very different from the expeditions I led to the Ak-Shirak range in Kyrgyzstan. There we travelled through the range on ski, exploring the major glacier systems, making multiple first ascents of peaks around 5000m in single day "hits" from high camps.

What to do depends on the interests and abilities of the potential team. The whole team has to understand and be committed to what is planned, not only to the objective but also to the style of the expedition, as well as being qualified to make a real contribution to it. Without that common commitment, Shipton comments, 'I have suffered agonies of ennui and self-righteous disgust on an expedition that has appeared to me too large and clumsy, and I have made myself an infernal nuisance in consequence.'

It helps if all members know each other and have confidence in their abilities. On an Antarctic expedition where one member was known only to one of the team, we were all impressed with his CV but he rocked up for what was predominantly a ski-mountaineering expedition without revealing that he had no previous experience of off-piste skiing. He ended up carrying his skis down from the warm-up route and spent the rest of the trip plodding along on snow-shoes; not such a problem in ascent but a liability when skiers began to display symptoms of hypothermia while waiting for him to catch up with them on the descents.

On the other hand, when climbing Mount Logan, I found that a team snow-shoeing could successfully share camps with a team of skiers but travel independently from camp to camp. There we had to evacuate two members of the team owing to medical problems and then lost a third who decided he'd had enough, but soon after we acquired an addition to the team when a Canadian asked if he could join us after his partner had also joined the "had enough" team to descend to base camp. Competence and commitment had to be assessed pretty damn quick on both sides together with making clear, witnessed statements on liability. To be successful, the whole team needs to sign up for the objectives and the methodology of any expedition.

Of course, another way to go about this could be for an individual to decide where and when he or she wants to go and then select a team for the expedition, although a large club or circle of friends will be needed to interest enough suitable people.

As far as the size of the team is concerned, this can also depend on the objective. There was a tradition of huge Himalayan expeditions that followed a pattern set by the early Everest expeditions and continued with others like Bonington's to Everest's south-west face. Eric Shipton was one of the first to question that tradition, quoting a friend's view that: 'Three constitutes a large expedition, a party of one may be considered a small expedition.' Chapters eight, "Large Expeditions" and nine, "Small Expeditions" in *Upon that Mountain*, are seminal reading on this issue, while Tilman's book *Everest 1938* is a sustained presentation of the case for small expeditions.

There were eleven climbers, including three Sherpas on the Pokharkan expedition and six or eight of us on my ski-mountaineering expeditions but a sensible minimum might be four. That means if one person picks up a bug on the plane or the trek, or suffers some minor injury it doesn't mean that the expedition is over. Also, with two climbing pairs it's possible for each to offer support to the other if necessary. Larger

Landscapes can be very different; Peru.

numbers can provide strength in depth but may also create communications problems and a tendency for splinter groups to form, so it's more difficult to recommend a maximum number. Having said all that, a glance at the record of Piolet d'Or awards reveals that there have been some remarkable mountaineering achievements by teams of just two. These tend to be highly experienced climbers and Paul Ramsden reminded me that there were a lot of failures behind every success.

Once you have some idea of who might join the team, what they would like to do and when they would like to go, then you need to work out where to go in more detail.

Chapter 3: Research phase 1; finding an objective

There are a number of sources for information about potential expedition areas and objectives, largely based on reports from previous expeditions or reconnaissance in the area. Reports are particularly valuable in that the photo-record of a climbing route can yield pictures that may be of use to a ski-mountaineering expedition and vice versa. Potential lines of routes can be traced and, of course, the appearance of a mountain can be a great motivator. In some accounts there may be comments about the winter potential of the area or the quality of the rock that can inform future plans.

It is often possible to contact the authors of the reports or the expedition leaders to request further details but responses are variable. Mick Fowler was a great help with access to Szechuan but a guide who regularly visited India couldn't be bothered to elaborate upon the ski-mountaineering potential of an area which he'd noted in an *Alpine Journal* report. Personally, I've always felt that having received a grant from the Mountain Everest Foundation (MEF) or Alpine Club (AC) implies an obligation to respond to enquiries following up on reports published after those expeditions, although the fact that I have climbed in a country by no means implies a thorough knowledge of all its mountains as some queries have assumed. One ought to be able to expect similar co-operation but some enquiries I've made have resulted in a cursory response or none at all. A notable exception was a generous packet of pure gold information on the Icefields Ranges in the Yukon from a Canadian contact.

Sources:

1. The Press

Even the travel pages of quality broadsheets can be useful when, for example, an article on ski-touring possibilities in Afghanistan is featured, but realistically those occasions are going to be few and far between.

More useful might be the climbing magazines, although in the UK most editions tend to have more to do with "celebrities" and rock climbing than mountaineering and expeditions. Scanning the contents pages can turn up the occasional useful article but don't hold your breath. If an area you are interested in is featured you may get lucky and find a suggestive photo or two that starts you thinking.

Americans are better at covering the ground, particularly in their Alaskan "back yard", in magazines such as *Climbing*, and *Rock & Ice*. Spanish and French offerings such as *Desnivel* and *Montagnes* seem to pay more attention to the mountains, sometimes devoting whole issues to a particular range. *Alpinist*, published quarterly, is another promising source with quality photos of less frequented areas.

2. Club journals

The *Alpine Journal*, first published as *Peaks, Passes and Glaciers*, is the original template for sharing the pioneering efforts of members, at first in the Alps, but later in the greater ranges. It continues to publish articles and "Area Notes" on new routes and discoveries but is less comprehensive or authoritative than the *American Alpine Journal* (AAJ) which claims to cover 'the most significant routes'. There are features on highlights of the climbing year but summary reports cover a huge range of other expeditions in valuable detail. The AAJ alone is worth the cost of membership of the American Alpine Club for any serious expeditioner although the submission of a report to the journal is usually rewarded with a free copy of that edition.

The Eagle Ski Club (ESC) publishes an annual yearbook with a wealth of up-to-date information on a wide range of ski-mountaineering destinations as well as maintaining an on-line record of its expeditions. The *Himalayan Journal*, modelled on the *Alpine Journal*, is produced by the Himalayan Club, based in India, while the Japanese Alpine Club (JAC) also produces a news journal in English.

The JAC published a landmark issue in *East of the Himalayas: the Alps of Tibet* when Tom Nakamura edited a volume that directed attention to this major area that had hitherto been largely unvisited. Subsequent editions revisited the area and updated developments until ethnic unrest resulted in a shift of focus to other areas. Repeated visits to the mountains of Szechuan and Eastern Tibet meant that Tom contributed a very influential collection of photos that enabled expeditions to be planned with at least some idea of potential lines to climb.

3. Grant-awarding bodies

Organisations like the MEF, and the Scott Polar Research Institute that administers the Gino Watkins Memorial Fund, make it a condition of any award of a grant to an expedition that a report should be lodged with them as soon as reasonably possible after completion of the trip. Photocopies can be requested from the Alpine Club Library for a price.

4. On-line sources

The internet has revolutionised research for expedition objectives, although, as with much web material, there can be little independent verification of what is posted. Cross-referencing is essential.

Most of the club journals mentioned above have the facility for on-line searches of their archives and for downloading articles, while the AC website hosts the Himalayan index.

Scouting for a route onto Pokharkan, top right, Nepal.

At the time of writing, only the MEF supplies on-line summaries of expedition reports but the Gino Watkins Memorial Fund has full reports linked to its website.

The BMC has some reports on-line as well as useful summaries by Lindsay Griffin and a comprehensive list of grant-awarding bodies.

UK Climbing has a searchable section on articles about members' trips and useful links. For something similar for Russian climbers and the Commonwealth of Independent States (CIS) area there is www.mountain.ru.

5. Networking

Some reports are going to be available by word of mouth only and this is where networking comes in.

Clubs with members who are actively organising expeditions can be a mine of information as well as a reservoir of potential expedition team members. A few words at a meet can sow the seeds of an idea in a context which makes follow-up enquiries possible. The UK national clubs (including Alpine Club, Climbers Club, Scottish Mountaineering Club, Fell and Rock Climbing Club (FRCC) of the Lake District , Rucksack Club and Eagle Ski Club) are the obvious ones, although some smaller local clubs have a tradition of running occasional expeditions. Most clubs also organise lectures for members during the winter months which may suggest objectives and offer opportunities to garner information by networking with the speakers.

Guides may have expert knowledge of certain areas that they may be willing to share. Rob Collister, for example, has an authoritative background in Indian mountaineering. Owen Day was very helpful when I was planning a ski trip to South America. Others have seemed to guard their knowledge more jealously, either not responding to requests for information or replying in the curtest fashion. 'No answer is also an answer', but you'll have to work it out on your own. Guides' and agents' websites may offer some suggestions about logistics even for areas that only neighbour those that they are offering to clients.

At this level the mountaineering world can be quite a small one and a friend of a friend may be just the contact to crystallise an idea for an expedition. My first expedition to Peru happened in exactly this way at Waters Cottage, the FRCC hut in Kinlochleven, when a fellow FRCC member invited me and my partner to join his team after learning we were very interested in climbing in South America.

6. Guidebooks

With the increased popularity of more challenging climbing areas there has been a tendency to publish guidebooks to the more visited of the greater ranges. Climbing in the Andes is a good example where the style resembles a kind of super-alpinism that locals term Andinismo. *Classic Climbs of the Cordillera Blanca* by Brad Johnson shows how such guidebooks can describe remote and challenging routes that can no longer be termed exploratory. Such a book is also useful to those planning exploratory expeditions if only by indicating unclimbed lines and logistical possibilities. Nearby, less explored areas might also be referred to in ways that suggest possibilities for expeditions. Harish Kapadia has written extensively about the Indian Himalaya and guidebooks are emerging relating to North America and areas of Russia and the Pamirs.

The twin peaks of Huascaran Norte (left) and Sur, Peru.

Chapter 4: Research phase 2; developing the detail

Once you have an idea the next step is to go into more detail principally on the logistics of approaching the mountain or range to give the greatest chance of success.

1. Google Earth

This can be really useful to help visualise the terrain you are going into or travelling through. I can remember cresting a rise to get my first view of the Tavn Bogd range in Mongolia and being struck by how accurately Google Earth had represented it on-screen. Google Earth has also been useful to obtain latitude and longitude details for key waypoints (such as passes or campsites) to add to a GPS device.

Having said that, there are a few cautionary notes to sound. Different areas have different degrees of detail: in some it seems like you can see every rock and fissure while in others the images are very blurry. Even in the same area it is as if you cross a boundary and the quality of the image immediately deteriorates. Even when the images are detailed a search can lead to the wrong point: some huts in the Pyrenees are not the buildings indicated on Google Earth and this could be serious when navigating in a white-out.

It's always worth working out some alternative routes, just in case that pass you were hoping to haul your gear over turns out not to be an easy snow slope but a steep rock passage. There may be an easier option just around the corner.

Google earth representation of the glacier approaches to Khuiten, Mongolia.

15

Satellite or aerial photos may be available from other sources such as government records; Baffin Island is an example.

2. Maps

Unlike Google Earth, these will be available in the field, and will provide more accurate detail for planning your access and exit strategies. When I first visited Peru, I was surprised to learn that I had to present my passport and purchase maps in person from the Instituto Geografico Militar. In fact, it should not have been so surprising as the military tide had only just turned against the Shining Path guerrillas. I had not tuned in to the different social context in which the expedition would be operating; it's easily done!

In some countries the military still control cartography on the principle that knowledge is power where the deployment of troops or ordnance is concerned. British readers should know that; it's in the title of the Ordnance Survey! In India the Army still limits access to the most up-to-date maps, but with security problems on its borders with China as well as Pakistan and an ongoing Naxolite insurgency that's not surprising.

It's better to obtain the best maps that are available at home in order to get as much forward planning done as possible. In the UK, The Map Shop (https://www.themapshop.co.uk/) and Stanfords (https://www.stanfords.co.uk/) are among the best retailers while Eastview Geospatial (https://www.geospatial.com/) offers a very comprehensive on-line service.

Other sources include The Royal Geographical Society and the Alpine Club. Both hold copies of maps relating to less explored areas that are available to members.

Again, a cautionary note should be sounded. The Russian map of the Ak-Shirak range in Kyrgyzstan that I used from 2006 to 2009 had not been revised since 1976. The pace of climate change means that the accuracy of such maps has to be questioned and indeed the amount of glacial recession significantly affected our plans in the field. Settlement patterns may also have changed with some villages abandoned or others more populated. Equally, Canadian maps operate on a 40m contour line division, which means that a 30m cliff could be lost between the contours. Be wary.

3. Local knowledge – agents

If you get to know local climbers who invite you to their area that can be a fantastically useful stroke of luck in that they will be so much more aware of what has been done and what could be done. Realistically that's not going to happen very often so most of the time your local knowledge is going to be supplied by an agent in the process of negotiating a logistics package that will get you from your arrival airport to your chosen area and back.

A good agent can be an incredible asset but a bad one a real liability. A recommendation from someone whose reputation you respect can be helpful but not infallible. Someone else may have taken over the business or hijacked its name. A good agent will understand the rationale of the expedition and anticipate your needs whereas

Trekking around the South side of the Yangmolong massif
confirmed our impressions from the research we had done

a bad one sees you as sheep to be fleeced. Rich western tourists who will tip a porter more than a teacher earns in a month have contributed to undermining the values of indigenous societies and created an expectation that western visitors will pay exorbitant prices so unscrupulous agents can get rich quick.

When I attempted to organise an expedition to the Chinese Tien Shan, an agent showed absolutely no understanding of our wish to explore two glacier systems on ski and tried to reshape our itinerary to conform to his concept of tourism which emphasised seeing the sites of Central Asia after "a whole day walking on a glacier!" His prices were high, but when I questioned this he kept stressing that they were what we would pay in Europe, without realising that that was just the point! Perhaps it was a language thing. It must be admitted that this expedition was organised at rather short notice after Tibet was closed and I had to find an alternative objective. Third choice was Kyrgyzstan and the agent there put together a superb logistics package in just three weeks, justifying my faith in her. She asked the obvious question about the Chinese agent: 'Didn't he realise that you are mountaineers?' A certain reputation for stinginess may go before us!

Always ask for a breakdown of costs. In most cases if you are paying what you would pay at home for accommodation, vehicle or animal (horse, mule, yak!) hire, then you are probably being overcharged. If an agent refuses to supply a breakdown of costs then they have something to hide.

A Greenland agent attempted to hold me to ransom over arrangements he claimed to be exclusive to his organisation while refusing point blank to itemise costs which were higher for my unguided and self-catered expedition than one he was offering commercially with guide and including catering. I found a better agent.

Sometimes it's just incompetence. One Mongolian agent had multiplied the cost of cook, cook boy and base camp services by the number of people on the expedition instead of dividing it between them. Always check the maths! Differences can usually be resolved amicably and you might still choose to use that agent while keeping a close eye on arrangements, and the bill. In that particular case I chose to use another much better one, although both had been personal recommendations. There may have been personnel changes.

The devil is often in the detail. Does the vehicle hire include the driver's wages? Is a permit required to enter a militarised zone? A good agent will help sort all that out beforehand rather than ambushing you with extra charges once you are there and with few or no alternatives available.

It's not as negative as it might seem. There is an incentive for bona fide expedition agents in that if they give a good service you are likely to use them again. If you don't visit the area again you may still refer enquiries from others to them. I used the same effective agents in Kyrgyzstan and China over several years and referred a number of other expedition organisers to the Mongolian and Iranian agents I had worked with when visiting those countries. Of course, the internet and email are indispensable tools to manage the search for and negotiations with an agent.

Language may tip the balance in favour of engaging an agent. Without at least a translator it will be hard to manage in Russia or China and an agent makes sense, whereas with a good Spanish speaker in the party it is possible to make use of the local infrastructure, however limited, to service an expedition in most South American countries.

By the time you have finished both stages of the research phase you should have an overview of what you are planning to do together with a workable logistics package to enable you to do it. The degree to which that has been finalised or paid for will depend upon where you are with the team. Unless you are very sure of your team don't part with money until everyone has paid their share. This is probably the stage at which formal meetings of the team will be held and commitments made.

Chapter 5: Preparation; funding, permits, supplies, insurance

Now is the time to focus on detailed preparations for the operation of the expedition in the field. It is also the time to make applications for permits, grants and sponsorship.

Funding

There should be a clearer idea of costs by this stage and applying for grants and sponsorship will clarify how much of those costs will have to be borne by individuals. The fund-raising aspect of the expedition could be assigned to one of the members rather than shared among the team so that someone has a good overview of the finances. It is worth going back to the most recent reports of expeditions to the same or nearby areas, if necessary, contacting the leaders of those expeditions to gain the latest information on costs as well as other changes, to access arrangements for example.

In 2010, the joint Chinese–American team which finally climbed Yangmolong (6066m) in Szechuan, approached by a much more circuitous route after reading reports from my expedition and another American one that had both suffered harassment from locals. The same local people, of ethnic Tibetan origin, had been very helpful in 2007 but there seemed to have been a profound shift in attitude after the unrest in Tibet associated with the Beijing Olympics. The valley, that had been empty of Buddhist monks and nuns on our first visit, was full of their robed figures in 2009. People were materially better off, using motorcycles rather than horses to get about and electricity had reached the village on brand-new pylons, but there were thefts from base camp and extortionate demands for money accompanied by the threat that they would just take all our equipment if we did not comply; they all had pictures of the Dalai Lama on their cell phones. There was a certain vicarious satisfaction that the successful expedition had followed the route that Steve Hunt and I had attempted three years earlier, particularly as we no longer had any intention of revisiting the mountain. However, our difficulties in 2009 increased costs for us and for the Chinese–American team significantly!

The BMC can supply a list of grant-awarding bodies although in practice it often comes down to the MEF and the Alpine Club, and/or Austrian Alpine Club if you are a member. The MEF stipulates that applicants should be citizens of the UK and New

Zealand, reflecting the composition of the original successful Mount Everest team. It was the subsequent fund-raising activities of that team which provided the financial foundation of the organisation. The Alpine Club and Austrian Alpine Club (British Section) only make grants to expeditions organised by members although in the case of the Alpine Club some non-members of the club may now be members of the expedition. Women and young climbers are helped by positive discrimination and a wider range of grants for which they can apply, such as the Julie Tullis and Alison Chadwick memorial awards for women and the Georgina Travers and Mark Clifford awards for young mountaineers.

I should also add a cautionary note about grant applications: some experienced mountaineers have advised me not to put too much detail in a submission. The panels that scrutinise applications are made up of other mountaineers who just might be tempted to use that detail to tip off their mates or mount their own expedition to your chosen mountain or even to climb your carefully worked out route. There has to be enough detail to give an application credibility but not so much that you may be handing over your hard-earned research to another team. It's an outside chance, but pretty crushing if you find it happening.

Whether for grant applications or sponsorship, it will help to have photos of previous trips to show that you can hack it out there, that your planning is credible, and what sort of pictures a sponsor might expect from your expedition (the sponsor may be a magazine, for example).

Sponsorship has declined from the heady days when Barclays Bank would stump up megabucks for a Bonington expedition. Nowadays equipment manufacturers might slip you a bit of kit but real money is hard to come by. It's a tough business world out there. Creative thinking can help or the ability to produce a film that can be used for product placement although the additional funding might only cover the production costs of such a film.

Having a look at the website of a "target" company may provide some ideas about their thinking on sponsorship. A member of an expedition I organised to Tibet was introduced to the DIY manufacture of pulks. He approached the plumbing company that manufactured some of the components for the hauling assembly with a possible marketing pitch they could use with photos from the expedition. The company liked the idea and sent a cheque for £1000 while we promised to provide the necessary photos. Unfortunately, permits for Tibet were not forthcoming that year so I returned the cheque. The company responded with appreciative surprise at that, but as a result turned out to be happy to sponsor a similar, later expedition. For me that arrangement was acceptable with mutual benefits and no problems about how the sponsorship might affect the conduct of the expedition, but that might not always be the case.

Walter Bonatti provides an interesting perspective on the issue:

Sponsorship is not something to be condemned out of hand. It is invaluable if well used, and also very ancient. But at present it is rampant. Almost always it comes down to a veritable shop, a marketing of ideals that changes the rules of the game, and at times changes history itself.

For those who benefit from it (and are its prime cause because of their weakness), modern sponsorship often ends up becoming a sort of coercion. This further aggravates its already enormous, implicit responsibilities. With bargaining and marketing, the sponsor exerts pressure on the sponsored, and they in turn can find themselves in a situation where they have to push themselves beyond sensible limits. You can die on a mountain this way.

So we have come to this: the sponsor no longer merely supports the undertaking, rather the undertaking is at the service of the sponsor, thence of his business, and must subject itself to all manner of implicit distortions. But what is no less worrying is that people in general have a tendency to compromise both for themselves and for others, to go easy on themselves for the sake of some advantage or other. Undeniably, this also represents a subtle malady that corrodes human dignity.

A strange psychological reaction often sees a man at fault spring to his own defence to the point of self-deception. As a result, the beneficiary of a sponsor, however exploited and reduced to being a seller of lies, nevertheless insists he is free and independent. But what really awaits him is a vicious cycle of debasement from which it will prove difficult to escape. Then, if luck is not with him and he fails to achieve what he has clamourously announced beforehand, his undertaking is even worse off, because it has been presold and has now depreciated in value. He must resort to some contrived account of the affair when the time comes for him to tell his story, not to mention the risks he may feel compelled to run so as not to compromise his long-awaited reward. It goes without saying; all this scarcely provides the best conditions to guarantee purity of purpose and idealism in conduct. Nor do I think it possible in these circumstances to speak of 'freedom of choice and action'; it would be in poor taste at this point. In fact, those who put themselves at the service of a salesman, perhaps with the illusion that they can thus enlarge their range of action, soon see their own freedom of movement become more restricted and conditional.

This is from a keynote address given at the 1989 International Mountaineering Convention, but while the focus has tended to shift to "celebrity climbers" it seems little has changed today.

I recall one speaker at a film-makers' convention sharing her sense of being used by a sponsor when the film made of one of her projects gave the impression that the climb had been achieved whereas in reality it had not. If anything, the emergence of "professional climbers" presented as marketable commodities with the collusion of the media and even the BMC has emphasised the points Bonatti makes. You have to decide if you want that sort of pressure: after Christian Stangl faked his speed ascent of K2 he wrote: 'I suppose that I came to this from a mixture between fear of death and

Language problems are more acute when there is no common alphabet and usually means enlisting the aid of an agent as here in Pakistan.

even greater fear of failure. Achievement and success were and are the determining factors in my sport…My sponsors did not pressure me into doing this. This pressure came from inside me. Fear of death is bad enough, but the fear of the failure in an achievement-oriented society is worse.'

In the end, despite the claims of the usual suspects for the cutting edge status of their climbing proposals, the value of any climb or expedition is going to be essentially subjective. Lionel Terray put it in a nutshell with the title of his book *Conquistadores of the Useless*. Why should anyone else pay for your holiday? And let's not get into the issues around sponsored charity events. As David Hillebrandt, medical adviser to the BMC, put it, 'If you run charity climbs please stop it: the health risks for the participants are unjustifiable.'

Permits and visas

The first thing to note is that if a permit is required, get one! There has been quite a bit of climbing without permits in the past, but it was very much off the record and in one sense for the purest of motives since the climbers would keep it to themselves afterwards: it was purely for their own satisfaction, not for glory. Now with professional climbers and Facebook, never mind the increased opportunities to track people by various gizmos, such activity is far less likely to escape official notice. A Japanese couple who made a fake claim to have climbed Everest were quickly rumbled.

Martin Szwed has claimed the speed record for skiing to the South Pole in January 2015 but he didn't have the required permit from his government. The claim has been strongly disputed by the polar community. Szwed's response has been that he is currently the subject of two investigations: a public prosecutor has accused him of fraud, on the grounds that the South Pole expedition never took place, and Germany's Federal Environmental Agency is pursuing a claim against him for travelling to Antarctica without permission. Conveniently, he claims that he could face jail and a fine of 50,000 euros if he divulges any details about the timing of his trip. It's a classic lose-lose situation!

When Yannick Seigneur climbed Taweche, a major peak in the Khumbu region of Nepal, after applying for a permit 'to explore the skiing potential of the Khumbu' then left Nepal without explaining himself to the authorities, he was never allowed to climb there again. But he also caused a lot of problems for those who wanted to climb there afterwards. In China, after a similar infringement in 2004, the authorities simply closed Shishapangma and sent expeditions home with no refund of their permit expenses! 'The mountain was not in condition!'

It's never a good idea to try to dispense with a permit. There may also be restrictions on the export or import of medical supplies, particularly controlled drugs such as morphine. It's worth avoiding such drugs by using alternatives and checking other possible restrictions with appropriate embassies. Prior written approval may be obtained from the embassy of the country you intend to visit by submitting a list of drugs in the expedition medical kit to the embassy. Such written approval may be very useful at military checkpoints!

Plenty of time needs to be allowed for visa applications to be processed by embassies or their agents and any permits to be obtained by agents or directly by the team. There is always a chance it won't happen. Passports have been lost by embassies and permits have been refused, so don't stop organising the expedition but minimise cash paid up front and have some contingency planning to fall back on.

People who travel a lot often decide to apply for a second passport for added security or to facilitate travel when one passport is with an embassy, although it's not easy to justify and is usually only successful if linked to one's work. When visiting Israel, a second passport can be useful because so many countries view Israel as a pariah state and have no qualms about interviewing you at length as to why you made your visit. Equally, I have been interrogated at length by two Israeli military personnel before flying out of Israel after visiting Jordan to climb in Wadi Rum so I suppose it is a quid pro quo. Another solution used by people who have only one passport is to ask Israeli entry officials to stamp the passport on a semi-detached additional sheet that can be removed after leaving. Two passports may also be a way around the restrictions imposed by the US government since ESTA (Electronic System for Travel Authorization) was set up, although in a digital age there are no guarantees and getting those passports mixed up doesn't bear thinking about!

Agents may have additional paperwork to complete to conform to the rules of their country. It all takes time and, as with much bureaucracy, procedures may change from year to year in a Kafkaesque way: Russia is a good example of a country where the application form has become more, not less, complicated to complete, since the process was outsourced to a private company (someone must have made a lot of money in that deal!)

In India at present a visa cannot be applied for before a permit has been given for the expedition and no one would buy flights before such formalities had been completed: this can become a stressful business. It's easy to criticise such apparent bureaucratic complexity yet as Indian and Pakistani officials have told me, 'You British taught us all we know about bureaucracy!' while a friend who had to apply for a visa to enter the UK described the process as more bureaucratic than the US.

Mountains designated "trekking peaks" in Nepal and Pakistan have greatly reduced bureaucracy yet can be challenging climbing objectives with some potential for new routes. The name does not mean that these peaks can be trekked up!

Supplies

Every expedition needs adequate supplies of food and fuel.

1.Food

Early expeditions to the greater ranges ran into problems with food that were particularly acute on Everest. One theory was to overcome the loss of appetite by providing expensive luxury delicacies. However, Tilman summarises the problem in *Everest 1938* when he states:

> It is at altitudes above 22,000 or 23,000 ft that the problem of what to eat becomes acute, more especially if a week or more has to be spent at such heights. This admission may please the 'caviare and quails in aspic" school of thought, but the fact is that so far it has been found impossible to eat enough of any kind of food in those conditions – even the supposedly tempting foods out of tins and bottles for which the shelves of high class grocers have been pretty well ransacked. Owing to its weight the pressure cooker has to be left behind so that cooking, apart from frying or merely heating things, becomes impossible. One is therefore driven back upon preserved and processed foods out of tins and jars, and the disinclination to eat anything which is already making itself felt thus becomes stronger. Eating is then a distasteful duty rather than a pleasure, but whether food eaten under such circumstances is of any benefit is a question for physiologists. It is the absence of hunger which makes the problem of Everest so different from that in the Arctic where the sledging ration, within the necessary limits of weight, has only to be designed to maintain the bodily heat and energy of hard-working men. There, concentrated foods rich in fat are the solution which any dietician can work out, and there such foods can be eaten with gusto; but a way of maintaining the heat and energy of equally hard-working men who are not hungry, and to whom the thought of food is nauseating, is less easily found. If you do succeed in getting outside a richly concentrated food like pemmican a great effort of will is required to keep it down – absolute quiescence

Waiting out bad weather at a high camp is a lot more cheerful if you have sufficient supplies of food and fuel.

in a prone position and a little sugar are useful aids… The loss of weight and consequent weakness which follows a stay at high altitude is probably due as much to lack of food as to the effort expended.

I should emphasise that the problems Tilman refers to are most acute at high altitudes. Modern advances in the preparation of freeze-dried and dehydrated meals must be, in part, responsible for the increase in expeditions both at high and lower altitudes. There is no longer any need to suffer the dire effects of poor food or to have to carry loads of heavy undehydrated packages.

Instant soups, add-boiling-water-to-the-bag (seal and cook) meals, and hot chocolate all operate on a clean-pot principle that keeps cooking simple and a lot less messy than it used to be. I have been told that some old expeditioners can't drink their tea unless it tastes of pasta but that's a taste I've never acquired. Add muesli/porridge for breakfast, washed down with tea or coffee and a flapjack for lunch and you'll keep going for weeks. It's operating on a calorie deficit but not an extreme one and we all have enough reserves to lose a bit of weight without harm. Technically, you can survive for three weeks with no food at all, although that is bound to be reduced by factors like altitude and cold. See Appendix 1 for a suggested daily ration example that will keep the weight of your food on the mountain down to around 500gm per day.

It all depends on your priorities: do you want to spend time hauling loads of food and fuel or climbing? Whenever people on my teams have held up their hands in horror and added more food to the basic allowance, they have usually ended up throwing most of it away uneaten. Altitude and exertion depress appetite and your body will soon get into the routine of accessing its reserves when it needs to. A bit of variety can help and the odd treat, but I'm only talking about something like a packet of biscuits over a two-week period.

Of course, this only works if there are no communal supplies.

I decided this was the way forward after hearing of expeditions coming close to grief owing to disputes over rations. It's the perennial problem of the kitty: far easier to measure input fairly than it is to ensure fair distribution of outgoings. There can be greedy people and trying to keep up can scupper any sensible rationing. I was told of an Alpine Club expedition where one of the team brought along his son who got bored at base camp and ate all the treats brought for the whole team while they were away for a couple of days on the mountain. It did not go down well. The problem was compounded when a local herder's dog managed to raid the stores and eat all the meat and cheese. It's never a good idea to have all your eggs in one basket.

Providing communal rations means shopping for all and usually within the country being visited, which won't necessarily have lightweight rations. This invariably means time lost shopping that could have been spent climbing and generally results in massive over-catering. On an expedition to Pakistan the result of over-catering was that we paid a large number of local porters to carry huge loads of food up to base camp then paid them again to carry most of it back down to their village… where we gave it to them!

If each tent team is responsible for its own rations then there can be no argument. If they want to carry more food, they can do so and they are the ones to benefit or to suffer, just so long as it doesn't stop them keeping up. This is where the idea of the whole team signing up to the style as well as the objective of the expedition is important. Moreover, it's part of taking responsibility for oneself, within a co-operative framework, that is fundamental to expeditions working well.

Of course, all this only really applies when the teams are self-sufficient on the mountain or otherwise in the field. If there is a catered base camp supplied by an agent as part of the logistics package then it's just a question of adapting to what's provided by the cook until the team moves onto the mountain. Do make sure the cook knows of any special dietary needs though. Cultures which have been based on nomadic herding, as in Kyrgyzstan for example, simply have no concept of vegetarianism – Why wouldn't you eat the animals? That's the point of having them!

2.Fuel

Stoves need fuel and the choice of both can be crucial. Gas is clean, easy to manage and gas stoves are generally lighter, but gas may be unavailable in some areas, like parts of Greenland, where liquid fuel might be the only certain option. There's no doubt that liquid fuel stoves can produce a fierce flame that will boil water quicker in colder or high-altitude conditions, although that may mean paying a weight penalty. One experienced expeditioner told me that if a stove was supplied with a maintenance kit it was a sure indication that it would have problems in the field and I only know of liquid fuel stoves that do so.

Compatibility of stove and gas canister can be an issue. Blue Camping Gaz canisters, which are penetrated by a bayonet or spike to release the gas when the canister is fitted to the stove, are still popular in some areas. These are undoubtedly cheap but the canister cannot be disconnected without releasing all the gas so once fitted they have to be carried assembled. This can result in gas leakage around the bayonet with movement of the stove, sometimes considerable gas leakage in response to the inevitable knocks and bumps in transit. Self-sealing canisters were developed that screwed on to newly designed stoves and could be disconnected for transport without mishap. It seemed that the bayonet mount was finished but Camping Gaz kept the faith and responded with screw-on canisters of their own just to confuse the issue. I remember one expedition to China where Dick Isherwood turned up very proud of his new stove only to find it simply would not connect with the only gas canisters available.

It's very important to make sure canisters and stoves are matched up correctly when ordering gas for collection in another country because you certainly won't be allowed to carry gas on your flights. Fortunately, you can email digital photos of what you want to an agent or other supplier just to be sure.

There can be some surprises though. I planned to rely on screw-on gas canisters for a ski expedition I organised in India, having had no trouble obtaining them on another expedition in June, but we were too early arriving in April. The plane-load of gas canisters bought in for agents by the Indian Mountaineering Federation (IMF) had not yet arrived and there weren't enough left from last season. We were reduced to using pump gasoline with all its impurities: most of our liquid fuel stoves played up and one was unusable by the end of the trip.

One of the advantages of using gas stoves is that their manageability means they can be used in the shelter of the tent when it would be impossible to use a stove outside because of the weather. Hanging stove kits can be bought for some stoves that make that arrangement even more convenient. Of course, I'm well aware of the dangers of carbon monoxide poisoning, which means paying scrupulous attention to ventilation. What may not be so well known is the greater danger when using a stove or pot with a heat exchanger. That vastly increases carbon monoxide output, particularly at altitude, making the practice much more dangerous. (See Paul Ramsden's article, "The Silent Killer" in the *Alpine Journal* volume 116, 2012.)

Heat exchangers are just as dangerous on liquid fuel stoves but such stoves would only be used inside a tent *in extremis* as there may simply be no room; flaring during priming risks burning the tent down, although SOTO claim to have produced a liquid fuel stove that does not require priming. A friend of mine was stuck in a small single skin assault tent for eight days on a peak in Alaska during a blizzard that put down 5m of snow. He and his climbing partner could not make their liquid fuel stove work outside the tent and had no room to try inside. The only water they could produce during that time was what they could melt by the effect of body heat on plastic bags of snow kept under their clothing. They came very close to death from hypothermia. Nevertheless, there is sometimes a preference expressed for liquid fuel stoves at altitude or in extreme cold when gas performance can become sluggish, although I've used gas with patience but no trouble at well over 6000m. Gas performance can be enhanced by taping an activated handwarmer pad to the base of the gas canister or using a simple stand that places the canister over a candle flame. Stoves with a new type of valve that maintains a constant gas pressure even when the gas canister is nearly empty have been developed by Jetboil and SOTO and can largely overcome the pressure problem. In the end the choice of fuel is still a matter of making a good judgement call.

With efficient stove practice a 450gm gas canister or two 250gm canisters should last two people three days, but it's always worth taking a bit more for extra brews or in case of emergencies. Stove manufacturers like Primus have produced fuel consumption charts comparing gas canisters with liquid fuel and one has suggested that a liquid fuel stove uses only 0.2l litres of fuel per day. Best practice is probably to test drive the rig

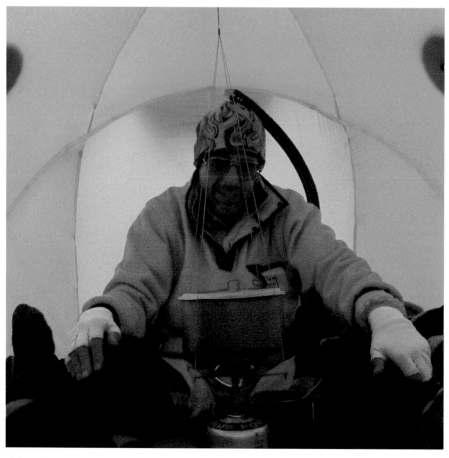

A hanging stove in action.

in summer conditions so that you know how your usage affects your supplies, then at least double the figure for winter/expedition use. It's also worth mentioning that access to a water supply reduces fuel consumption whereas having to melt snow or chips of ice will increase it.

Insurance

And so we come to the thorny issue of insurance! When I first went on expeditions, BMC expedition insurance for a full year cost something like a few hundred pounds. That is no longer the case. There have been some very large and questionable claims and in Nepal there was something of a scandal about agents advising inexperienced clients that they could be flown out, funded by their insurance, if they didn't want to go on with their trek or climb. Whether it's been bad judgement calls on claims or the temptation to maximise profits and minimise risk, there has been a general increase in premiums and exclusions applied regarding all currently available policies. The more remote, in terms of altitude or area, and exploratory an expedition is the costlier will be the insurance. It has almost reached the point where it is cheaper to take a chance on climbing without insurance and pay the costs of rescue oneself, although that might mean losing your house! Such a gamble will be very dependent on where the expedition is going and should never be even considered if climbing in the US and Canada, and also many parts of the Arctic or Antarctic where the cost of rescue and medical care can be astronomical, hence the exclusions applied to those areas or at least the hefty supplements charged to cover them. India requires a bail bond of £50,000 just to cover military evacuation from the mountain.

Generally, there are two types of insurance: the comprehensive travel insurance that includes hazardous activities, and the insurance that covers search, rescue and repatriation for mountain activities which is intended to supplement basic travel insurance that does not include such cover. The BMC provides the best example of the former and the Austrian Alpine Club the best example of the latter. That's why the costs are so different. Both can be almost worldwide in their cover but standard travel insurance will be necessary to cover loss of baggage or flight delays, for example, that are not covered by the Austrian Alpine Club. At the time of writing both will quote for additional premiums to cover excluded areas or altitudes. Global Rescue is an alternative.

There was an issue with the AAC in Austria changing the wording of its cover in the German language documents which had not been revised in the English language documents. I learnt of this from a friend whose expedition, he had been informed, was not covered because it did not comply so I took it up with Section Britannia and the officers initiated negotiations with Austria that led to a reversion to the original provision.

The devil is in the detail as always, and if you have any doubts about anything in a policy it's worth checking up on it before shelling out your hard-earned cash. In Kyrgyzstan I had asked all members of the expedition to make sure that they had insurance cover, but when we were discussing this on the glacier it emerged that one member had a particular BMC policy that a BMC representative had described as inadequate to another member who had therefore gone for a more expensive package. Had that been queried, and an assurance obtained in writing, I would have had no problem but as it was, there was the distinct possibility that I had an uninsured member of the team who had only a verbal confirmation that he was covered.

On another occasion with an American company that covered Greenland I asked for detail as to what was meant by "evacuation to hospital". Was it evacuation from the scene of the accident, having found that location or only from a roadhead? A written assurance generated a lot more confidence in the cover and would have been invaluable if it ever came to a court case.

There is an argument that with modern technology there is no longer any reason to have "search" but just have "rescue". An insurance company could be sent one's position every hour using a Garmin InReach Mini, so long as there were sufficient power supplies, therefore rescue cost would just be a matter of the cost of the nearest helicopter. Perhaps some broker needs to look into this and it could become part of the contract.

Contingency planning for rescue might be worth documenting and leaving with a responsible adult who can act as a central contact in the event of an emergency with all the insurance and personal details of the expedition team to hand.

Insurance is always changing so up-to-date information should always be sought. Both the Eagle Ski Club (https://www.eagleskiclub.org.uk/plan-your-trip/insurance-advice) and the Alpine Club (http://www.alpine-club.org.uk/eic-insurance) have insurance information on their websites which is updated from year to year and is in the public domain.

This is the ESC advice at the time of writing:

The Officers and Committee of the Eagle Ski Club wish to remind members that ski touring, ski mountaineering and related activities contain, by their nature, a degree of hazard and risk, and despite the greatest care accidents may still occur.

All participants in any Club activity should be aware of and accept the inherent risk associated with the activity, be responsible for their own actions and involvement, and ensure that they maintain adequate insurance cover for the activity being undertaken.

It is also worth participants considering how much additional insurance they would like in order to cover risks such as cancellation of travel arrangements and accommodation bookings. It is important to bear in mind that not all policies cover these risks in the same way and each policy should be checked to ensure that it provides the cover required. This has been a particular problem with cancellations due to the COVID-19 outbreak, which some policies covered and others did not. EACH PARTICIPANT MUST CHECK THEIR OWN INSURANCE TO ENSURE THAT IT IS ADEQUATE FOR THEIR NEEDS.

Personal and Other Insurance

All Members taking part in Club meets involving ski touring or any off-piste activity are required to have adequate personal cover to pay the cost of "getting them off the mountain", by helicopter where necessary. Members are also strongly urged to have additional cover to pay for possibly extended local hospitalisation and/or repatriation. Such cover should extend to all medical emergencies and not just accidents.

Given that levels of cover provided by policies vary, members are advised to read policies carefully to check exactly what activities are covered, what search and rescue costs are covered and that levels of cover provided are deemed to be adequate. It is the Member's responsibility to ensure that their insurance provides cover for all the intended activities.

Non-UK Resident Members are not covered under the Club's Combined Liability Insurance which is secured through the Club's affiliation to Mountaineering Scotland. Therefore, they will need to make individual arrangements for third party liability cover, should they wish to participate in the Club's activities. The level of cover carried should be at least £2,000,000.

The range of policies available is too wide for the Club to make specific recommendations and Members are urged to do their own research. It is hoped that the following notes, though not exhaustive, will be helpful to that end.

The policy/policies needed will depend very much on personal circumstances, existing cover, age and activities foreseen. Some otherwise good policies become uncompetitive for members who have passed 60. Some annual policies can be a bargain if you get away a lot and climb etc in the summer too. Many policies have specific exclusions or limitations, for example in terms of geography or altitude.

What is absolutely essential from a ski mountaineering and touring point of view is that adequate cover to get a Member off the mountain (i.e. helicopter rescue) and provide urgent medical support. For example membership of the Austrian Alpine Club UK (which also gives you reciprocal rights in most Alpine Huts) includes this sort of basic cover worldwide without age restrictions, but medical insurance costs are limited to 10,000 Euro (Dec 2019).

It goes without saying that cover for areas outside Europe, particularly North America, will need to be very significantly higher. You might also consider obtaining cover against loss of a deposit or other non-refundable payments for a Tour from which you had to withdraw late because of injury on a previous trip, for example.

Other insurers you may wish to consider might include the British Mountaineering Council (BMC), Snowcard, and Protectivity.

Check for updates!

Finally, porters and other local personnel need to be insured for the duration of their time serving the expedition. That may be organised in your home country or there may be local arrangements that a liaison officer or agent can organise.

Chapter 6: Preparation; Equipment

Equipment

Every expedition will call upon equipment related to the specific objectives of the expedition and it would be pointless to attempt an exhaustive list, but exploring remote locations means that there are some common threads.

1. Camping

Tents are the most flexible and adaptable means of providing shelter on an expedition. Igloos or snow caves are possible alternatives but take longer to construct and are not often as comfortable owing to the disconcerting habit snow has of melting when the temperature rises. At best that can result in a continuously damp atmosphere while the worst-case scenario has the snow cave or igloo collapsing. It can be damp in tents too when frozen condensation melts, but they soon dry when the sun comes out.

Specific tentage depends on the type of expedition. Flying in to a base camp from which the surrounding mountains can be explored in no more than a day's travel means a big base camp tent can offer communal facilities, even a wood-burning stove! The whole group can then cook, eat and socialise together, although sleeping arrangements may still be back in smaller two- or three-person tents. If that option is not offered there is no escape from the heavy snorer or relentless joker or storyteller. We all need space, and some privacy.

If travelling is involved or the need to set up high camps before making a summit bid, then smaller two- or three-person tents are going to be essential; the lightest possible given that they *must* be able to stand up to mountain weather including storms. Two-person tents such as the Terra Nova Quasar are ideal for a climbing pair, but the Super Quasar can take three people without the additional weight penalty of more substantial, three-person tents like the Mountain Hardwear Trango 3+.

Although three-person tents inevitably weigh more, the advantage is that the total weight can be shared between three people, not two, with one taking the inner tent, one the flysheet and one the poles and stove kit so that personal loads actually weigh less. It can be a good idea to rotate the allocation of communal loads just to ensure a sense of fair play. As you might expect, careful thought about who shares with who will be necessary for such arrangements to work.

Tents with inners and flysheets tend to be better ventilated and more weatherproof, but there's no doubt that single skin tents of Gore-tex® or similar material have their place when both lightness and compactness are required. The big base camp tent can be supplemented by single skin assault-type tents like the old Bibler I-tent, for sleeping at base camp or for travelling to less accessible peaks in the area. They shed snow easily but tend to be less effective in heavy rain and are colder in windy conditions. Somehow, sometimes, it seems like the breathability goes into reverse and the wind filters through the fabric. Still, we can all put up with a bit of hardship for a night or two to achieve our dreams!

For those who dislike camping in fields it's worth noting that snow camping is much cleaner. Guying out the tent can be trickier though. On Denali I was shown some home-made bamboo tent pegs by a Korean party. Wood doesn't heat up and melt out of the snow as quickly as metal pegs do and a broader profile can be produced to hold better in snow. It's easy enough to buy some bamboo poles of 8–10cm diameter, saw them into appropriate lengths, then split the tubes into four or six tent pegs, shaping them to a point with a spokeshave. There are broader metal tent pegs sold for use in snow but they need burying deep enough for them to be less likely to melt out. With the advent of bio-degradable plastic bags it's now possible to fill such small bags with snow, tie them to the guys then bury them in the snow. When moving on, just cut the plastic bags off the guys and leave them buried in the ice that the snow will have turned into in the interim. At the next campsite you can use new bags. Such an approach needs thinking through carefully though. Any plastic left blowing about because it's melted out won't do wildlife much good if they ingest it, no matter how bio-degradable it may be. It's worth having

A tent modification in the field.

A misbehaving pulk, Kyrgyzstan

sufficient means of anchoring the tent because bold claims about using skis or ice axes to peg out flysheets look a bit silly when those items have to be used for a day's climbing or skiing. You could come back to find your tent missing!

I'm not a fan of snow valances on tents as the snow spread over them tends to freeze the valance in to the compacted snow below. You can do a lot of damage trying to break them out of the ice when you need to move on.

Tent design is important not only with regard to valances, as I found out when purchasing a new tent, mail order, before an expedition. I unpacked it to find half the front door of the inner tent was simply a mesh panel with no option to seal it up with a zipped flap as you can with Quasars. In the field it was cold as the warmth generated in the inner tent by our bodies was quickly lost through the draughty mesh. It became so bad that I cut the hood section off my Pertex® sleeping bag liner and duct-taped it over the mesh. At last we had a warm night! Subsequent discussions with the manufacturer revealed that the designer had a somewhat simple-minded theory about condensation: that lots of ventilation would stop it.

Actually, lots of ventilation does stop condensation but only because the air in the tent never gets to warm up enough for the water vapour in it to condense on the cold inner tent surface. In practical terms that almost means you might as well be curled up in your sleeping bag on the snow outside. Condensation occurs when warm air meets a cold surface. Now that may be on the underside of the flysheet if the tent warms up enough to push the dew point out beyond the permeable inner tent, but more often it is when that air meets the inner tent fabric which becomes damp and, as the temperature drops, freezes. If you let a lot of cold air into the tent that won't happen because warm air is confined to your sleeping bag. Consequently, the dew point where condensation occurs gets pushed back into your sleeping bag, which becomes very damp and will need to dry out during the day. Wet down is a less efficient insulator so you will be colder. That becomes less and less reasonable as conditions become more and more extreme. An expedition tent should not have mesh panels that cannot be covered. In extreme cases the finest spindrift can leak in through the mesh. Eventually, in my case, the tent manufacturer agreed to modify the tent with a zip cover for the mesh panel, but I had to use the term "not fit for purpose" before he agreed.

I've already considered stoves when discussing fuel choices but one way in which a tent can be warmed up is by cooking inside, which saves heat loss to wind chill although adequate ventilation is absolutely essential to avoid the dangers of carbon monoxide poisoning mentioned earlier. Jetboil and Primus both have hanging stove kits for their stoves but the best one I've used was made by MSR. It was a simple, titanium flip-out "spider" that locked around the "neck" of the Superfly stove suspending it from four wires, which, of course, stabilised the pot between them. Sadly, MSR make it no longer, but it may be possible to construct a DIY job with aluminium alloy.

Liquid fuel stoves usually mean digging a stove pit in the tent porch, to avoid flare-ups damaging the flysheet, particularly when priming. SOTO make a liquid fuel stove that it is claimed doesn't need priming, offering a very much safer alternative.

A "clean pan" approach to cooking whereby the pan is used only to boil water simplifies cooking and makes the use of titanium pans safer. Titanium absorbs heat quickly but doesn't transmit it very well so titanium pans heated without water in them or used for traditional cooking have actually melted.

Sleeping needs can be catered for with an appropriate sleeping bag constructed for the expected temperatures. Down is the obvious choice for warmth without too much weight unless really damp conditions are expected when a synthetic filling would be better. A thermal inner and/or vapour barrier inner can extend the temperature range of a sleeping bag if necessary. The Rab vapour barrier sleeping bag liner that I used on Denali had a brushed interior that felt comfortable to the touch and never resulted in any sweatiness. Most sleeping bags now have a Gore-tex® type shell fabric which generally sheds drips from the tent roof.

Ground insulation is provided by sleeping mats and/or inflatable mattresses. Personally, I take a short Therm-a-Rest mattress and a long mat. That way if the mattress is punctured there's still some insulation from the mat. I've never actually seen a successful inflatable mattress repair in the field.

2.Load carrying

Issues about load carrying usually begin with flights. Air freighting is a risky business. A French team at Constable Pynt airport near Scoresbysund in Greenland was leaving as my expedition arrived. They had spent two weeks at the local "Hilton minus one star" waiting for their equipment to arrive. It helps if your kit can fly with you and with the minimum of connections that afford opportunities for it to be lost in transit. Hold luggage up to 23kg can be supplemented by a substantial weight of hand luggage squirrelled away in clothing as well as carry-on bags. One team member once invested in an under-jacket that offered lots of large "poachers' pockets".

Before reaching base camp, it is likely that animals or porters, motorcycles, skidoos or helicopters will have transported the loads. It's worth negotiating a fixed price for the journey rather than a daily rate if you don't want porters or muleteers to have a vested interest in extending the length of time spent getting to base camp. Porters are normally self-sufficient in basic equipment and food for the journey, although there can be differences in approach from country to country. Pakistan, for example, has government regulations. Just don't expect porters to tackle technical terrain without appropriate equipment trusting to some "innate ability!" A Peruvian porter I saw being hauled up a vertical ice step with no ice axe on the approach to Alpamayo Col camp repeatedly cried out in fear and was thoroughly wasted at the top. I have no idea how he was expected to get down on his own unless he was spending the duration at Col camp while his employers climbed and he would return with them.

Most expeditions require self-sufficiency in the field so more issues around load carrying begin above base camp. From then on, the team has to organise itself for load carrying. The time-honoured means has been a very large rucksack on one's back and, in many locations, that is all that will be necessary, but not everywhere or for every trip.

The "expedition rucksack" can be anything up to 100 litres in capacity but the larger they are the less useful they are for actual climbing: great for trudging up a glacier but hell on technical ice pitches! Smaller rucksacks are more versatile but carrying less may demand a higher level of hardship, and there are limits to how long one is prepared to put up with hardship. Some rucksacks have been designed to become more streamlined when side pockets are folded in, but that doesn't reduce the weight of that additional material and there remains an argument for detachable pockets. Others have "floating lids" that can be completely detached and do service as a small rucksack on summit day. Again, it's worth being aware of the options and making your own judgement call.

With longer expeditions or those involving greater independent travel, such as the ski exploration of a range, more capacity may be required than is provided by a rucksack alone. Enter the trusty pulk!

There are ready-made pulks available at fairly eye-watering prices, which, bearing in mind their potential expendability, is a powerful incentive for DIY efforts. Another disadvantage of the commercially available pulks is their sheer size and weight, particularly if travelling by air. I've used lighter, cheaper alternatives on trips of around four weeks duration with no problems beyond those that are endemic to pulks (more later!) The simplest of kiddies' sledges is robust enough for most trips but it is the hauling modification which takes the effort. Having said that, an afternoon's work with an electric drill and a screwdriver can produce a workable pulk from a kiddies' sledge needing only short lengths of bungee cord, climbing accessory cord and some plumbing pipework and connecting fittings. A waterproof bag, roll-top closure or waterproof zipped, to be strapped to the pulk can be found in a yacht chandler's catalogue.

The rig to haul the sled has been a recurrent problem. I remember trying to use plastic waste pipe and fittings for the first pulk I made only to find that the plastic became brittle and shattered at low temperatures so that any benefit from the rigidity of the rig was lost. With only a haul rope, the pulk has a nasty tendency to catch up with the haulier and, when skiing, wrap the rope around the legs of the skier! Later models have used bamboo poles or more flexible and durable plastic piping and compression fittings that don't shatter, thus adding effective additional control to pulk management. This increases the cost but poles are reuseable and can be carried home in ski bags so still keeps it down to a level at which scrapping the pulk is not a daunting prospect and, hey, any local kids will love them!

I won't try to give a blow by blow account of pulk building but the series of photos in Appendix 2 should make the principles clear. To avoid shock-loading the system it's wise to incorporate some stout bungee cord in the traces for shock absorption. When travelling roped up in crevassed terrain, the pulk will also need to be attached to the safety rope using a Prusik loop, so there needs to be a loop of cord to which that can be attached at the rear of the pulk (see photo in Appendix 2).

Pulks will always be difficult beasts to control. On a traverse a pulk will tend to slip away downhill instead of holding the line of the haulier, and threaten to take him or her with it. All efforts that I've witnessed to devise a "keel" to avoid that tendency have resulted in unacceptable drag. Heading downhill, the pulk picks up speed and either pushes the haulier over or threatens to overtake and roll on the turns. The only successful method to slow its speed to something more manageable is to have a loop of thickish rope attached to the nose of the pulk that can be flipped under the front when descending to increase drag (see photo in Appendix 2).

There is another alternative for trips of around two weeks that involves travel continuously on snow: the haul bag. The lighter weights involved in shorter trips mean the load can be shared between haul bag and rucksack so a simplified system can be used. Tough, waterproof, roll-top tubular bags can be attached to a single pole equipped with swivels to avoid the attached rope kinking with the inevitable rolling of the bag (see Appendix 3). The original pole I tried was bamboo and had the added advantage that I burnt it at the campfire we made in our first camp off the snow so I didn't have to carry it out. The joints within the bamboo pole do have to have a steel concrete reinforcement rod driven through them if the pole is going to have the accessory cord run through it. Bags need to have a smooth rather than textured surface if they are to run freely and should generally be of around 35–40 litres capacity. The larger and heavier they are, the more likely they are to break free from the system. There always needs to be some shock absorption built in to the system by having a two-point attachment to the bag; one of accessory cord should be longer than the other shorter one of stout bungee cord which will stretch and absorb energy before the weight is shared with the other. Swivels range from big wall haul bag swivels such as the rotator from Black Diamond to less refined swivel snap links from ships' chandlers or karabiners usually attached to ice axe leashes: it depends what levels of reliability and expense you want to work with.

Haul bags are generally easier to manage in the field than pulks owing to their smaller size and weight. They won't hold a traverse line any better than a pulk but are less of a threat to the haulier. On the downhill, they can run ahead of the pedestrian but a skier can ski the fall line in shorter runs, taking brief breaks whenever the bag threatens to overtake.

3.Communications

In practice there are two requirements for communication in the field: with the outside world and within the team.

The first requirement can be satisfied by a satellite phone. Inmarsat operates with geostationary satellites which means that if you cannot connect to a satellite you are unlikely to be able to do so at all whereas the Iridium system uses polar orbiting satellites so that you are more likely to catch a passing signal, even if down a crevasse! Satellite phones are becoming more reliable and lighter year on year it seems but do have their limitations and if you have a second one for back-up make sure that they are compatible. In Greenland I was only able to communicate

Haul bags in action, Antarctica.

intermittently, by text, because of such limitations. However, the continuing development of locator beacons with a variety of features is extending the range of options available in the event of an emergency or a necessary change to plans. The Garmin inReach location beacon also allows texting between teams on the mountain as well as reaching the outside world. Again, it is worth checking that there are no restrictions regarding such equipment; at the time of writing satellite phones are not allowed on expeditions to India.

Two-way radios are still an effective means of communicating within the team in the field. The number depends on the number of people in the team and the likelihood of divisions within the team to pursue different objectives.

As always in expeditions, weight remains an issue and it's not just the weight of the equipment but also the batteries to power it. Solar chargers offer some hopes of keeping that weight down but they too have their limitations. The wire connections become more brittle in the cold so it is worth taking a spare connector or making sure that the connection point is unable to wiggle using some extra protection at that point. Attempts to use them while travelling, attached to a rucksack or pulk, are generally less effective than at base camp. An alternative might be a lightweight power pack to top up devices, but there's no doubt that more gizmos mean more power consumed and more concern about replenishing it.

One of the most valued elements of the expedition experience for me has been the simplicity of self-sufficiency; a leaving behind of the complexities and artificiality of first-world life. There is less time spent faffing about and more opportunities to relate to the natural surroundings. So I've usually been content to pack a couple of spare batteries and leave it at that.

4.Navigation

I have to confess to being a bit old school about map and compass work as the first resort when navigating. However, the points noted earlier about the unreliability of maps in more remote areas should be remembered and a couple of GPS units, to check on each other as well as the route, can be invaluable. Again, GPS is not infallible. I use bamboo marker wands at each waypoint on an out and back trip and the GPS unit has often insisted that I'm at the waypoint when I can see the marker wand some 50m away. If I was relying on GPS only, the accumulated error involved from point to point could lead to dangerous inaccuracies in navigation. Using the wands to correct deviation as it occurs, it's possible to limit that. Nonetheless, in a white-out or severe weather a GPS can be a lifesaver.

5.Medical equipment and supplies

If you are lucky enough to have a medically qualified person on the team this area can be delegated to that person, but if not, there should still be a designated team member taking responsibility.

Like any first aid kit the contents of an expedition medical kit are dependent on:

- The nature of the activity and its specific risks – for example an expedition requiring a long trek in through jungle will be different from one which flies the team onto a glacier.

- The number of expedition members

- The duration and remoteness of the trip – Isolated = medical help within hours; Remote = medical help within a day or two; or Wilderness = medical help several days away or is unreliable

- How much you can carry – porters or not

- The medical expertise available on the trip

It is still advisable to have a modular approach to the Expedition Medical kit:

- Personal first aid kit – for every member to carry and administer their own first aid and minor illness self-treatment. Depending on the trip this might include antimalarial prophylaxis; Diamox for first stage altitude problems (although there may be ethical questions if it is used as a prophylactic) and a broad-spectrum antibiotic. In addition, members should carry sufficient supplies and spares of their own personal medications. Appendix 4: ESC Mount Logan medical kit includes a recommendation for a personal medical kit.

In addition, the RGS Expedition Medicine Manual suggests the modular expedition first aid kit might include:

- Field kit – a basic kit containing limited supplies of first aid equipment to be carried for a small group of people while away from base camp for the day.

- Mobile camp kit – supplies for each group camping away from base camp a few days at a time.

- Base camp kit – the main medical kit for the trip. Also used to replenish the other kits and provide a reserve stock of medicines for individual members.

- Accident kit – part of the base camp kit – a pre–packed emergency kit in case of a serious accident. This needs to be portable and available quickly to team members.

Appendix 4 consists of two examples of group medical kits; the first an advisory document, the second an actual kit taken.

All medical equipment and supplies need to be protected from contamination by water or other sources of infection. Packaging in resealable bags or boxes that are transparent enough to be able to identify the contents without opening is standard good practice. It's also worth remembering that there is an understanding that no NHS prescriptions should be written to be used for treatments overseas so private prescriptions will need to be secured for supplies that can then be bought.

Sources

- RGS–IBG *Expedition Medicine* handbook, David Warrell and Sarah Anderson (eds.), Profile Books, 2002. This is now a little out of date on specifics but the general principles still apply.

- *Oxford Handbook of Expedition Medicine*, Eds. Johnson C, Anderson S, Dallimore J, Imray C, Winser S, Moore J, Warrell D. Oxford University Press, 2015 (2nd edition).

- *Pocket First Aid and Wilderness Medicine*, Drs Jim Duff and Ross Anderson, Cicerone, 2017 (3rd edition). A favourite resource as it's very succinct, pocket sized and has a good appendix listing medications and quantities required for:

> Large group =10–15 people away for one month
>
> Small Group = 6 people on a one–week trip
>
> 2 people travelling in a developing country
>
> Minimalist kit – e.g. for a mountaineer

6.Wildlife protection

Depending on the area that is being visited, it may be necessary to take specialist equipment for protection from wild animals.

Simba Col on Mount Kenya is at 4600m yet it gained its name because the skeleton of a lion was found there, and on the walk up the Chogoria Gorge we were warned about elephant that are such powerful creatures they can kill with a careless swipe of their trunks. At around 2000m on the Ngorogoro Crater rim we had braziers burning all night because the previous night a lion had come into the camp. However, there's not much else that can be done: rangers may carry guns but you aren't likely to be issued with a rifle.

That's not the case with Greenland and other parts of the Arctic where a rifle or shotgun with specialist rounds is going to be standard issue, sometimes together with flare guns and/or "bear bangers" and bear spray. Polar bears are at the very top of the food chain and anything moving is a potential meal to them. Musk ox can also be dangerous if spooked. We were advised by locals to take a dog which would warn us of bear presence as well as putting off polar bears by its scent and barking but that was in an area where polar bears were hunted so they had reason to fear the presence of dogs. In national parks, where polar bears are protected, they are less likely to be deterred. The Inuit had no faith in tripwires and perimeter alarms which depend on chancy

Rifle training in Greenland.

electrical connections in sub-zero temperatures. Rifles are less easy to use at close quarters than a hand gun but for various reasons handguns are less easy to obtain.

Further south, grizzly are more of a problem than black bears in North America and there have been a number of fatal attacks, whereas there are no records of fatalities resulting from wolf attack. Most expeditions are unlikely to carry firearms unless they intend to supplement rations by hunting: the weight factor is generally unjustifiable. However, some travellers put their faith in bear spray, while others follow advice to bang pots and pans when travelling through dense forest where they could take a bear by surprise and provoke a defensive attack. Most bears will flee from unusual noises but there have been attacks by sick or injured bears that have not behaved normally so bear spray is worth considering. The main limitation of bear spray is that it's only really effective at close range.

7.Personal Equipment

Personal equipment is always a personal choice and is most likely to be based on whatever Alpine equipment has been found to be successful for that person as they acquire the skills to qualify themselves to take on the additional challenges of expeditions. Insulation may be uprated, hardware lightened, but the principles of Alpinism can still be applied.

If there is a long trek to base camp then a set of appropriate kit (clothes, boots, daysack, umbrella for rain and sun) should be sourced for that: don't expect to walk in wearing high-altitude boots! Some treks feel like they begin in the tropics and end in the polar regions so be prepared.

Chapter 7: Team-building

Selecting a team

Sometimes a team will select itself in that a bunch of mates will decide on an expedition and those who can make it will be the team that goes. There is a question of size though. A large group may fragment and lose focus as personal agendas begin to influence the functioning of the team. In Cathy O'Dowd's book *Just for the Love of It* she describes how personnel difficulties on the walk in to Everest base camp almost did for the expedition that eventually put the first South African on the summit, Cathy herself. In that case, team selection included a qualifying climb on Kilimanjaro yet the team didn't gel in the field until a dissident group left after failing to take over the leadership.

In the Everest example above, one of the factors involved in the fragmentation of the team appeared to be the development of a relationship between a married male team member and the female expedition doctor that hinged on her efforts to be added to the expedition permit rather than work out of base camp. In an adventurous environment it's perhaps not surprising that in a team of men and women there might be some romantic adventures and this may account for the unwillingness of some expedition leaders to include women members in their teams. Of course, there are bound to be issues around privacy and personal space but Arlene Blum has detailed some of the obvious prejudice she encountered. Clare Roche has also revealed how the very considerable achievements of female alpinists such as Lucy Walker were studiously ignored by a male-dominated establishment that was still denying membership of the Alpine and Climbers' clubs to women as recently as 1973. H.W. Tilman was only deterred from resigning from the Alpine Club after the vote to admit women when he was offered honorary membership. The response of women climbers historically had been to climb "manless" and the all-female Pinnacle Club still thrives today. It's sometimes not recognised how revolutionary manless climbing was originally, because since there were no women guides it necessarily involved guideless climbing. Even men could suffer establishment criticism for climbing guideless. Perhaps male discomfort arose because women climbers were challenging stereotypes whereas men were often conforming to them.

I've been lucky to live through a period which has seen women shake off any suggestion of being "belay bunnies" to take their places at the forefront of the climbing world, and can honestly say that expedition team selection for me has never been

Iona Pawson climbing the Grunegghorn on an evaluation
week in the Alps before confirming team selection.

influenced by gender issues. Sometimes my partner and I formed the core of a team but it has been a privilege to climb and ski with all the women who joined my teams. All demonstrated the ability that fully justified their places, particularly a woman like Lizzie Hawker who won the Ultra Trail du Mont Blanc at her first attempt and went on to become the world 100km champion. That equal partnership in the project has been the key to successful mixed sex expeditions. The single occasion on which I vetoed a wife accompanying her husband was based on roles more than gender as she would have been operating as an unequal partner, stuck at base camp as expedition doctor while he was on the mountain. I'd already seen the problems that had generated on a previous expedition; it was a question of focus. No expedition can afford to simply ignore gender issues.

If more people want to go than is likely to be practical, some selection process is going to be necessary. Both the Eagle Ski Club and the Alpine Club organise, and support financially, expeditions that are open to all club members: they both use standardised application forms before less formal assessment takes place. Up-to-date references are also required as is found with applications to the Mount Everest Foundation for support. That's one way of managing a selection process, although by no means foolproof. I recall a certain sinking feeling standing on a glacier in Mongolia when a member of the expedition, who had been described as possessing "sound mountaineering judgement" in a reference, looked a bit lost when I suggested roping up and he asked, 'Can you just go over how to tie a figure of eight knot please?' At least he asked.

A change in context can affect performance. I remember teaming up with a fellow Chester Club member for his first Alpine route. Simon was climbing in the E grades on British rock but we set our sights low for the North-north-east Ridge of the Aiguille de l'M at just D, pitches of five. I led the first pitch, expecting to alternate leads from pitch to pitch but the sheer scale of this mountain territory was new to him and just too intimidating; I ended up leading every pitch but one, an enclosed corner crack where he could feel a bit more at home. Even sound alpinists can find the rigours of snow camping and the need to be well organised in such a situation just too much for them.

It helps to know people, or to know people who also know the applicant and whose judgement you trust. Even if a person has been involved in previous expeditions, the fact that no one has ever gone with them twice can be useful to know. A lot can be read between the lines of expedition reports. The donation of expedition diaries to the Alpine Club archive has revealed that in the past there have been some remarkable efforts to paper over the cracks that have riven certain expeditions when it came to the official accounts. Gradually more candour has encouraged self-analysis to become almost confessional at times.

With a decent selection process, it should be possible to avoid the situation where an excellent rock climber made his first snow and ice ascent but then was too intimidated to reverse the route in descent. In that particular case the pair took a huge diversion via an entirely different valley before they rejoined the team at base camp, absolutely exhausted. There are, however, no guarantees. Eric Shipton comments that, 'the choice of companions for an exploration is ... something of a lottery, and my experience has taught me to mistrust my judgement in the matter'. On one of his Patagonian expeditions one of the team returned to England rather than continue with him so that comment should not be too surprising. He continues:

Normal acquaintance with a man, however close, is a very poor guide to whether or not he will be a suitable or even tolerable companion on an expedition. Faults that may normally seem utterly trivial often become nagging irritations in the enforced intimacy of an expedition; characteristics that may never appear in ordinary life can be distressingly or splendidly revealed in conditions of hardship, danger and physical or nervous strain. Some men who will rise magnificently to a crisis, may yet wilt under the stress of enforced inactivity. Then there is the diverse interplay of characters upon one another. A man may find himself with two companions, both of whom he likes very much, but who cannot tolerate each other. One of my most successful and delightful expedition partnerships was with a man who, I had been warned, was generally regarded as impossible to travel with. The argument of those who believe that an "arranged" marriage has at least as much chance of success as one based on a love affair, seems to be applicable here.

Interestingly his views reflect the fact that although his wife accompanied him on trips he made with Tilman in Xinjiang, she made few excursions above base camp

Pre-departure activities like shopping in-country can focus the
mind on personal supplies and help a team gel; Mongolia

and his climbing experience gave him little expectation of opportunities to explore the
dynamics of a mixed gender team.

Stakeholding

One obvious qualification for inclusion in an expedition team is a medical qualification,
and I don't mean just a first aid certificate. But don't expect too much of even an A &
E junior doctor. On expeditions there is none of the support provided in a hospital
such as blood tests, X-rays and MRI scanning that they could expect in their normal
working conditions. It's a bit like an airline pilot flying without radar. A Rescue
Emergency Care (REC) or Far from Help course can qualify another member of the
team to give invaluable support to the medical lead and it could be that one or two
amateur but trained team members is the best you'll get. If you're going to expect
responsibility for medical matters from a member of the team then it's sensible to give
them the responsibility for organising medical supplies both centrally and those to be
carried by individual members for emergencies.

Equally a team member who has financial expertise could be invaluable in managing and raising funding. However, that's a specific job. All members of the team can
be stakeholders in the process of reviewing the access arrangements and logistics that
have emerged from the research as they move into the preparation phase of expedition
planning.

Communication is crucial; all members should at least have phone numbers
and email addresses although many will also use Whatsapp and Messenger or other

message systems. Email, in particular, has revolutionised the capacity to share ongoing information about planning and involve team members in decision making. Even so, meetings can be useful for more active and sustained stakeholding. I always organised at least one weekend meeting to review the planning and clear up any misunderstandings which might have arisen from hastily read emails after a hard day's work.

Weekend meetings were two-part: a day spent working through the details of the planning followed by social interaction, eating and drinking, and having the following day out on the hill together. That way the planning is embedded in the socialisation of the team. That socialisation can be structural too. On one occasion, three of the team had never participated in an expedition before so those less-experienced members shared tents with others who were more experienced. Once a member put in a request to share a tent with another because, as he put it to me, 'He's the one I think I have least in common with so I'll make more effort to make it work.' Owning that sort of decision making means members have a definite stake in the planning and style of the expedition.

At the point where the details of access and provision in the field have been established it is well worth engaging the team with contingency planning, examining "what if …" scenarios, as well as considering the options for exit strategies. There may be alternative routes to return to the roadhead or similar issues to explore. Contingency planning and exit strategies are sometimes assumed to be self-evident but some team forethought can be very valuable. As the planning issues become more

Getting to know the locals is also teambuilding; Mongolia.

complex the input of team members not only checks what planning has been done but also contributes to improving the quality of further decision making as the ownership of the organisation is shared among the team.

It's a moot point as to whether it was team building or management in the field but crewing a yacht from Ushuaia to the Antarctic peninsula provided good opportunities for the team to get to know each other in a situation where they had to solve problems and take responsibility before tackling the mountaineering component of the expedition. The yacht also functioned as a kind of floating hut in which to take refuge between excursions onto the ice. During those rest days it was possible to share photos and compare impressions jotted down earlier in tents for later reporting. Other opportunities can be found while approaching the mountains, involving the team in sightseeing, shopping for in-country supplies, or organisation of transport or permits.

Of course, there are leadership issues involved here. A leadership style that has difficulty with involving the team in planning, perhaps taking criticism personally rather than seeing it as a way of improving the quality of decision making, will not result in the sort of ownership of the expedition that can produce a cohesive team approach. It's like the situation where a guide takes on all the responsibility for leading a group: if he's avalanched, who organises the rescue?

Chapter 8: Management in the field

Management of the expedition in the field essentially comes down to the management of people and resources, although situation sensitivity will always make such management a lot more effective.

This can begin on arrival in India or Pakistan to climb any mountains that require a liaison officer (LO). Welcoming an LO, who may be of military rank, into the team is not going to be easy because he or she has not been part of the team building that has taken place back in the home country. Similar problems can arise for the same reason when members resident in another country only meet fellow expeditioners when they arrive in the country in which the expedition will take place. With an LO though, there can be an accumulated resentment owing to the requirement to equip the LO for high-altitude climbing at the expense of the expedition; in India $500 is paid to the Indian Mountaineering Foundation (IMF) for equipment the LO checks out from IMF stores in Delhi. Some LOs are keen to get onto the mountain but others may not go beyond base camp, or even the roadhead, and can be more interested in selling their equipment, unused, than putting it to good use, although in India it has to be returned to the IMF.

Be that as it may, an LO is potentially a valuable resource. They can help with language translation and local protocols unknown to team members, such as sensitivities about photography of local people, or militarily significant features like bridges. During a long approach march, they may seem to be enjoying their "little brief authority" by visiting the headman of every village, but that headman may well come in useful if there are unforeseen problems like thefts from the expedition's baggage. On such marches, the LO can facilitate food purchase from local villages, which can save money or avoid carrying in additional supplies, although in the Karakoram, for example, the land may be so barren that buying local supplies is not possible.

In places like India and Pakistan, there is a more or less formal caste system and even junior military officers will often never have cooked their own food, so it might represent a considerable loss of face for them to be asked to do so. Normal life for an LO may be far from solitary so they might never have been left on their own for very long. In that context, it's not unreasonable for an LO to expect a cook/companion to be employed who will be at base camp when the climbers are away on the mountain. A bit of consideration for the LO as a person will maximise their usefulness as a human resource.

During an approach march or with a catered base camp provided by an agent the agency staff are responsible for managing their resources but they are accountable to the team and issues should be tackled as they arise rather than left to fester. If food is not meeting expectations either in the cooking or quality then that needs to be discussed with the cook. I recall a team becoming restive about a ceaseless stream of bland curries but on taking it up with the cook learnt that he thought that was what we would want. As a result of that discussion he began to include more spices and diversified to include Chinese cuisine; everyone was happier.

I suppose one of the most important lessons that I've learnt from expeditions is to assume nothing. The location is likely to be remote and the cultural context very different from that of home. Rather than ignoring any potential problems they need to be sorted out at the earliest opportunity. This often involves making that extra effort to understand a point of view that is literally foreign to one's own. This is a particular responsibility of the climbing team: apart, perhaps, from an LO, cooks and porters are unlikely to raise issues because they see themselves as not having the authority. In some societies there is even a tendency for local people to want to please visitors so much that they will tell them what they think the visitors want to hear rather than

With one of the team at the top of the mast, another at the helm and others at the bow, navigating through ice was a real team effort in Antarctica.

disappoint them with the truth. On my first expedition to Peru we spent several days at the roadhead being told that pack animals would arrive '*mañana*' although the truth was that it would take several days to round them up.

Sensitivity to local feelings is appropriate too. No matter how interesting you find a "sky burial" in Tibetan or Nepali areas, don't be surprised if villagers take exception to you taking photographs of their relatives' bones.

In some areas there may be an expectation that the expedition will dispense medical care to local people. The team needs to be prepared to carry additional medical supplies if that is the case. However, great care needs to be taken in this area as locals can hoard drugs against a rainy day and nothing powerful should be given unless by a medically qualified person. Referring locals to their nearest clinic will avoid over-extending the resources of the team although that's not advisable, of course, in the case of a medical emergency.

Within the expedition team, as Shipton states in *Upon That Mountain*:

> One of the most acute problems of expedition life is the difficulty of preserving harmony amongst the members of the party… and the personal relations between the individual members of an expedition can, more than any other single factor, make or mar the success of the enterprise.

On most expeditions members of the team will suffer from stress of one type or another. Smythe comments on the effects of sleeplessness brought about by altitude on Everest:

> The most disagreeable effect of sleeplessness is a host of trivial yet worrying thoughts which are sometimes concentrated into fancied and absurd grievances. These in their turn are responsible for a deterioration of judgement and an upset of mental balance which can be a serious menace to the smooth working of an expedition. Such deterioration – 'bloody-mindedness' is cruder but more descriptive – is best countered by experience and knowledge of high-altitude conditions, for this helps to maintain a sense of proportion. Thus, instead of loathing the method by which your companion imbibes his soup, you merely tell yourself that your own method is probably just as disgusting to him. Once this idea is planted in the mind, it will never cease to bear the fruit of tolerance, sympathy and understanding.

I suspect there may be an element of irony in that last sentence.
Eric Shipton is also aware of these dangers:

> …every man should feel that he has an important part to play. Nothing is more conducive to bloody-mindedness than the feeling, even for a short time, that one is superfluous or redundant…. For this reason, the expedition should be divided as much as possible into small, self-contained units, each with its special task and responsibility.

I have already indicated that I think delegating responsibility for their own resources to tent teams simplifies the business of resource management as soon as the team becomes self-sufficient (usually above any catered base camp, if you have one). Each tent team will monitor its own fuel and food consumption, source its own supplies of water or snow to melt for water, and in the process inevitably check out, to a greater or lesser extent, how each person in that tent is getting on. Teams of two or three are usual since larger numbers create problems with the fair allocation of tent components when load carrying.

A roomy three-person tent can be useful to squeeze everyone in for full team meetings when necessary, although often meetings can take place outside. When meeting outside it may be that everyone is wearing sunglasses, or with impromptu meetings en route in poor weather they may be muffled and goggled. This will mean that cues as to how people are feeling through facial expression will be missing. In particular, research has shown that not being able to see people's eyes tends to undermine confidence in what they are saying. Being aware of that means that everyone should do more checking and allow more time for discussion, inviting comment from those who have been quiet. It is important to ensure that tent teams do not become isolated from one another and to respond to requests to mix and match partners when possible, always remembering that neither of a pair of tall team members sharing a larger tent may physically fit into some of the small ultra-lightweight tents that other pairs may have opted for.

If such a delegated approach is not adopted then there has to be delegated responsibility for monitoring food and fuel that may involve a dedicated member of

Squeezing into the biggest tent for a group meeting, Kyrgyzstan.

the team. As an extreme example, some members of British teams attempting Everest in the 1920s and 1930s were only there to manage supplies, transport or porters. Given the numbers involved, that shouldn't be surprising, but it's no argument for adopting such an approach today.

Enduring hardship is an inevitable part of expedition life and it can be a dour business. People can tend to shut down and retreat within themselves. Keeping communication channels open is crucial to the effective functioning of the team. A morning summary of what's planned for the day and an evening check on any issues arising is a baseline minimum, but everyone can monitor how things are going and there should be no impediments to raising issues in the course of the day. Taking a break for a sit down and a snack can be a useful means of keeping a team together; it's not easy to quarrel with someone who offers to share their trail mix with you. It can also be an opportunity to check with someone who might be having problems with boots or rucksack. Sometimes a tendency to want to keep up can mean that systems maintenance is ignored until a minor niggle has become a repetitive strain injury. People may have reservations about route or conditions but not raise them because of an unspoken peer group pressure: 'If everyone else is keeping going why should I feel concern?'

Recently, in December in the Canadian Rockies, my team was battling against a headwind that was reducing the temperature to something like minus 30°C. The leader called a halt to check navigation and I said, 'I'm beginning to doubt the wisdom of this.' Immediately others voiced their concerns. It was not that we were incapable of going on but that any accident, a crevasse fall for example, could rapidly escalate into a life-threatening situation. A broken leg in those conditions could be a death sentence. We turned back, but it took my comment to trigger the sharing of concern that led to that group decision.

The freedom to make such comments is essential to the group dynamic. There may well be disagreements and wherever possible these should be resolved by building consensus, letting people have a fair hearing and taking their views seriously. Ridicule, anger or personal attacks should never be part of the debate. Only if there is no time to build consensus or a consensus does not emerge after a discussion should a decision be put to a vote to avoid the "not in my name" situation arising when people basically don't support the democratic decision. In this context the leader acts very much as facilitator of the decision making process although as a kind of chairperson he or she may well have a casting vote.

There may also be occasions for swift action when no debate is possible and the leader needs to have the authority to make decisions and expect the team to follow his or her lead. That will always depend on the leader gaining the confidence of the team not by asserting their position as leader but by the way the expedition is run.

Eric Shipton had a great deal of experience both as a leader and as a member of an expedition team. He also had decided views on leadership:

In my opinion far too much emphasis has been laid on leadership in connection with mountaineering and exploratory expeditions, for this led to an exaggerated notion of the importance of the leader and the difficulty of his task. How often does one hear the word 'brilliant' applied in this connection, when in fact all that was called for was the exercise of a little tact and common sense? In ordinary mountaineering the man who has had most experience on the particular type of ground to be covered generally assumes tacit charge of the party: the more evenly experience and skill are distributed among the members, the less obvious is this assumption of charge. Anyone who tries to play the dictator in the lower valleys is likely to become very unpopular. As far as possible the same principle should be applied in the whole conduct of an expedition. A leader should make his position as inconspicuous as he can, and he should certainly avoid the appearance of taking his responsibilities too seriously. His primary task is the selection of his party. In the field his main function is to see that every man is placed in a position which gives him the widest scope for his particular job and for the use of his own initiative. Heavy military discipline, obviously necessary when vast armies are involved, is wholly out of place when dealing with a handful of carefully selected and thoroughly competent specialists. When it ceases to be laughable, it becomes intolerably irksome.

I suppose this is close to the Taoist view:

> The best of governors
> Is a rumour to his subjects.
> Next comes one they love and honour,
> Next one they fear,
> Next one they scorn.
> (When there is not enough faith
> There is a lack of good faith.)
> Tentative, he makes no snap decisions.
> When his work is done
> The people say,
> 'All this happened naturally.'

Two other factors contribute to a healthy group dynamic: informal monitoring of everyone in the team by everyone in the team and a willingness to do something about issues arising from such monitoring. That sounds incredibly formal. It's not. Basically, it's the foundation of what makes a good team player. It's a consideration for others that becomes part of the way people work with others. If team members have difficulty with this approach, they will need coaching and some of that may be by example. Even if there's a storm coming in and it would be much nicer to curl up in one's own tent, a good leader will go out and check that everyone is OK at the end of the day. That can be contagious but if anyone turns out to be immune then someone who stands the best chance of getting through needs to have words with that person; team playing again.

It's surprising how unreceptive some people can be. When sharing a tent with two other guys it gradually became noticeable that one of them was never around when any hard work was required. A team member from another tent diplomatically pointed out to him that the other two of us were working hard to build snow walls around the tent and perhaps he could help. 'Oh, I think they have it under control' was his reply before strolling off to chat to someone else. I had to have words with him but little changed so I never considered any further applications from him for subsequent expeditions.

But a team can be unaware of problems. There were plenty of opportunities for social interaction and the exercise of group responsibilities crewing a yacht sailing to Antarctica. However, two members of the team who had never met before until they flew in to Ushuaia ended up sharing a tent and managed to use up three days' fuel supplies on the first night. To recoup their losses, they ate cold food and had cold drinks for a day or two before the rest of the team realised what was going on. We had assumed from their expedition applications that they were experienced snow campers but neither had ever really managed a stove properly. They were not removing the condensation resulting from adding too much snow to the water in the pot so the heat was simply evaporating that condensation and, of course, cooling rather than heating the water by that evaporation. To compound that, they were putting the pan down

Teamwork solving an equipment problem, Antarctica.

on the snow, further cooling it and finding snow sticking to the outside of it together with the condensation. We only worked out what was going on when one of the pair was questioned about why he was spending so much time in another team's tent. The two unfortunates had to have a crash course in stove management and cadged hot water from other tents until they had made good their losses. It solved the problem but meant that we all had to take some of that pressure on our fuel supplies. If no one had noticed they could have been in serious trouble with dehydration.

Monitoring health is obviously the most important consideration for any expedition. Frank Smythe comments, 'Sore throats, coughs and "'tummy troubles" are tremendous hindrances to climbing at high altitudes. The foul dust we had breathed for weeks on the march, combined with the cold, dry air and the necessity for breathing quickly through the mouth, had wreaked havoc on the membranes of our throats.' And, 'The intensely dry air and the hot sun were already ravaging our countenances. My lower lip had cracked so badly that I was careful to avoid hot condiments and food.' Later, 'My heart and lungs might be acclimatised to 17,700 feet, but not so my digestion. We had curry for dinner and it gave me hell.' He is acutely aware of how other team members are doing and when they need to go down to recover. The seriousness is emphasised when one of the Sherpa porters tries to tough it out and ends up in a coma being given oxygen. Modern medication can deal with illness much more successfully today than in the 1930s, but if symptoms are ignored there can still be deaths from altitude sickness and as antibiotic resistance increases we don't know how long that success will continue.

Much of this chapter has concentrated on managing the team but there are also factors related to the environment. Most climbers and skiers will be used to assessing snow quality and its effects on progress but in remote settings there may be other factors. Wildlife is one and has featured in the equipment section earlier. I've seen bear tracks in the snow in Nepal and Canada and snow leopard tracks in Kyrgyzstan, but if all your experience has been in areas where there are no potential problems with wildlife it may take a deliberate conscious effort to appreciate the risks in areas of North America for example.

On an expedition to Mount Logan, Anna was so anxious to avoid meeting a bear that she and George spent most of their time bashing pots with spoons whenever they left the road, yet they were the only ones to see a bear, fortunately always beating a retreat, before we flew in to the mountain. The rest of the team were quite disappointed so, after we had descended, when a bear sauntered along the lake shore not far from our camp, we all set off after it with our cameras. It ran and we chased. It stopped and we realised that chasing after it might not have been such a good idea. We did get a few pictures but none were close-ups!

More scarily, we came down from a traverse of the Coast range in Canada from Bute Inlet to Knight Inlet just at the time when bears were waking from hibernation. At our last camp on the snow we dis-covered bear tracks. When the snow ran out there was an opportunity to sample British Columbia's world-class bushwhacking. Temperate rain forest is particularly dense. In one area we counted ourselves lucky to

Improvising a bear alarm at the camp perimeter, Canada.

find tunnels forced through the bush until increasingly fresh bear scat not only testified to the creators of the tunnels but also made us question the nature of our luck. Fortunately, we never came face to face with a grizzly but the thought was pretty daunting as we didn't have any bear spray. We made a lot of noise!

It is important to be prepared and avoid confrontations with animals that could lead to tragedies. Planning routes and assessing situations to do so should be part of contingency planning. In Greenland we had planned to travel along valleys running more or less parallel to the coast, camping on the sea ice in fjords where these intersected with our route. According to our research, at that time of year polar bears would be miles out on the sea ice where there was open water in which they could hunt seals. Then we learnt that if hunting was bad at sea the bears would come inland to hunt musk ox, using the fjords as highways to the interior. We camped higher up the valleys and kept a keen lookout while crossing the fjords. A bear with cubs, for example, is going to be acutely sensitive to any perceived threat to those cubs. If one is sighted then the family should be given a very wide berth.

Human beings are not used to considering themselves as food for other animals and some of us may find that a hard concept to grasp and/or suffer a very emotional reaction if we have to do so in the field. Most animals will prefer flight to fight since there's less risk of damage and more chance of survival but we should always remember that it is their land and we who are the intruders. Real respect for wildlife means considering the interests of our fellow creatures. Burying rubbish in snow pits may seem to be removing the signs of our passage but that snow may thaw in summer sunshine to leave plastic blowing about the glaciers and moraines for animals to choke on. Carry it out.

I suppose all the strategies outlined above are in the end an attempt to provide a framework to deal with the unexpected. But even when the leader exercises good leadership and the team exercise their skills as good team players it is always as well to expect the unexpected.

Chapter 9: Reporting

On a ski expedition to Kyrgyzstan my team had left the roadhead and skinned across a frozen lake to set up camp just below the snout of one of the main glaciers in the Ak-Shirak range. Later that afternoon we were surprised to see a pair of skiers following our tracks across lake; this was a remote area and on a previous visit no other people had been seen in the mountains. I waved, but gave them time to set up their camp a short distance away before I went over. They were Netherlanders who had read the report that I'd written for the Mount Everest Foundation (MEF) which is a condition of grant aid by that organisation. Standing on the snowy moraine, we had one of those awkward conversations about intentions, trying to work out if we were going to be in competition. Fortunately, they were heading up a different branch of the glacier so we parted amicably enough, having exchanged email addresses.

That was the last I saw of them, but much later I emailed from home to find out what they had done. The response was that they didn't bother recording any of their first ascents, they just left a cairn and liked the idea of someone else reaching the summit and finding it. No information was forthcoming, partly because they were self-funding so had to provide nothing for any sponsor, but partly, I got the impression, because they just couldn't be bothered. However, if I hadn't recorded the first expedition they wouldn't have been there. How many more have followed I just don't know but the area is home to snow leopards and wolves that would probably not respond well to the disturbance of their habitat so there are more than purely selfish issues to consider about putting such information in the public domain.

Local people, however, might welcome an increase in visiting tourists whose spending could be a useful additional income. On another occasion I encountered a group who were hoping to see snow leopards, led by a local hunter who had realised there was more money in preserving the snow leopards for visitors than selling their skins.

Reporting at its best includes an element of review so that lessons learnt during the expedition can avoid repeating mistakes in future expeditions. Perhaps a certain tent had particular drawbacks, certain brands of freeze-dried foods turned out to be tastier than others, or certain stoves failed when others continued to function. Perhaps individuals responded differently to altitude or to medication for "tummy upsets". All members can contribute to such a review and leave the expedition with their stake in it reinforced and perhaps an appetite to return on another.

The Netherlanders camping on the glacier lake shore after learning about the Ak-Shirak range from a report I had written about Kyrgyzstan.

The reports I have prepared for the MEF certainly recorded the expeditions and were supported with a view to providing enough information for subsequent visitors to visit the areas with less trouble and to be aware of what had been done so far. No one wants to be in the position of the team who claimed to be making the first winter crossing of Iceland simply because they hadn't done enough research to know that it had been done more than once already! On the other hand, it can be particularly galling to find that another team is a week ahead of you on the mountain for which you have secured grant aid (while they haven't) and are planning to climb one of two possible routes that you were intending to climb and had noted, in perhaps too much detail, in your report of an attempt the previous year. In the end though, a good detailed report for the MEF at least means that subsequent applications for grant aid will be taken seriously.

Other reporting may be a commitment to sponsors who might have particular requirements for photos that they can use in marketing campaigns for their products or more general publicity through exposure on their website, or wanted you to field-test their products. Clubs can be prepared to support their members' expeditions but will usually expect at least an article for the club newsletter and/or a lecture about the expedition that might be delivered at the Christmas dinner or AGM. The Austrian Alpine Club, Alpine Club and Eagle Ski Club are just three that run programmes of local lectures in different regions so lectures may have to be repeated according to demand. These needn't be onerous if it's recognised that one picture is worth a lot of words!

The idea of making a film of the expedition is often floated, by sponsors in particular. It's worth weighing up the pros and cons very carefully. I first encountered a

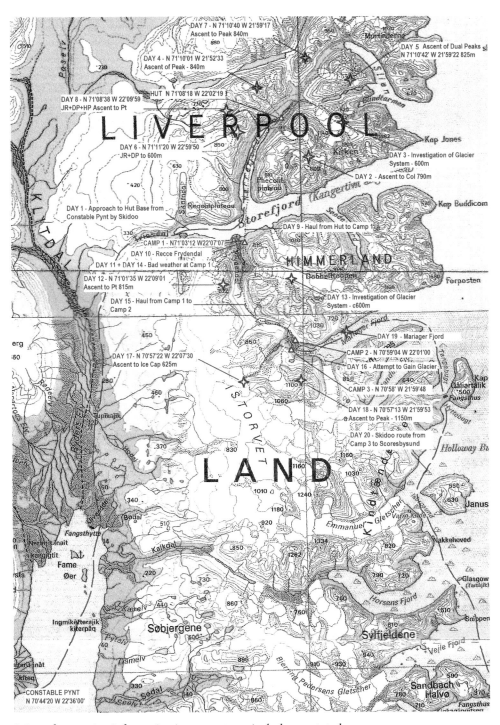

Ways of presenting information in a report can include annotated maps like this one from Howard Pollit relating to our Greenland expedition.

film-making enterprise when I was invited to join an expedition to ski the highest ski peak in the world. The guy in charge of the filming had very definite ideas of what he wanted, which tended to take over plans for particular days. Filming the crossing of a glacial torrent had to be done in the late afternoon when it was at its most torrential, not early morning when it was easy (and when it was mostly crossed!) Other film clips had to be shot when the light was at its best, which might not be at a time of day when anyone would normally be in that position on the mountain. On one occasion I found him well away from the actual route filming one of the team making spectacular jumps over a crevasse. We had some debate about whether the resulting film would actually be misrepresenting the climb. I go on expeditions to make contact with a reality beyond the artificiality that influences so much of our lives back home, not to construct a virtual reality that conforms to the expectations of sponsors or vicarious thrill tourists. Needless to say, I did not appear in the film!

On a later occasion I tried to make a film about a Greenland expedition that I also led. The demands of trying to perform both roles effectively were extraordinarily stressful. A good place to film could place me at a point where I was unable to catch up with decision-making on the ground or offer support to anyone having difficulties. Then again route-finding might place me in exactly the wrong position regarding the light for filming. I succeeded in making a film, however amateurish, but would never try to combine those roles again.

Having a clear idea of the audience is important for filming. The idea of taking a film to a festival like Kendal or Banff actually shapes the kind of film you can make: festivals won't show long films by newbie film-makers. The pressure to make short films for festivals or competitions, like those run by the BMC, also poses an artistic problem. Too often complex issues are oversimplified because there just isn't the time available to explore subtlety.

Even longer films can run this risk. Andy Kirkpatrick is right to say that the *Psycho Vertical* film is Jen Randall's film and to note the lack of humour when humour forms an integral part of Andy's life and is embedded in the way that most climbers respond to the risks they take. There's an undeniable truth to the film but it's a partial truth that never encompasses the whole man.

Whatever the form of reporting of the expedition there should always be a responsibility to accuracy and some thought given to the effects on those whose lives may be impacted upon as a result of the report.

Keeping a journal is much more comfortable on a yacht in Antarctica but has more distractions than a tent.

Chapter 10: Health issues

1. Acclimatisation

Acute Mountain Sickness (AMS) can begin to affect some people as low as 2000m with symptoms including irritability, headache, dizziness and nausea. As height is gained atmospheric pressure is reduced which makes it harder for your lungs to obtain the oxygen your body needs to operate at cellular level. Short term your body will adapt by increasing the rate and depth of your breathing and increasing your heart rate, which won't feel pleasant. Long term the body will increase red blood cell production although this brings associated problems with thickening of the blood and may result in circulation problems, particularly where a pre-existing condition exists: most deaths in the Alps are due to heart attacks happening too far from help. Left untreated, AMS can develop into High Altitude Pulmonary Edema (HAPE) affecting the lungs, or High Altitude Cerebral Edema (HACE) affecting the brain, both of which can be fatal. Treatment is simple: reduce or reverse your rate of ascent. Acetozolamide (Diamox) and other drugs can treat the symptoms *in extremis* but dependency on the drug to allow continued ascent can create its own problems.

To avoid AMS it is necessary to gain height gradually. In the Alps valley bases are usually around 1000m so training walks to 2000m fulfil the "climb high sleep low" formula and can be followed by training climbs on peaks around 3000m from huts around 2000m before setting out from huts around 3000m for peaks of 4000m. Such acclimatisation enables your body to cope with the demands of altitude and to recognise those demands and respond more efficiently in future. Even then it's likely that your performance will be inferior to what you would expect at below 2000m so it's worth adjusting your ambitions accordingly.

The situation can be more complicated regarding expeditions because the altitudes involved can be greater, much greater. Do the maths; an 8000m peak is double the height of the majority of Alpine peaks. In the Himalaya, historically, a long trek in from a valley base could allow acclimatisation to take place gradually and naturally. This is still possible, but I can remember in India Harish Kapardia stopping the vehicle in which we were travelling. Just off the road was a monument dedicated to Jim Corbett's shooting of a man-eating leopard on that spot. Roads have been driven through what was jungle, up increasingly remote valleys and over passes as high as 5000m as the population has increased and primeval forest has been cleared for farming. Given the traffic nowadays, a trek along such roads would be a profoundly unattractive prospect.

Flying into La Paz in Bolivia puts incoming mountaineers immediately at 3650m and the effects can be dire. Lima in Peru may be more or less at sea level but the long coach journey to a mountain centre like Huaraz is no preparation for the altitude of 3000m. The same applies to days spent cooped up in a Landcruiser travelling from Chengdu to northern Szechuan. You may be spending time at altitude but an almost complete lack of exercise in the process simply doesn't permit acclimatisation to occur.

It is important to recognise the problem of travel to instant altitude and take sufficient time after arrival to rest and adapt gradually to the height. AMS symptoms can be controlled by Diamox but it's not a good idea to become dependent on the drug instead of allowing your body to acclimatise naturally.

For many people who earn enough to be able to afford to participate in an expedition, workplace constraints on time may apply. As the business world has become increasingly competitive employers have become more inflexible. Extended leave without pay is no longer the option that it was and even the self-employed cannot absent themselves from their work programme for too long without the risk of losing clients to competitors. Two weeks' leave may be all that people can manage.

For those who are "cash rich, time poor", there are expedition destinations that offer fine adventures without going to any great altitude; the polar regions are the most obvious, with Alaska, Greenland and Baffin Island providing some suitable objectives. In my view that is preferable to dosing oneself with drugs such as Diamox. I know many competitive athletes have disgraced themselves proving that drugs can enhance performance but once you start messing about with your metabolism in a potentially hostile environment who knows where it will end? There's also a double standard being applied by those who resort to drugs: if drugs are cheating, in athletics for example, then surely it's cheating to climb a mountain by using drugs.

Many climbers at the higher altitudes accessed by expeditions will experience symptoms of AMS in the process of acclimatisation but even when apparently acclimatised the body can succumb to pulmonary or cerebral oedema surprisingly quickly. Tablets of nifedipine, for pulmonary oedema, and Dexamethasone, for cerebral oedema, should be routinely carried by all at high altitudes in order to have the drugs to hand to address these problems promptly in oneself or one's climbing partners. And don't leave it too late; collapse due to cerebral oedema can result in the loss of the swallowing reflex so that Dexamethasone can only be administered by injection and you may not be carrying the necessary equipment.

Of course, everyone is different. Some will acclimatise quickly but find they have an altitude ceiling above which they don't function very well. Others take more time to acclimatise but then go well at increasing altitude. You just have to listen to what your body is telling you and, as always, err on the side of caution.

2. Dehydration

Lower humidity and the increased breathing rate at altitude causes you to lose more moisture with exhalation than you would at lower levels. This can lead to dehydration which can trigger AMS or produce very similar symptoms. The problems associated with thickening of the blood owing to increased red blood cell production are also linked to dehydration. You need to compensate by drinking more.

That's fair enough but the Hydrate or Die! slogan seems to be trying to make a fortune out of frightening people and it's wrong. The case of a marathon runner who collapsed and died with ridiculously low sodium levels in his system makes it clear that hydration can be taken too far. I have a labelled water bottle that confidently asserts that I need 500ml per hour when climbing. For a twelve-hour route that is six litres of water; six kilos of additional weight! If I carried that lot I'd never get up anything. Early experiments on Everest established that at altitude the body requires a minimum of three litres of water per day to operate. I've climbed 7000m peaks and never carried more than one litre of water but made sure I drank at least a further litre at both the morning and evening camps. Of course, it's necessary to have a bottle that you can check easily in order to ration your water, so hydration bladders can be a problem even if you escape their inconvenient habit of leaking into your rucksack. I've also climbed with Russians who carry no water at all at high altitude because they reckon it just gets pissed straight out. They seem to pace themselves to avoid water loss through panting and sweating and to make sure they are fully acclimatised before making a summit bid.

You will know you're dehydrated if you've stopped urinating or your urine is dark yellow. Back at base camp you can easily rehydrate until your urine is clear and copious. Avoid alcohol and caffeine-based drinks including energy drinks, tea and coffee that act as diuretics. There is some evidence that small amounts of complex carbohydrate additives in water may help rehydration. Certainly, after a lot of sweating it's a good idea to replace lost electrolyte salts. Bananas are a good way of topping up electrolytes but don't travel well so stick to the dried flakes and drink plenty with them. Maintaining hydration is one of the best ways of preventing altitude illness and it is far easier to prevent AMS than to treat it once it has happened.

3. Sun damage

At higher altitudes a thinner atmosphere filters less ultra-violet radiation. With every 1000m increase in altitude UV levels increase by about ten per cent. Exercise in strong sunshine can increase the effects of dehydration and damage skin and eyes. Early alpinists wore veils or smeared grease on their faces to protect their skin. Light-coloured wicking clothing can protect the skin and reduce sweating but any exposed skin should be protected by sun-block to avoid sunburn and potential skin cancer. It's not just that you don't want a nose that looks as if it's had a close encounter with a blow-torch; melanoma can kill. If you develop any unusual raised moles when you return home check them out with your doctor ASAP.

Rescue helicopter arriving at King Col, Mount Logan, Canada. Casualties suffering from cerebral oedema and slipped disc."

Eyes also need protection from ultra-violet light which can cause snow-blindness even in cloudy conditions and accelerates cataract development. Sunglasses should be a hundred per cent effective in blocking UVA and UVB radiation. Glacier glasses with leather side attachments or sports glasses with a wraparound style will also prevent reflected light reaching the eye from the side. Polycarbonate lenses of 3mm thickness are recommended as they are highly impact and shatter resistant.

4. Cold damage

High mountains involve lower temperatures which decrease at a rate of between 5 and 10°C per 1000m of ascent, depending on moisture (i.e. dry air gets colder than moist air). High mountains are also more likely to be exposed to strong winds, producing a wind-chill factor that becomes more severe the lower the air temperature and the stronger the wind. Look up the National Weather Service Wind Chill Chart (https://www.weather. gov/safety/cold-wind-chill-chart) for more details.

Frostbite damages the extremities: fingers, toes, ears and face. The body reacts to cold by constricting blood vessels in the extremities in order to retain heat and to warm blood in the essential body core. Cooling of the extremities as a result can then cause tissue to freeze or become starved of oxygen. In extreme cases tissue dies and may have to be surgically removed to prevent infection and potential gangrene. Symptoms are progressive, beginning with pain and numbness (frostnip), continuing with a white waxy appearance to the affected areas, finally resulting in a hard, frozen feel to underlying tissue with a very white or blueish tinge to the skin that may turn black if exposure to cold continues. Deep frostbite may include damage to bones or tendons and requires professional medical attention.

Frostbite has occurred when winter climbing in Snowdonia as well as in the greater ranges, so symptoms should never be ignored. Warming the body core can gradually reverse the process of shutting down circulation to the extremities, but rewarming the extremities should never be undertaken if there is a danger of them refreezing and causing more damage. It may also be less damaging and painful to walk out of the situation on frozen feet than it is on rewarmed feet. When the patient can continue to be kept warm, affected areas can be rewarmed with warm, not hot, water, although they may need painkillers to cope with the

Seasickness is a grim business.

consequent severe "hot aches". Even with severe frostbite there is no hurry to amputate; antibiotics being the preferred option. Rather than undergo amputation under third world conditions it will usually be better to get home and consult a specialist.

Sometimes the appearance of frostbite can seem more serious than it is in reality as in the case of two of my team who summited Mount Elbrus in a very strong cold wind, returning with black skin on their noses and cheekbones: within a few days the dead layer had peeled off, leaving sensitive pink skin behind but no lasting damage. Numbness can last for some time without becoming serious and there are cases of climbers, months after the event, suddenly suffering an attack of "hot aches" in a frost-nipped toe while dozing in front of a roaring fire. On the other hand, long-term sufferers of frostbite have complained of continuing sensitivity to cold, impaired sense of touch, persistent numbness and/or pain in the affected parts.

An irritating condition resulting from cold is cracking of the skin, particularly around the nails of the hands. Splits in the skin can extend into small wounds that bleed persistently and seem to refuse to heal. A simple plaster may help but can be easily lost in the course of a day's work on snow. A Scottish lass put me on to Snowfire, which usually needs to be ordered from a pharmacy south of the border and is a remarkable balm that not only halts cracking but also fosters healing of the cracks.

Hypothermia is when the body core temperature drops from a normal 37°C to below 35°C. Symptoms develop progressively from shivering, goose bumps and numbness, through intense shivering, lack of co-ordination, sluggishness, violent shivering, difficulty speaking, mental confusion and stumbling, to slurred speech, difficulty seeing and finally unconsciousness and death.

Exercising in cold conditions requires conscious and careful thermoregulation to avoid hypothermia. Exercise generates heat which can stimulate sweating to cool the body but it's a delicate balance to prevent over-heating or over-cooling. Wet clothing significantly increases heat loss so wicking base layers and removing or adding insulating layers are ways of managing efficient thermoregulation. However, it's worth monitoring yourself and your climbing partners for symptoms of hypothermia to be sure you haven't made any mistakes. If the body core loses more heat than exercise can generate to compensate, the increased blood flow involved in exercise can continue to cool the body to a hypothermic level, while you may still feel you are just "running cool". Monitoring is made more difficult by the likelihood that hypothermia may involve mental confusion. Personally, I've found that slurring my speech has been the warning sign I have to recognise. On Chimborazo I was breaking trail through thigh-deep snow, finding it hard work but not feeling worried until I turned to talk to my climbing partner and couldn't get my words out. We turned around.

Dehydration affects the body's capacity to regulate temperature yet cold drinks can be unacceptable so a flask of hot sweet juice can be effective both in maintaining hydration and blood sugar levels as well as directly adding warmth to the body core. A hot drink can rapidly reverse the effects of hypothermia but, despite the legends of St. Bernard dogs with brandy barrels attached to their collars, alcohol can be a killer since it may dilate the capillaries and increase heat loss from the skin.

Treatment of the hypothermia victim is simple in theory but more difficult in a hostile environment: warm them. Having spare, warm clothing can make all the difference to a hypothermia victim. Techniques include, drying the victim, re-insulation with dry insulation, insulation from ground cold, covering and protecting head, hands and feet from further heat loss, feeding warm sweet drinks if conscious and, if unconscious, evacuation with very careful handling. Surrounding the victim with a windproof and waterproof layer like a bivvi bag or bothy bag can create a warmer micro-climate and placing another person or persons in there with them can significantly raise the temperature. If there is no sign of breathing or pulse and the victim is cyanotic, CPR should be added to rewarming. Remember: 'They are not dead until they are warm and dead.'

What follows is a note on heat loss from the head in this context since various myths and debunkings have rather muddied the waters. At rest the head loses about seven per cent of total body heat loss but when exercise begins the increased cardiac demand increases blood flow to the brain and heat loss also increases to about fifty per cent of the total. As vasodilation responds to the demands of the muscles for more blood flow, the flow to the brain proportionately decreases and heat loss from the head reduces to about ten per cent. However, a hypothermia victim who is shivering is exercising without any vasodilation so the heat loss from the head is back up to around fifty per cent of total body heat loss and consequently needs to be reduced by insulation; get out a woolly hat!

5. Carbon monoxide poisoning

This has been referred to earlier in considering fuel and stove choices but it is worth repeating the warnings. The British Antarctic Survey was so concerned about the danger to their personnel that they funded research into this problem which revealed the additional levels of carbon monoxide production resulting from the use of stoves with heat exchangers. A hanging stove used inside a tent may well overcome the problems of wind and weather that could make cooking outside impossible but vigilance is always necessary to ensure that there is sufficient ventilation bearing in mind that the effects of CO poisoning may well be dulling the senses and confusing the judgement of those affected. It remains the nearest that I have come to death.

6. Arthritis

The oldest remains of a mountaineer are those of Ötzi, the 5000-year-old ice-preserved body that emerged from the Similaun Glacier in 1991 and redefined the dating of the use of Copper in Europe; he was carrying a beautifully made copper axe. Ötzi's joints show evidence of arthritis, and skin tattoos in the region of those joints suggest that tattooing may have been a form of treatment. Our bodies do their best to heal joint damage but joints do wear out and high levels of use, such as in mountaineering and in particular carrying the large loads involved in expeditions, contribute to that. Cold conditions may also make a contribution.

The use of trekking poles cannot be recommended too highly to help avoid impact damage that can lead to arthritis. It is a source of considerable regret to me that such information was not available when I began mountaineering and indeed not widely known well into my mountaineering career. I can recall making long descents to the valley with a heavy rucksack full of climbing gear, wearing boots with little in the way of cushioning, having missed or been unable to afford any cable car that might have been available, and racing to get down before full darkness. That was a forlorn hope sometimes, but on many occasions I remember my knees were hot from the activity. I'm now unable to run without pain.

On the plus side, remaining active can reduce the pain of arthritis and increase joint mobility, even for those whose joints are more damaged than more sedentary sufferers. There is no cure but there is some evidence of the benefits of taking glucosamine sulphate and cod liver oil tablets. Joint replacement can also extend active mountaineering.

A lot of old climbers are hard of hearing and we've all experienced that deep chill in the ear in bitter winds, so it's worth protecting the ears with a headband to avoid any chance of arthritis of the bones of the inner ear.

7. Diet and hygiene

There is a lot of information and a wide range of specialist products that will provide for nutritional needs on an expedition. Some of that information may seem confusing or simply an attempt to sell a particular product. While some expeditions may have base camps complete with more or less "normal food" others may be entirely self-sufficient and involve extended periods away from such supplies. It's possible to tolerate a calorie deficiency for extended periods by accessing the body's reserves. You will lose weight but even the thinnest of climbers has enough reserves to survive for about three weeks without food whereas we are unlikely to survive more than three days without water (and no more than three minutes without oxygen, to complete the "rule of threes"). To avoid overloading yourself with food it's only necessary to supply enough calories to enable your body to access its reserves. Those reserves can then always be topped up when you return home. The trick is to make sure you have enough reserves and that the period of calorie deficiency is not too extended.

We used to carry high-sugar rations and I remember evaluating the difficulty of a route by the number of chocolate bars consumed while climbing it. Today we know more about nutrition and are aware that sugar concentrates are likely to raise blood sugar levels too high too fast. A sugar spike stimulates insulin production which can then reduce the blood sugar level to a point lower than it was before the sugar was ingested. That may account for some of the sudden mood swings that have been experienced in teams of climbers. The way to avoid a sugar spike is to include fibre in the input which spreads the burn and avoids stimulating insulin production. Blood sugar rises more slowly over a longer period to less extreme levels. Flapjacks don't

Iona, Dave and Howard, the day after the close call with CO poisoning, keeping cheerful in a snowstorm on the top of Friendship Peak in Mongolia and still determined to ski off it.

freeze solid and fulfil the role of hill rations more effectively for me now than my past dependency on chocolate bars. Complex carbohydrates and sugars in gel form of the type used by endurance trail runners may also have their place as weight-saving snacks if you can stomach them (best test drive a few!)

Being away for weeks rather than days means that the normally varied diet one would expect at home is limited by the harsh nature of the environment. Fresh fruit and vegetables may be non-existent so vitamin and mineral supplements may need to be taken. Severe cramp can result from a day of hard work with inadequate replacement of salts sweated out in the process. Again, supplements of salts may be necessary.

Despite all the thought put in to dietary requirements, reading over my journals has revealed the inevitability of stomach upsets. I don't think there's a trip where no one suffered. Hygiene is always an issue, especially when water for washing is in short supply and having "the shits" can be extremely debilitating. Wind can blow contaminated material around a campsite and bacteria can "hibernate" for years in snow to be reactivated when that snow is melted for drinking water. Be particularly careful about regularly used campsites, especially on snow. Bacteria may well not be killed even though the water appears to have boiled because of the lower temperatures of boiling point at altitude. A good rolling boil and sterilising pills or procedures should deal with the problem, but only if it's recognised and at a catered base camp where the fate of the whole team is in the hands of the cook!

8.Mental health

Climbing can be a stressful activity, both bodily and mentally. The mind is continually required to assess risk in what can be considered a hostile environment. There are also the strains that such stress can put upon a climbing relationship: you or your partner may react in ways that are difficult to anticipate under pressure of circumstances. And expeditions extend the time spent with one's climbing partners in a hostile environment far beyond the lengths of time experienced in an Alpine season. Surviving depends as much on keeping one's mental balance as on keeping the more obvious physical balance. DON'T PANIC. When difficulties are encountered it may be necessary to react quickly but there will also be times when a hasty response can cause as many problems as it solves. I recall Gordon Nuttall's experience with a ski-tourer whose wife fell into a crevasse. The man kicked out of his skis and rushed back to the crevasse screaming her name. Unfortunately, he failed to assess the stability of the crevasse edge and pitched in after her. Both died before they could be rescued.

Familiarity with the proposed line of your route can help anticipate where problems may arise, and sensitivity to your surroundings will mean fewer unpleasant surprises than plodding along in a world of your own, listening to a podcast. Snow conditions change during the course of a day as can the quality of the rock being climbed, and a seemingly simple snow ridge may hide lethal cornices. Respect any uneasiness you may have about your situation: your unconscious mind may be registering things your conscious mind has missed.

Self-awareness is also important. Not only how tired or irritated you may have become but also whether attitudes to risk have become modified by your drive to succeed. Summit fever is catching, but there are other heuristic traps for the mind that may be just as dangerous. Just because you chose the route does not mean that you have to stick with it if a better prospect looks possible. Getting away with crossing a doubtful snow slope on one occasion doesn't mean you'll get away with it on another. Keep checking yourself and your partner for any oddness about your thinking. When in doubt stop, take stock, talk over the situation.

When I was climbing a steep snow slope in Mongolia in full sun, I discovered there was no resistance to the insertion of my ice axe shaft for its full depth. Below there was no safe run-out apart from a drop over a cliff: I called a halt. Derek and John, both experienced alpinists and ahead of me on the rope, then admitted that they also had doubts about the slope's safety so we decided to retreat. Until I stopped all three of us had kept our doubts to ourselves perhaps in response to an unvoiced peer group pressure and/or an excessive focus on the objective, both potentially lethal heuristic traps.

On another occasion in the Caucasus an avalanche swept across the line of the route ahead of us that my team was ascending on ski. Careful examination of the track of the avalanche, once the air cleared, revealed that it had been powder snow filling the very cold air. Only a dusting of snow was actually deposited so the team was reassured enough to continue without anxiety, checking all the time of course.

Rest has an important place in expedition climbing. After two or three days of climbing, a day or two of relaxing and catching up on sleep pays dividends for the next outing. There's also a question of balance here. Expeditions are not only about gaining summits but also about experiencing the picturesque valleys, hot springs and yak or llama pastures. Frank Smythe's *The Valley of the Flowers* is a moving testament to this. Many climbers have agreed with Ruskin that the best views of many mountains are from the valleys and such diversity itself is a source of recuperation as much for the mind as the body.

Recovering from a dislocated shoulder in the Caucasus.

Part Two: Case studies

I've tried to illustrate some of the points made in Part One with brief anecdotes. However, there's no doubt that I learnt multiple lessons from certain key expeditions and it was the context which was often important so I have decided to include several case studies that provide those perspectives. There are certain issues that are emphasised but many additional insights into tangential issues which may be considered useful. All the expeditions described were valuable learning experiences and enjoyable both for the climbing and for the opportunities they provided to encounter new places and people. That's important to remember when what is described may seem to imply criticism of individuals.

Where possible I have quoted people's own words to describe the problems they experienced, taken from the reports of the expeditions, and to avoid any tendency to personalise those problems I have supplied the minimum of personal detail, including the use of first names only. I can only add that I don't believe anyone deliberately caused problems and where matters could have been better managed, people showed a willingness to learn from that experience as I did myself.

1. Communications issues in Peru and Pakistan

Peru, Cordillera Central

A chance meeting at Waters Cottage, an FRCC hut in Kinlochleven, resulted in an invitation: would Pam, my partner, and I like to join an expedition to Peru led by fellow Fell & Rocker, Paul, for the following summer? It was to be our first, full-on, MEF-supported expedition.

Paul had discovered an area of the Cordillera Central that had never been visited by a British expedition and its highest peak, Ticlla, was a respectable 5897m. He had compiled an impressive folder of documentation including maps and travel details since the area had not been visited by any non-locals since a Spanish expedition 35 years earlier. There was a reason for that; the Shining Path Maoist insurgency. Peru's president, Fujimori, had succeeded in a campaign against the rebels which culminated in the capture of their leader and the re-establishment of government control of areas like the one that we were visiting. We had been warned that there were still security issues in Peru but that the situation was much more stable.

Flying into Lima we transferred immediately to a quiet suburban *pension* in Miraflores, an area with little street crime, where the whole team gathered. From there we planned to take a Cruz del Sur bus to Huancayo, but our arrival coincided with a national holiday that Paul's research had somehow missed; seats were scarce and we had to travel in two groups of four, two days apart. Not a good start. The bus station was a crowded, confusing place and the team's Spanish speaker had left with the first busload. We had been warned about the bus station being dangerous and our worst fears seemed to be realised when amid the noise and stink of diesel, a van rolled up and four men sprang out brandishing pistols. Were we about to be caught in crossfire? It turned out that the firearms were to defend whatever was contained in the boxes, which they transferred to a waiting bus and then stood guard over. It was a salutary reminder that we were operating in a very different social context.

The journey was uneventful except for a long delay while passports were examined at a checkpoint; we never found out why. The landscape was also very different from anything we had seen before. Unrelentingly arid, there were places in the dusty hills where it seemed truckloads of powdered poster paints had been randomly spilt across valleys and ridges; colourful metallic compounds were being leached out of the rocks and soil. Wildlife was thin on the ground but that was hardly surprising given the size of our bus roaring down the road, although near a remote brackish *laguna* we surprised a small group of very woolly llamas.

In Huancayo, despite the holiday crowds, we eventually managed to secure a bus to transport the whole team, our equipment and multiplying amounts of supplies, to the village at the roadhead, also confusingly named Miraflores.

Life was slow-paced at Miraflores village and we spent a couple of days carrying loads to a campsite about three hours' walk from the village before burros actually turned up to carry the rest of the kit for the simple reason that we didn't seem to be able to get through to the locals. They nodded an understanding of our requests but the burros would always be arriving *mañana*. Paul reckoned it was appealing to the women that finally cracked the problem, although perhaps the men became suspicious of him repeatedly accosting their wives and girlfriends and decided to get us out of the village ASAP!

Meanwhile, we discovered that the people were kind, helpful and honest while the children were keen to pick up a few words of the language spoken by these strange foreigners. I remember one evening tracking down the haunting sound of Andean pan pipes to a solitary lad on a street corner making music entirely for his own pleasure in the dusk. High above, the mountains were still alight with the last rays of the setting

A view of Ticlla, centre and Nevado Padrecaca right of the figure, Peru.

sun. Although the village was at 3700m, the depth of this valley meant the villagers never actually saw a sunset. Even at base camp, at 4390m, the surrounding rock walls continued to deprive us of the sight.

Once established at base camp the teams set about acquiring some acclimatisation by walking up easy peaks and cols. Our significant ascents were all to be over 5000m. It became clear that we were a loose association of climbing pairs that might or might not end up on the same route together depending on rather piecemeal exchanges of ideas about objectives. In some ways that accelerated our exploration of the surrounding mountains since we often headed off in different directions and were able to compare what we had seen with our somewhat out-of-date maps on return.

The team rapidly concluded that the glaciated terrain marked on the old maps had dramatically retreated. One team, fully equipped for ice climbing, found nothing but a 10m step in a remnant glacier to amuse themselves on a training peak, although the resulting instability of the rock was anything but amusing. Most ascents of these lower peaks were no more than loose scrambles, although one team was to turn back from a ridge they were climbing when it seemed as though it might collapse under them. Only on the higher peaks and the south faces was there enough snow and ice remaining to offer more solid climbing. That was another re-orientation; in the southern hemisphere it is the south faces that are cold.

Droving trails ran over cols and into adjacent glaciated valleys, very reminiscent of Scottish glens complete with ribbon lochs and blunt rock outcrops. Higher slopes tended to be composed of a jumble of broken rock and screes where the ice had retreated. We had to remind ourselves that we were a long way from a hospital so an accident could mean the end of the expedition, but we all experienced enough mileage and altitude to be ready to look for objectives that required more real climbing.

We needed a proper training peak before tackling Ticlla and there had seemed to be an interesting face and ridge route on the south side of Nevado Padrecaca, 5362m. Pam and I joined forces with Stuart and Ken "Grande" to carry kit over a pass and bivouac among sheltering rocks not far from the glacier at the foot of the face. Next morning was cloudy and threatening so we delayed departure until an improvement in the weather encouraged us onto the face. We climbed trending left, then further left along a snow band between two rock bands to gain the left-hand ridge. Skirting the crumbling rock further left, where the mountain turned its west face to the sun, we climbed the snowy ridge, weaving between rock outcrops and taking short ice steps. Then, with a suddenness we had not expected, we were on the almost flat summit where we all posed for pictures and took in the cloudswept view.

Stuart and Ken raced off down the ridge, intent upon getting back to base camp before dark, but Pam and I went rather too slowly and steadily so that by the time we had reached the bivouac site there was little option but to spend another night out. At least we had company since the other four had arrived to make their ascents of the peak. This they did next day while Pam and I packed up and walked back over the col to base camp. Snow had begun to fall by the afternoon and it continued to do so for the next three days.

Paul reported, 'The morale of the group plummeted at this point; bad weather itself is bad enough but there were thoughts and fears about future climbing if the snow dumped any significant amounts on the mountain.'

In the conditions most of us only left our tents to huddle over food or attend to the call of nature. The locally purchased stoves played up and tempers frayed. We escaped into our books and communication between tent pairs became sporadic. Later in his report, Paul was to comment that, 'Base camp needs somewhere that all the members can congregate together [*sic*]. We had difficulty in arranging this so in future we will be considering taking a large cheap tent or a lightweight tarpaulin from the UK.'

Paul was very much the leader but his leadership style involved a lot of mockery, not least of himself; he adopted a studied eccentricity that extended to wearing a tie up to base camp and tut-tutting the bad language of some of the team like a comedy maiden aunt. I suppose it was a strategy to avoid anyone taking anything too seriously; after all, climbing has a tradition of understatement and irony as the means of coming to terms with risk that goes back to the 19th century.

Pam and I felt like newbies among the rest of the group who all either knew each other or had been on expeditions together before. Photos show us in our colourful Alpine clothing, standing out from the others predominantly in traditional British navy blue or khaki. Paul's insistence from the start of addressing us with the exaggerated formality of "Pamela" and "David" rather than the Pam and Dave we were used to, while he never addressed the Kens, "Grande" or "Chico" as Kenneth or Chris as Christopher, tended to reinforce incipient feelings that we were outsiders. We had both made the point that we

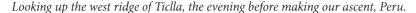

Looking up the west ridge of Ticlla, the evening before making our ascent, Peru.

Pam making herself comfortable in the assault tent, Ticlla, Peru.

preferred to be addressed by the names we were used to but to no effect. Perhaps he thought it was funny but as prospects soured it became simply irritating and put a distance between us that was reinforced by the isolation of each tent imposed by the weather.

As the weather gradually improved an impromptu plan emerged to establish an advanced base camp (ABC) in the valley beneath the west ridge of Ticlla, and tent pairs began to carry equipment and supplies over the pass to a suitable campsite. Chris and Peter stayed there in order to sort out the camp and Ken Grande, Pam and I planned to follow them. Meanwhile the attention of Stuart, Paul and Ken Chico had shifted to the south-east face of Ticlla which offered a steeper challenge.

We all sat out a day of dubious weather at base camp (BC) before departing in our separate directions. Descending from the pass to ABC, we met Chris and Peter on their way back to BC having climbed the west ridge of Ticlla the previous day, despite the weather. It had taken them four hours to get onto the ridge and seven hours actually climbing it. In order to complete the route in a day they had left their rucksacks halfway up the ridge yet still descended to ABC in darkness: and they were the fast team!

Ken Grande, Pam and I settled into ABC and worked out a game plan: pack the assault tent up to the col on the ridge then do the route next day, either returning to the tent or bringing it down with us. However, next morning there was fresh snow, and cloud came and went, lifted and swirled back, as we brewed up and ate a scratch breakfast. We hung around indecisively, then Ken decided to return to base camp and give it a few more days for the weather to settle. For some reason I felt less pessimistic and glimpses of the col shifted me out of the contained balance of waiting; suddenly I was very sure that we would get to the col that day, if only to set the tent up for a future attempt.

The tracks Chris and Peter had left helped us to find our way to the col but the final slope looked steep so I left my rucksack and went ahead to look for a campsite. The slope would have been awkward for us, heavily laden, and there was scant shelter for a single skin assault tent on the windswept col. I climbed back down and we set about stamping out a tent platform in the shelter of a nearby rock buttress. The snow was so deep and soft that stamping it into a firm base also created sheltering, although less substantial, walls of snow around the tent. Pam and I settled in and spent a reasonably comfortable night.

The morning was cold and very clear. So cold that boiling enough water took a couple of hours and the sun was striking the tent as we left. We climbed easily up to the col where the west ridge of Ticlla rose ahead of us in ragged steps to the ice cliffs guarding the summit dome. Tracks could be seen where the steeper slopes raised themselves for our inspection but as we climbed they were often lost among penitentes infilled with new snow and spindrift so that we soon had our share of trail-breaking.

This was my first encounter with penitentes, those strange fields of snow-ice spikes, pointing in the general direction of the sun, so characteristic of South American mountains. They are formed by differential ablation dependent on a dew point that is below freezing and I have seen some in Chile four or five metres high. They can slow the pace of climbing to a crawl. Here they were brittle cowled puppets that fell apart at a touch, or on steeper slopes a dense crop of hard ice blades. The snow between them was unpredictable too; sometimes taking our weight, sometimes letting a foot jerk through knee-deep, but all the time we were conscious of the surrounding peaks falling away beneath us.

We climbed a steep slope to the left of ice cliffs which were tumbling massive blocks of ice down the west face to the right whenever the urge took them and found ourselves on a kind of serac balcony. Scoops and ridges of snow steepened above to more ice cliffs draped with huge icicles and wind-sculpted flutings. It was very beautiful but distinctly threatening since we had to thread our way between crevasses, over hollow-feeling depressions, and under the fall line of semi-detached ice blocks, to break out onto a hanging snow slope further left which could be traversed to the summit ridge. Below that slope the mountain broke up into a chaos of crevasse chasms and seracs ponderously poised in the act of falling. The only consolation was the cold wind that, coupled with the altitude, was hopefully continuing to freeze these snow structures into immobility.

We had roped up and now made a point of moving together as little as possible through the treacherous territory. Pam was rattled by the terrain at times but that was only to be expected since she had survived a crevasse accident in the Alps which had claimed the life of her husband. Gaining the summit ridge, we plodded up its broad and friendly back on snow beginning to be softened and rotted by the sun so that our crampons balled up and it felt like lifting several extra pounds of attached snow with each step. The toil contributed to the high-altitude delusion in which distances appear greater than they are, lowering our spirits so that we stepped onto the summit dome with some sense of surprise mixed with relief. The dome had a mirror image around 50 metres away so we climbed that too just to be sure. Having stared up at them for so long, it was exhilarating to look down on so many snowy summits. Beyond Nevados Acopalco and Cullec, the northern peaks of the Cordillera Central drew the eye to distant snows that might have been the Cordilleras Huaywash and Blanca.

The wind had increased tremendously on the summit and cloud was blowing in so after the obligatory pictures we hurried down to shelter for food and drink. But not for long. Gingerly reversing the softening snow of the hanging snow slope, we were acutely aware of the broken instability below and the difficulty we should have in regaining safety if we had the misfortune to slide off into it. We crept under the seracs, then quickly on down the steep snow in what was almost a controlled slide amid a flurry of shattered penitentes. Back on the easier-angled ridge, we stowed the rope away and strode back to the col, racing the setting sun.

At the col at 6 p.m. we looked behind in utter stillness to see the summit was turning pink with reflected light. To the west the sun was a glowing ball layering the sky with shades of red as it lowered itself over the horizon; it was the first sunset we had seen in a long time and we drank in the sight before plunging down off the ridge into the shadows.

Another night in our assault tent was troubled by the impression that there were voices outside and the sound of something heavy being dragged across the snow, but perhaps it was just our minds responding to the stress of the day and the cold night that had us repeatedly rewarming our feet with vigorous toe-wiggling. We eagerly anticipated the opportunity to get going in the morning to generate some warmth, leaving the tent and sleeping mats for the next team to attempt the route.

Advanced base camp was warm and sheltered. We enjoyed the luxury of water, brewing and washing (especially our feet!) before packing huge sacks for the return to base camp. Just as we were about to leave, we were hailed by Paul and Ken Chico who had finished their route on the south-east face in darkness, but could not find their way

Descending through the ice features that barred access to the summit of Ticlla from the west ridge, Peru.

off the summit so had been forced to bivouac on a ledge among the seracs. Had Pam and I known that they intended to descend by our route, we might have been able to assist their descent, perhaps by carrying marker wands to help them find their way through the summit difficulties; it had been a total surprise to see them crash into camp looking very rough. After sharing a brew with them, we shouldered our loads and walked back to base camp, sighting four huge condors en route, wheeling lazily, as vultures do, despite being harassed by a solitary falcon.

Paul and Ken Chico were to spend the next couple of days at ABC, recovering and using up some of the excess supplies there while Stuart and Ken Grande passed through on their way to the assault tent and their turn to climb the west ridge. Next day, Paul and Ken Chico waited until the others reached the safety of ABC before setting off on their return to base camp. Meanwhile Peter and Chris attempted Llongote and Pam and I climbed Quepala Sud (5360m), fast and light.

By 18 August there had been more free-wheeling and fragmentary discussion as we floated ideas inconclusively about when to leave base camp now that we had pretty much run out of climbing objectives. Pam's flight from Lima was on 24 August so she and I were committed to leaving earlier than the others but we were not alone in considering that option.

That morning Paul and Ken Chico decided to walk down to Miraflores and see what the chances were for an earlier departure; then Ken belatedly confessed to Paul that he had a frostbitten toe. The thing was black and leaking pus, though Ken tried to make light of it. Stuart, who was in charge of medical matters, immediately put Ken on a course of antibiotics and anti-inflammatories; standard treatment. Paul rushed off to Miraflores, though no one, including Paul himself, seemed to be quite sure what he was going to do. He spent some time looking for a telephone or at least someone who could help him arrange to evacuate base camp (without success), contemplated walking to the next village to try there, then gave up and walked back to camp.

In the absence of any clear team plan, Chris and Peter had decided on a night ascent of Ticlla by the south-east face and were explaining this to Paul when he let them know that he felt really fed up about being left to sort things out on his own. He reported that, '... no one [was] wanting to help with the organisation. This may have been my fault as I did not get people together and put the situation to them and organise what needed to be done.' After discussing the situation with Chris and Peter over a brew in the cook tent, they agreed to give up their plan to climb and would return to Miraflores with Paul to see if burros could be organised. He notes that, 'I cannot recall why I did not go round to see Ken Grande and Stuart; perhaps I felt they were tired and needed the rest.' Pam and I only learnt of the change of plan next morning too. We duly packed up and twice shifted 25kg loads consisting of all our personal kit down to Miraflores.

It was unfortunate that the only Spanish speaker was banished to his tent nursing a frostbitten toe, but Chris produced drawings which in turn produced a positive response and burros were promised for the next day. No telephone communication was possible but after bringing the loads down Peter and Paul continued to the lower village of Tinco Alis and discovered that there was a scheduled bus we could catch in two days' time on 21 August. It was a stroke of luck just when we needed one. Chris was going well and even managed to carry a third load down from base camp although probably only because he was worried about the lack of any action from Stuart and Ken Grande.

It seemed that while Paul was seeing the evacuation and hospitalisation of Ken Chico as an urgent emergency, Stuart thought that he had followed standard treatment and it was unlikely that the hospital would do much more. I suppose he and Ken Grande, as the oldest members of the expedition, didn't really see the point in carrying heavy loads down from base camp if burros were going to be hired to do it anyway. The bottom line was that people had different perceptions of the situation and nobody arranged time to share them and reach a consensus.

The rest of us stayed the night at Miraflores then set out to pack up the rest of base camp while Paul waited for the burros to arrive then accompanied them on the trail up to camp. There was even a horse for Ken Chico to ride to save damaging his toe any further. By the time all the kit had arrived in Miraflores, Chris and Peter had set off for Tinco Alis to hire the taxi/truck that had brought Peter and Paul back from their earlier foray. Paul and Pam spent the time distributing the burro loads of excess food and equipment to the villagers who must have thought Christmas had arrived early!

It was dark by the time Chris and Peter got back, fortunately with the truck, but we did succeed in catching the bus to Huancayo at 7 a.m. next day! Two things remain with me about that journey. The first was after we waved the bus to a stop in the dark; the door swung open and I stared into the barrels of two automatic weapons held ready for action by the bus guards. The second was later, in daylight, when a shepherdess flagged us down in the middle of nowhere. Assisted by a couple of travellers from the bus she then hog-tied her small flock of sheep and bundled them into the luggage compartments in the lower sides of the bus. An hour or two later she got off, untied her flock, and walked away into the empty landscape, the sheep apparently none the worse for the experience.

Ken received further treatment in Huancayo and made a full recovery after flying back with the rest of the team.

Pakistan, Hindu Kush

Despite our misgivings about communications, and somewhat to our surprise, Pam and I received another invitation, this time from Ken Chico, to join a similar team that he was leading to make the first British ascent of Saraghrar (7300m) in the Hindu Kush.

The mountain had been attempted by a group of students from Oxford in 1958 but was abandoned after the death of Peter Nelson. Paul had researched this very well and met with the former expedition member, Bill Roberts, who gave him copies of photos taken during the expedition and even made a donation to expedition funds. The plan was that we should complete the "British Route" via the Northern Cwm of Saraghrar, hopefully via the Nelson couloir down which Peter Nelson had fallen to his death when within striking distance of the summit.

There had been a number of climbers who had been interested in this expedition but subsequently dropped out, which may perhaps have accounted for the invitation to Pam and me. It certainly meant that we didn't have much opportunity to get to know each other at the group meeting prior to flying to Islamabad: there was just too much to be organised. Four of us formed an advance party to try to sort out in-country issues before the arrival of the teachers on the team.

In Pakistan the chickens well and truly came home to that particular roost: four of the team did not have permits to enter the closed, military-controlled area, while others who had dropped out of the team had permits that were useless to them and us. Worse, the documentation that we thought had been submitted to obtain the necessary permits had been left in the UK under the impression that it would not be needed.

Even our agent, Maqsood al Mulk, who was a member of the former Chitrali Royal family, was worried. Despite the slightly disturbing reverence with which he was treated by his retainers, worshipfully bowing foreheads to the ground, he was not convinced that even his influence would help the expedition to get beyond Islamabad. Days passed in fruitless visits to the Ministry of Tourism involving long waits punctuated by occasionally sallying forth to buy supplies of food and more equipment for the Liaison Officer (LO), all of which might never be used.

The vanguard of the expedition, Ken, Karl, Robert and I, was booked into a hotel in Rawalpindi yet the ministry offices and our agent were based in Islamabad so it seemed, to quote our leader, 'that we spent those first few days chasing around in taxis going from the hotel to the ministry and back again', although not before the false economy of a bus journey had left us desperate to find our hotel at 11 p.m. one night.

Our LO, Captain Bhutt, told us he was 'on the case', but with little discernible effect. He called in at the hotel for a long chat on one occasion that revealed a yawning culture gap. He couldn't believe 'you people' would be climbing what we proposed to climb 'at your age', and was very dubious about the inclusion of a woman on the team: 'Men are superior to women; Adam and Eve started it all, as it says in the bible, man being made first.' In an attempt to bridge that cultural gap we all bought shalwar qamiz, the local flowing shirts and baggy trousers that seemed to cope with the appalling heat better than any clothes we had brought with us. Unfortunately, this tactic turned out to have little effect on the captain's mindset.

One chore was to register as foreign nationals with the police. This was a Kafkaesque experience as we wandered around blocks of buildings, signed only in Urdu, looking for the right office and being constantly misdirected. People sought legal advice from stalls in a square surrounded by lawyers' offices at Ayub market, while others queued and argued at hatches and doorways. Some officials were friendly and helpful, others completely uncomprehending. Finally, we discovered the correct office, only to be told that we didn't need to register if we had visas, which we did.

Despite having contracted with an agent to supply a cook and base camp facilities, team members wasted a lot of time in Rawalpindi shopping for stoves and base camp pots and pans, without success. Perhaps it was the urge to compensate that led to increasing purchases of foodstuffs. When we did meet the cook it was clear that he spoke no English so all communication occurred via our LO. There were frequent misunderstandings.

The advanced guard had all been suffering from bouts of sickness and diarrhoea, while an attempt to have a little laundry done resulted in the plastic zips on the pockets of my shirt being permanently ironed shut at the Paradise Hotel. Trouble in Paradise meant that when Paul, Brian and Pam arrived, we all booked into the Capital Hotel which provided much better service.

Eventually, paperwork in order, we were able to set out for Dir in our air-conditioned mini-coach. Driving etiquette was distinctly un-English with lots of hornblowing to persuade other drivers to give way. Karl became increasingly distressed by the experience and began to deliver a critical commentary on driving technique in hopes of dissuading the driver from riskier manoeuvres. It didn't make any difference.

At Dir we hired three jeeps for the rough onward passage over the Lowari Pass to Chitral, bouncing and rattling up 45 hairpin bends to a height of 3118m. This all took longer than expected and a 10 p.m. arrival at the darkened Mountain Inn revealed that they had no record of rooms being booked. After some haggling, twin rooms became available at £12 per night. With several members of the team suffering from stomach trouble, the journey had been endured rather than enjoyed. Then calamity; as we tottered off to bed, Paul discovered that his treasured planning folder of maps and pictures had somehow gone adrift.

Miraculously, the folder was waiting in the lobby the following morning; the staff must have phoned ahead to the jeep drivers and not only located it but also arranged for its return overnight: a great relief. It was a relief too, to breakfast in the cool morning garden of the inn surrounded on three sides by the verandahs of the hotel but with expansive views down-valley from the open fourth side. At this height temperatures were far more acceptable in true hill station tradition. A tame bird took to Brian and perched on his shoulder.

After this peaceful start to the day, the hassle reasserted itself. To quote Paul: 'The morning in Chitral was spent shopping and trying to get Saegal, the cook, to take charge of anything at all. In the end we marched him round a variety of places, eventually getting him to purchase cooking equipment and stove spares for the trip. Arguments ranged over amounts, why some things had not been got in the capital and who was to take charge of what.' People were tired and ill, so the arguments were no surprise, nor that 'some members [got] more stuck in than others' before 'all was accomplished' to Paul's satisfaction and he had even started to make up 25kg porter loads, although it turned out that insufficient petrol was purchased.

Before leaving Chitral next day Ken planned to change money into smaller denominations to pay the porters, while Brian had stayed up the previous night writing postcards to send from the post office. Unfortunately, no one had realised that Sunday in Pakistan had been adopted as the weekly day off at that time so neither banks nor post offices would be open.

Our purchases in Chitral meant we needed not three but four jeeps to carry ourselves and our kit to the village of Zundrangram (2700m) at the roadhead below the Rosh Gol glacier. On arriving we set up camp in an orchard and found the people very friendly. They were delighted with copies of photos from the 1958 expedition showing the younger versions of friends and relatives that Paul had thoughtfully brought along. We left them with the families of those who featured in them and arranged to visit Peter Nelson's grave.

Pam was able to visit the local women and involve them more in the proceedings otherwise they would have continued to hover uncertainly on the fringes of things. She even managed to take a few pictures of them. Later on, Janine, an Australian trekking in the area with her partner, confirmed that, although segregated, the women were quite capable of having a party of their own with foreign women visitors and were much more relaxed about the presence of the expedition as a result.

Then negotiations began in earnest over porters and loads. To quote Paul again, 'As always sorting porter loads became a mixture of organisation and high farce.' To me it defined the term "organised chaos!" Up at 6 a.m. next day we left the village with relatively light loads while around 34 porters carried 25kg each. There was a well-marked path more or less following the river that flows down from the glacier since the villagers drive their bulls up to pasture as the snow retreats in the spring. When we found the bulls they showed some impressive nimbleness for such powerful animals as they grazed the moraine slopes below the glacier.

Negotiating rates for porters at a village at the roadhead, Pakistan.

We all camped halfway, overnighting at Druh, where a spring sustained a grove of Himalayan paper birch trees. At 3450m it was delightfully cool in the shade they afforded. Their papery bark made fire-lighting easy, but despite the spring the ground was very dry and fires that seemed to be out smouldered underground to break out in fresh flames metres away. It took a lot of stamping and dowsing to be sure they were extinguished in the morning. The porters celebrated a night out with drumming and dancing in the light of a great bonfire. Saegal took a lead in the dancing after distributing lots of rice and chapatis from what we suspected was some deliberate over-catering before they all retired to substantial stone-built shelters.

Next day the expedition team became strung out along the trail as illness and altitude took their toll. By 1 p.m. all the porters had reached Totiraz Noku, a convergence of streams that was to be our base camp at 4200m; they were expecting to be paid off in time for them to return to Zundrangram or at least overnight at Druh. The faster expedition members were also there but Karl, Bob and Ken were missing, along with the cash to pay the porters. The wait became embarrassing and the porters began to view us with some suspicion until Bob arrived having been sent on with the cash. There was some awkwardness about the large denomination notes which meant that several of the porters had to share bills between two or even three of them, but they all knew each other so did not seem to be too fazed by this. Six of the porters were to make a further carry to a higher camp, later designated the Dump, on the way to the Northern Cwm and some of the others decided to stay to keep them company, perhaps with an eye to further employment.

Those of the team who felt fit enough busied themselves with getting tents up and organising the camp. Others nursed headaches and took aspirin and Diamox or repeatedly relieved their suffering bowels. Paul notes in his report that, 'Robert came up too quickly and is now suffering! … I suppose he should have gone straight down again – our fault for being too consumed with the task in hand and not thinking about people.' (As the youngest in the expedition Bob was getting the formal name treatment.) Paul later adds, 'Robert and Karl had developed headaches since their arrival at base but somehow it seemed too late to do anything about them; that, on reflection was a poorly judged lack of effort by the rest of us. The lack of action in getting them lower that night may well have caused their difficulties in acclimatising for the next three weeks.' Bob and Karl had never been above 4000m so it should have been anticipated that they might have difficulties with acclimatisation, but the focus on managing the loads was instrumental in creating the conditions in which a failure in "thinking about people" sufficiently could happen.

Ken was clearly unwell and Paul, taking on the organisational burden, was so intent upon making up porter loads for the morrow that when Pam and I were trying to sort out a load between us he simply lifted our rope from our pile and made off with it. I asked him to hold on and explained what we were doing only to be rounded upon with sarcastic comments about Pamela and David (still using the language of exclusion) not being part of the expedition. I pointed out that other members of the team had already been missing kit that had been taken from their bags and there was

Trekking in to base camp, Hindu Kush, Pakistan.

a danger of losing track to the point where the effectiveness of climbing teams could be undermined by misplaced equipment: 'You can't climb without a rope!' This led to a full-blown row that simmered on after Ken and Karl finally arrived, becoming both more or less heated or partisan by turns. Food and drink restored some balance but I turned in early and slept uneasily.

Pam and Paul seemed to have acclimatised better than the rest of us so headed up to the Dump with the porters. Karl was feeling rough but the Captain, Ken and Bob helped me dig out a toilet site and build a screening drystone wall, at least until they too began to feel rough and needed some recovery time, sunbathing, while I finished it off. Pam and Paul returned with horror stories about the trek up to the higher camp and arguing for employing porters for a further day to stock it. Although this seemed fair enough, I did wonder if we ought to be carrying out a reconnaissance of the route beyond before committing ourselves to this investment of resources into this particular route but I chose to avoid the possibility of further argument.

It's said that no battle plan survives contact with the enemy but that is as much a recommendation for flexibility in the application of any battle plan as a recognition that it is impossible to plan for every eventuality. We seemed to be attempting to make this plan work at all costs rather than testing its capacity to deliver, yet group interaction was creating an atmosphere in which such discussion could not take place.

I noted in my journal, 'It's worrying how Paul seems to want to lead by remote control, sending Ken over to pay the porters although he hadn't agreed a rate for the day. Ken seems reluctant to act as leader and I don't blame him when Paul later decides unilaterally to pay 450r for 20kg tomorrow rather than 25kg loads as carried today! Snap decisions happen "on the hoof" and are quickly lost track of as other matters interrupt. More thinking time is needed.'

The porters duly set out next day and delivered their supplies to the Dump. Brian, Paul, Bob and I never caught up with them despite our lighter loads. Brian and Paul went to scout ahead with some kit for a higher camp but the porters had gone back by the time Ken and Karl arrived. Karl went straight back with Bob, their headaches only worse from their attempts at acclimatisation, but Ken and I spent hours clearing tent platforms only to be informed by Paul on his return that we wouldn't be camping at the Dump. My annoyance was tinged with relief, having described the place in my journal as 'a dreadful pile of shattered rocks which was probably mostly snow before the glacial recession of recent years". Brian had gone on to find what may have been an Italian camp, judging from the discarded cans but could go no further, while Paul reckoned he had reached 5000m and dumped a tent for later use. Returning to base camp and without discussion, Paul led off down another moraine ridge which was not that of the ascent and the others followed him. I declined to deviate from the original route and, despite having to cast about for the trail through a boulder field, reached base a full 40 minutes before any sign of the others. At least we were able to test the two-way radios in the field and were impressed with their range and reception – much better than just line of sight. Their presence, it was hoped, would mean the team would stay more closely in touch with each other.

Bad weather more or less stopped any further progress for the next six days. Paul and Ken reached the Dump and camped but ran out of food and had to retreat in bad weather while Pam and I used brief fine-weather windows to get some acclimatisation by investigating alternative approaches to the summit via ridges and couloirs above base camp. It was good to be climbing and the cloud helpfully cleared at crucial points to give views of potential routes. I think Pam's trip up to the Dump had already sown the seeds of doubt in our minds about the viability of the northern approach to the peak. Karl, Bob and Brian stayed lower at Totiraz Noku, taking some time to recover from illness and altitude problems.

Paul, Pam and I then took the first fine-weather opportunity to get back up to Camp 1 above the Dump. There Pam's stomach kept her toing and froing from the tent all night so that only Paul and I pressed on next morning. Far from improving, the terrain continued to be difficult all the way to the Northern Cwm.

The Rosh Gol glacier rose in a series of steps through which we continued to find ways despite the contending insecurity of rubble on ice followed by snow on ice, both liberally lubricated by meltwater as the day wore on. Crevasses and rubble mounds gave way to slippery ridges and ice pinnacles, shrinking where they had lost their capping rocks and were exposed to the heat of the sun. On the threshold of the Northern Cwm a huge avalanche poured down a nearby couloir, triggered by a cornice collapse from the ridge above. We both took pictures, but Paul continued to do so as it raced closer until I suggested to him that we ought to take cover behind the biggest of the nearby boulders just in case any flying debris got this far. Minutes later we were enveloped in a freezing cloud of snow spicules that soaked the warm rock around us but adhered to our fleeces to leave us looking like snowmen. Fortunately, the heavyweight stuff had been channelled off down the glacier so that we were only caught in the blast on the margin of its passage.

Still we went on, traversing a snow slope below an ice cliff fringed with icicles to reach the base of a couloir debris fan, then across more chunky debris from serac collapse. Threading through the larger blocks, we reached the crest of an ice ridge and looked down into a yawning gap stacked with more ice blocks from previous serac collapses. I think Paul had cherished the image of a perfect campsite on a flat snowfield in the centre of the Northern Cwm with the Nelson couloir leading from it up to the summit above. Perhaps there had been a photo or a description which supported that image in his research folder; who knows? The reality was very different. There was no sign of any levelling in the surface of the cwm and while the way ahead might "go", by the time we had got through it would be late enough for our return to be continuously threatened by avalanche and collapsing ice. Moreover, it was very clear by then that this route would not function as a supply route for load carrying: it was some of the most inhospitable glacier terrain that I had ever experienced and it was only the hope of getting a picture of the Nelson Couloir that had kept me going.

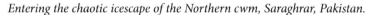

Entering the chaotic icescape of the Northern cwm, Saraghrar, Pakistan.

Defeated, we descended the chaotic glacier back to Camp 1 and radioed our news to base camp. Paul continued down to the Dump with the extra tent, Ken's axes and ice gear etc. I had to wonder why we had transported such kit up to that point before ascertaining that it would actually be needed. Pam was still too weak to walk so I sorted out some food and stayed the night with her and she was well enough to walk out next day.

Ken later summarised the position: 'Having made two camps and transported 250kg of gear up the Northern Cwm (route), we came to the decision that it was far too dangerous to climb the intended couloir … We decided to shift our attention to the southern part of the mountain, so we brought down around 200kg of equipment from ABC and this took us a week to complete the task.' Paul added that ' … it was a despondent group of climbers that left Totiraz Noku with empty sacks to start the reallocation of the gear.' It was lucky that two friends were trekking in the area and were able to give us a hand with the loads but not much fun for them.

Ashley and I took a few hours out to cross the glacier and scout out possible routes on Langar, a peak of around 7000m which dominated the upper Rosh Gol glacier. I think I was already beginning to feel that we had stacked the odds against ourselves and would be lucky to climb Saraghrar, but here was an opportunity to inform a return trip.

A Japanese expedition had approached Saraghrar from the south in the 1960s and this route now emerged as our alternative: not a first ascent but certainly a first British one; if we succeeded. We would have to be quick. As the relocation of the gear came to an end, Pam and I volunteered to start a reconnaissance of the southern approaches. Unfortunately, by the time we had packed up it was noon, the hottest part of the day, and the walk down to Druh blistered my feet mercilessly so, finding no alternative on the slopes above, we camped there for the night.

Back at base camp, discussions had confirmed the Japanese route as the favoured option and Paul now decided to join the advance team. Musharief, who had been helping Saegal, had portered for the Japanese so would be able to lead Paul to the site of their base camp at Warsing Gol where they expected to find Pam and me next day.

While Pam and I explored the course of a little river valley to the left, Musharief and Paul reached the old tent platforms near the snout of a glacier on the right of the valley above Druh. Pam and I had lightened our loads by leaving climbing gear below before scouting the drainage but found no better campsite so turned back to join Paul for the night after Brian had walked up with a stove for him. It was becoming clear that co-ordinating our efforts was proving challenging.

Because "Days had been lost in the north so there was no time to lose..." as Paul put it, he pushed for two teams, one to explore the watercourse on the left, the other the glacier on the right. Pam and I had been going for a week of continuous hard effort with no days off but despite this Pam and Brian set out. My blisters were a sticking point for me so Paul went up alone, although later that day I collected all the dumped kit from lower down and slowly brought it up to the camp. Pam and Brian succeeded in finding the Japanese ABC after following the watercourse to a drystone wall decorated with scraps of rubber hose, while Paul discovered his glacier was too broken to make a safe load-carrying route. The rest of the team, enlisting the support of the trekkers, Australian Dave, Ashley and Andy, began to carry kit up to Warsing Camp, then decided to bypass it and head to ABC direct which was only at 4300m. I reminded myself that that left 3000m to go!

Ken commented, 'I feel in a state of limbo, totally powerless in what the members of the group are doing.' At about the same time I recorded in my journal, 'Very undecided about what to do though most people want to "have a go". It's really muddled in terms of planning – just gungho!' There follows an exercise in day by day scheduling of stages in establishing camps and people so that everyone would have a chance to get to the summit: it would take ten days with no contingency days for bad weather. This was on 10 August It began to look like we were going to run out of time. Perhaps that was why no one else seemed to be interested in making such plans; they were in denial.

Pam decided to go back to base camp to collect our hill food while I was shifting all the rest of our kit up from Druh. Brian and Paul were relaying loads to the new ABC south while Ken, Karl and Bob explored the route above, relishing the opportunity to get some climbing done. In their absence Paul reckoned to have conducted an inventory of food supplies at the camp and reached the conclusion that there wasn't enough 'basic foods for the camp like pasta, cheese, biscuits, soups and noodles'. Perhaps vegetarians like Paul are more prone to anxiety attacks about food but nobody else seemed to have identified this problem. He enlisted Brian in support and they headed off to base camp with empty sacks to remedy the situation.

Food had become a bit of an issue. The sheer volume of food clearly came as shock to Brian when he saw it all piled up for portering: 'We've got enough food to feed an army!' Some of the food I considered entirely inappropriate for an expedition: time had been wasted decanting jam, pickle and honey from glass jars into plastic containers, which then leaked their contents all over the rest of the food in the porter load. Padding the glass jars in a plastic barrel might have been more successful although the fact that Paul had decided on the use of plastic containers indicated that there had been a problem in the past: they certainly weren't the solution.

Saegal's lacklustre performance in the kitchen added to suspicions that base camp cooking might be responsible for our continuing stomach upsets. Supplies of Wayfarer undehydrated, boil in the bag meals started to be used at base camp rather than in the intermediate camps as intended. Bob made list after list in his diary of 'food I want to eat when I get home'. The Captain resorted to ordering up live chickens from Zundrangram. No one was very keen on spending much time at base camp, which made it all the more puzzling why Paul decided to move base camp down to Druh. We obviously needed to supply higher camps with enough food to get us to the summit but a rucksack full of hill food can last a surprisingly long time; there seemed little point in expending all that effort to move base camp.

I worked on the campsite until Pam arrived from Totiraz Noku with all our hill food. Shortly after, Ken's team arrived back from a useful but inconclusive reconnaissance and remained puzzled by the disappearance of Paul and Brian. For some reason Paul had taken Bob's trekking boots so Bob had to descend to Totiraz Noku next day in his hot and uncomfortable plastic boots. He was not happy. He and Karl were determined to collect their hill food from base camp and stock ABC. By then Brian had recorded, 'Paul makes the decision to move base camp from Totiraz Noku to Druh.' When he arrived at Totiraz Noku, Bob was able to add, 'When we arrived at base camp there was utter chaos everywhere as Paul had decided to move base camp from here down to Druh… I went to lie down for a while as the commotion was all a bit too much to handle. Didn't get much rest as Paul was busying around trying to get us and things organised for the big move in the morning. He was really annoying and awkward. Brian went back to bed as he was really ill and tired.' Porters had been booked but Paul records, 'I had underestimated the number of porters needed by 33% so in the end we had to leave a number of packs in the camp for the porters to retrieve the next day. So much for my expertise on these expedition things.' Bob's diary adds, 'Woke up very early like a block of ice… Paul even more annoying.'

Paul had also decided to have Pam's base camp tent taken up to ABC south and was then surprised by her refusal to agree when she was told about it over the radio. More time was consumed by the formalities of clearing the base camp to the satisfaction of Captain Bhutt who had to approve the release of our environmental bond. He would welcome the change of scene, having been bored with his stay. It's worth mentioning that he never used any of his equipment in the field, his communications with the cook never succeeded in securing any variation in the bland monotony of the food, and he failed to provide even one radio weather forecast; all tasks he had been keen to take on!

Meanwhile Pam and I had been pushing the route out above ABC south. We had halved the time taken by the earlier team to reach the icefall but Pam hadn't liked the look of it and was feeling the altitude so dumped her load and went back after watching me solo to the top of the ice. I climbed up the debris of an avalanche of collapsed seracs from the upper icefall to the left, then went on, skirting crevasses while keeping on the safe side of a wall of debris bordering the avalanche trough on the right. Approaching the upper cwm I found a sheltered campsite below a rock rognon at the end of a low-lying ridge which rose to demarcate the left side of the upper cwm. Meltwater flowed down from the glacier to the right. At 5000m this was just the place for Camp 1; I levelled a tent platform in the snow. It felt right. Perhaps the Japanese had camped there too.

We returned to find a frustrated Ken, the only one in any position to provide support, had we needed it, while the others were embroiled in moving base camp. He told me, 'I feel like a manager with two strikers out on the field and the rest of the team back in the changing rooms.' Despite radio contact the situation was spiralling out of control.

While chaos continued below, Ken carried a load up towards Camp 1 and Pam and I spent the night there and climbed to various vantage points from which we could scout the route ahead. It was serious stuff with stonefall in a couloir in which the snow turned to sugar while the sound of running water beneath rose in volume through the course of the day to the point where we could not hear each other's climbing calls clearly. The ice screws I placed to secure the rope while I went ahead for a better view were melting out nicely by the time I returned. We narrowed the options down to three but all of them were steep enough to require fixed ropes for safe load carrying and we thought it better to wait for other views before fixing any of them.

Back at ABC the rest of the team was assembling various amounts of kit and having rows about who should be doing what based on complete misunderstandings. Paul commented, 'It certainly shows how easy it is to annoy other people without really trying.' I wondered if it was indicative of people turning in on themselves, shutting out the world outside as they increasingly felt themselves in the grip of adversity.

When Pam and I descended for a rest and briefed the others on what we had discovered they decided to go up and consolidate Camp 1 south and try to sort out options on the way forward. Unfortunately, rain and snow blew in. The team who were camped at Camp 1 south decided to sit it out and Paul tried to talk them into fixing the ice wall over the radio but with no luck. Bob got up to find, 'I almost had to dig myself out of the tent because it had snowed so much overnight.' Soon everyone was back at ABC south, except Karl who had shat himself during the night and had descended on his way to Druh by the time the others arrived. Paul commented, 'It seems we are doomed to make as little progress as possible! If it is not the weather it is our ills.' There were attempts to raise morale with card games and quizzes during breaks in the rain. It was cold enough to still the meltwater streamlets as their sources above froze solid.

Next day the temperature seemed to have gone up so Paul, Pam and I headed up to Camp 1, the soft snow balling up on our crampons on the glacier. Pam and I settled in for a reasonable night despite an elusive scent of petrol lurking about the tent that I blamed for my morning headache. Paul was ready first so led up the ice wall using two axes and fixing the occasional ice screw. It was gritty, rotten ice that would never have been safe for load carrying without the 7mm fixed line that I took up when I followed. I fixed the end to a substantial ice bollard where the angle eased back, then Paul and I climbed back down, retrieving the climbing rope but leaving the other in place. Cloud had obscured the sun all day but despite that the ice we climbed was running with water. My hands became soaked and as a result very cold, with a raw wind compounding the problem. Ken and Brian had arrived and Ken joined Pam and Paul to carry a load up to stash above the fixed line. I stayed with Brian, shivering while he levelled another tent placement and my hands agonised back to life. Brian's diary entry concludes, 'The weather is not good but at least progress is being made. Bob is at ABC and Karl is on his way up from Dru.'

In the morning, the weather was clear enough to keep pushing the route out. I set out with a heavy sack up the fixed rope, going well and carrying extra 7mm line. With the extra rope I set up a haul line and with this Brian and Pam were bringing up the other sacks with mechanical efficiency, broken only by Brian shouting at Paul who had for some reason decided to solo about on the ice still carrying his heavy sack. When he gained the top of the rope, Paul headed on alone, with Ken's sack, before we all went on to join him.

Paul had been heading for a small peak on a ridge to the right but as we approached him the clouds cleared enough for a view of the mountain to the left which offered a far better line of ascent. Brian and I indicated this to Paul, then Brian led off while Paul and Ken sorted out their sacks and traversed to join the new line. It was good to be gaining altitude and the weather continued to improve. We zigzagged up the slope to a narrow ridge or shelf behind a kind of ice bluff which looked like a suitable campsite. It was beneath some seracs but they seemed stable enough while if anything did fall from them it was likely to slide to one or other side of the ridge rather than directly down onto it. We started to level tent platforms until Ken arrived looking very worn out followed by Paul who had actually abandoned his rucksack, back down the trail. He was in no state to retrieve it so Brian went down for it while we made a brew. Paul seemed to be burnt out but still fussing and had to be told to sit down and take some recovery time.

Ken's stove wouldn't work so both tent teams shared mine. There was still no plan for the ascent. Despite the co-operative effort involved in fixing the ice fall, we were all still functioning as independent tent/climbing teams carrying everything we needed all the way to the summit; hence the huge rucksacks full of food and camping kit. We had 2000m of ascent to go and were booked to fly out of Pakistan in less than ten days. I think most of us realised that we would have to have an extraordinary run of good luck and perfect weather to get to the summit, particularly given the struggle some of us had experienced in getting to this camp at just 5300m.

During the evening the sun came out and at midnight the sky was beautifully starry with that liquid light so noticeable about the Milky Way in areas of low light and little air pollution, but by morning snowfall had gently accumulated to a depth of 13cm. Brian decided 'to call it a day and bail out'. He packed up and headed off. Paul recorded, 'I wondered if Ken and I should hang on to the Phoenix tent he was using but somehow we did not.' It seemed that, for the first time, he was beginning to think about tents for multiple camps. Karl and Bob made a carry of food and fuel for Ken and Paul who somehow hadn't brought enough. Karl and Bob seemed cheerful enough but were carrying far lighter loads than the rest of us had managed the day before.

Pam and I debated what to do, sketching out various scenarios in day by day plans but realising that so much of it was pure speculation. Then the patter of snow on the tent fabric increased its tempo. We peeped out into a world of whiteness. That was it. In these conditions avalanche would become a real danger and progress through deep soft snow would be painfully slow. We packed up.

Just before dropping the tent, Paul called out asking if I would leave my tent for Karl and Bob to use. For a moment I couldn't quite believe it. Now, when the strongest climbers had decided to bail out and the two who had suffered most from health and acclimatisation problems might possibly come up to this camp, he was asking me to leave my tent up here. The fact that we'd already had problems with kit going astray didn't encourage any confidence that the tent would find its way down again if they ran into problems, even if the weather cleared. I'd had enough. 'I'm going home and taking my stuff with me. It's that simple. If Bob and Karl come up they can bring their own tent, surely.' I packed up the tent and followed Pam down the line of descent.

Visibility was poor to white-out with continuing snowfall of varying intensity. Snow balled on our crampons producing some nerve-wracking moments on the snow-covered ice. Rappelling the ice wall was the easiest part of the descent although we had to wrap a lot of turns into the Prusik loops to slow down our speed on the thin wet rope.

Bob and Karl had arrived at Camp 1 and made us a brew, complaining all the while about the performance of Brian's stove. I couldn't finish my tea and felt oddly sick; it just turned my stomach and I felt ill all the way back to ABC. There, more digestible brews solved the problem and I ate normally later. It had been strange how so often one or other of us had succumbed to stomach upsets with such little warning. I had been lucky.

Brian, Pam and I carried load after load down from ABC to base camp at Druh, more or less clearing the site. It felt strangely autumnal walking down in the changeable weather and so much cooler than when we had sweltered up that track for the first time. The first leaves were falling from the paper birches. Paul and Ken stayed up at Camp 2 for another day while the mountain continued to accumulate more snow. Then, with Bob and Karl in support at Camp 1, they descended and de-rigged the ice wall in a lull in the weather. Meanwhile Bob and Karl had packed up Camp 1. There

Highest campsite before turning back on Saraghrar, Pakistan.

was still a lot to go down from ABC and Brian and I burnt a fair amount of rubbish and a lot of surplus supplies as we finished the evacuation. The petrol jerrycan melted in on itself as discarded lighters exploded in the flames.

On the way down to Druh, Ken twisted his knee and could no longer carry his sack. Fortunately, Pam was walking up to help and could take the rucksack while Brian and Paul took the pockets. A little lower down Karl appeared on his way to help out and again there was some redistribution of loads.

But there was no peace at Druh. Paul and the porters seemed to have reached an impasse over transporting the remains of the gear down to Zundrangram. They were not going to do it unless they were paid more was the message from Paul and Ken. I decided to sit in on negotiations with Ken while Paul took a back seat, just to see what was going on. It turned out to be another misunderstanding. The porters who had moved base camp from Totiraz Nok to Druh had never been paid and that had generated the suspicion that we were trying to take advantage of them. It was not that the porters were holding us to ransom but just that they wanted to be paid what they were owed. A few pointed questions managed to establish that and then it was all smiles and handshakes as we prepared to move out next day.

Language problems mean that much can be lost in translation but it might have helped to avoid these misunderstandings if there had been a negotiating team in the first place, rather than a one man show. Good relations were cemented when the team handed over a donation of £220 to the local school, a great idea of Paul's! Then there was the bonus for many of the porters; I summarised it as follows, 'We paid them to carry all this food up to base camp then we paid them to carry most of it back from base camp then we gave it to them.' Nonetheless, good relations were important. A couple of times lone figures had drifted through Druh with rifles over their shoulders. Hunters we had thought but the shepherds disabused us of that idea: 'Taliban; they are good guys! Fight Russians!' They never troubled us, but the turn of the century was to change all that and I'm not likely to return to that area any time soon.

When we reached Chitral I recall feeling relaxed for the first time in a long time over a meal in the hotel gardens with the whole team, Ashley and Andy. Then there was a shudder. It was as if the grass lawn had rippled like a carpet catching a draught: earthquake.

Brian, Pam and I found the Pakistan International Airlines (PIA) office to confirm our flights but it was late and they saw no point in wasting time trying to phone Islamabad; we were assured that it would be done next day. Brian wisely asked for the name and phone number of the official who made that assurance, 'Just in case we need to check.' He seemed to be a semi-retired airline pilot who had returned to his home town of Chitral and had a soft spot for the English. 'You taught us all this bureaucracy, you know. We had nothing before the Raj! And things have not always worked as well since!' He thought it a great joke.

Later, in Islamabad, PIA claimed to have no knowledge of this confirmation. Brian handled it superbly by getting them to phone the number, explaining the situation to the official in Chitral then simply handing the phone to the PIA clerk in the office. The blistering dressing down he received could be heard a metre away. Our flights were confirmed. A good communications strategy saved us a lot of trouble that time.

The Saraghrar expedition exposed how the problems we had encountered with the free-wheeling organisation of the Cordillera Real expedition became magnified in taking on a more ambitious objective. Far more co-operation was required and the opportunities for misunderstandings based on poor communications multiplied. Above all, leadership failed when it became telling people what to do rather than enlisting their willing support for a shared and agreed plan of action, founded on good communications and a sense of ownership. The two key mistakes were committing to the Northern Cwm route without adequate reconnaissance and the moving of base camp from Totiraz Nok to Druh; decisions taken by one person with no consultation within the team or even, as far as I was aware, with the nominated leader. Despite recognising the communications difficulties experienced in Peru, the response had been to put more faith in radios than in changing the culture of decision making. We got away with it in Peru but didn't in Pakistan.

2. Encounters with altitude in Peru

Following my first expedition to Peru I decided to return for another summer trip with an Alpine Club team of Pam H, Clive, and my partner, Pam C. Living just a little above sea level in the UK, we decided to acclimatise steadily on the Inca Trail to Macchu Picchu before travelling to Huaraz and higher mountains. The flight to Lima, on the shore of the Pacific, was no altitude problem but Clive's hold luggage was mislaid so he missed his flight to Cuzco and the opportunity to acclimatise on the trek.

Flying to Cuzco was a shock to the system. We jumped from 5m to 3400m, but it was either that or a very long bus journey with few opportunities to stretch our legs. We reeled drunkenly around Cuzco trying to take in the sights as our brain cells struggled with the thin air. The Church and Convent of Santo Domingo, built on the foundations of the Inca temple of Qorikancha, did nothing to dispel a distorted, dream-like quality to the experience. Unable to face walking up to the ancient fortress of Sacsaywumàn, we took a taxi and walked back downhill. Pam H was particularly badly affected and threw up into a succession of drain gratings as we walked the streets of the city.

After a few days the effects began to wear off and we caught the train to Kilometer 88 to start the Inca Trail even though Clive was still stuck in Lima awaiting his luggage. In those days it was possible to backpack the Inca Trail, an incentive to travel light with minimal impact, but now access is reserved for trekking agencies with teams of porters carrying luxuries like tables and chairs as well as trekkers' personal luggage. I hope it's still an adventure for the mind as trekkers try to make sense of the extensive archaeological remains that distinguish the route. With three high passes to cross before reaching Macchu Picchu, each a little more challenging than the last, it was a good plan for acclimatisation.

Successfully completing the trek, we flew back to Lima where Clive had been reunited with his baggage so that we could take an overnight coach to Huaraz where the climbing would begin. At just over 3000m, Huaraz was only a problem for Clive, but he seemed to be coping well and we all agreed Pisco was a suitable first climb. At the roadhead there were mules for hire to carry camping gear and the campsite, at a small moraine lake at 4700m, left us with less than 1000m of climbing the following day. The climbing was classic snow and ice with the only real problem an exposed step up onto the summit which involved abseiling from an ice bollard in descent. Of

Pisco 5752m

course, we all gasped a bit on the long summit ridge but felt much the same as on a first 4000m peak of an Alpine season.

The locals described mountaineering in the Andes as "Andinismo", and there are clear similarities to "Alpinismo" in Europe: walks in to a hut or established camp or bivouac site, one- or two-day routes, and mountain towns in which to spend rest days. The level of technical climbing is pretty much the same but it is the altitude that is different; mountains of 3000–4800m in the Alps but 5000–6900m in the Andes. Still, Clive kept up well and returning to the campsite said, 'If the rest of it is that good, well, you can forget the Alps as far as I'm concerned.'

A rest day or two planning for the next climb had produced a settled determination to climb Huascarán Sur, at 6746m the highest peak in Peru. There were four camps required for the ascent so there was time for gradual acclimatisation. A cheerful young camp guard, Edgar, was engaged, transport arranged, and, when we reached Musho, arrieros and burros hired to carry our kit up to base camp at 4200m. Unfortunately, we took the walk in too fast and without enough food or water, which left us dizzily setting up the tents when we arrived. Standing up unsteadily after crouching over tent pegs, I saw spots of intense light through a dull red mist before my vision cleared. Sometimes it was better to just have a sit down for a few minutes.

Edgar was kind enough to help carry some of the gear up to Moraine Camp across glacier-smoothed slabs, running with water in places. Rain showers blew in and the long traverse was sometimes delicate, testing our balance, unaccustomed as we were to the huge rucksacks. There wasn't much moraine left and we camped in gravelly scrapes among the rock. More rain meant that we hedged our bets by ferrying a load up to a deserted Camp 1 but spent another night at Moraine Camp: it was good acclimatisation: "climb high, sleep low".

Next day dawned cold and clear. A caracara, a handsome black and white Andean hawk, landed near to our tents, finding the cold air hard work. We took it as a good omen and set off for Camp 1. Perhaps it was: just after gaining the glacier, there was a rumble of broken ice blocks collapsing onto the slabs that we had just crossed below. It was another reminder of the seriousness of the route. A Spaniard with a broken leg had passed us on horseback just below base camp, and a rescue operation with dogs, sled stretchers, and a guy washing blood out of his hair in a meltwater basin was taking place as we moved up to Moraine Camp. On the first night there, we had heard the clattering of a sled being hauled past our tents in the dark and in the morning a neighbour asked if we had seen the dead Spaniard! We also met two English girls who had failed to summit because they were drawn in to the rescue of a couple who had slipped into a deep crevasse. The couple were both dead by the time they were extracted. A New Zealand pair told us about crosses placed on the edge of a crevasse that they could only cross by a narrow snow bridge, à cheval.

In improving weather, we had reached Camp 1 at 5300m and intended an early start the following morning, but that was not to be. Although Clive had seemed fine at Moraine Camp, now he was suffering from a cracking headache and becoming increasingly nauseous. We delayed our departure to allow time for improvement but instead his condition deteriorated so he and Pam H had no option but to go down.

Pam C and I set off for Camp 2 but heavy sacks slowed us as we climbed in and out of huge crevasses and between massive seracs hung with icicle columns, bent and folded by the wind. Then we ran into a 6–7m ice wall, just off vertical, barring the way. A French team was following their guide's lead, hauling rucksacks and porters up a direct line to embedded snow stakes hammered into the slope above. It was taking some time and after a brief conference they offered to let me lead up the side using the ice screws left in place by their guide.

I found Pam a good belay behind a snow pedestal from which I launched myself onto the wall. It was balancy and sapped arm strength so I decided to place an additional ice screw. I'd just clipped into it when I glanced down to see one of the French guys had climbed up to remove the screw below! A steep sequence of moves and I could clip the last ice screw just under the overhanging lip of the slope above. I reached up with some difficulty to lodge the ice hammer in the brittle ice of ground above the tip: the axe followed and then I was up and over. There was a bent snow stake in front of me but I didn't trust it for a belay. With the French party using all the other stakes there was nothing for it but to fiddle around with ice screws for some awkward sack-hauling before I could bring Pam up, collecting the ice screws as she came.

Unfortunately, we had not eaten or drunk anything while waiting below the wall and this was no place to hang around. We carried on hoping to find an easing where we could take a break but with no luck. My calves were tight and painful by the time we reached a levelling on the spur above. From there it seemed a short traverse to the tents of Camp 2, but as we rounded the spur the slope fell away into a hidden snow

Climbing up to the Garganta on Huascaran.

bowl scattered with fallen ice blocks and threatened by tottering seracs. It was the sort of place to run through but we could barely keep walking and the final pull out of the bowl was a real sting in the tail. The Garganta is the huge saddle between Huascarán Sur and Huascarán Norte and the views were stunning; we felt fully justified in taking a rest day at this camp!

We turned in early, but at 7 a.m. next morning I unzipped the tent and stumbled out into the windy glare; instead of finding a deserted camp, everyone seemed to be packing up. Some were already heading down. They couldn't all have summited yesterday! I collared a passing Italian and he told me that an English group had been turned back in the night when a snow bridge collapsed leaving an uncrossable 5m crevasse; the route would no longer "go" so everyone was bailing out. Guides from Huaraz would be up to place a ladder across the crevasse in a few days' time. All our efforts so far looked like they were wasted. Pam and I hurriedly conferred and decided to stick to our plan to take a rest day then climb next day, at least to get as far as we could. After all we might be able to find a way around the crevasse and it had taken us days to get into this position, so not to be thrown away lightly.

No, there was no way we were going down on the strength of someone else's failure. When the spindrift cleared there was only ourselves and a couple of Americans left at the camp. We went over to ask them what they planned to do and were told, 'We're gonna sit on our sorry asses all day then go up to take a look at that crevasse tomorrow morning.' They were both named Steve and both from Boston, although one had moved there from Canada so wasn't really American after all. We discussed possible rope manoeuvres to tackle the crevasse, but none of us was very happy about trying to sort out the problem in the dark. Not one of the guided parties had stayed to have a go.

I lay in the tent and dozed, then mid-afternoon took a hard look at Huascarán Norte. There was not the slightest sign of a track. We had no guidebook description but I thought it might be possible to pick out a line from the trail on Huascarán Sur. I walked up to 6000m and gazed intently at the south face. There was a line that looked as though it might "go". A snow chute in the middle of the face led up to a serac barrier but a ramp seemed to escape up left onto a glacier shelf leading to a levelling on a snow spur. From there it looked like steep snow slopes stretched all the way to the summit. They were cut by a few crevasses, but it looked as though it would be possible to find a way around them. Best of all there was no evidence of falling ice. Arriving back at the camp I was pounced upon by the Steves, who declared their interest in tackling the route when I explained it to them. Pam was quite happy for the four of us to try it more or less together; suddenly we had a new game plan.

The alarm went off at 11 p.m. but it was freezing and the stove took hours to boil water so that we didn't get away until 1 a.m. We plodded over a large crevasse via a bridge of precariously balanced ice blocks and on into the throat of the Garganta taking a wide arc to avoid possible hidden crevasses in the trackless snow. Odd flashes of light betrayed the Americans' position ahead of us but we only stumbled onto their tracks when we were well into the snow chute at the base of the face. A steep pull up

The camp on the Garganta with Huascaran Norte looming above.

variable snow, sometimes sinking knee-deep, brought us to the serac barrier where we caught up with the two Steves. They were preparing to pitch the escape ramp up to the left.

The ramp proved easier than expected with careful cramponning and a nearly full moon rendered head torches unnecessary except in the deepest moonshadows amongst the glimmering ice. Emerging onto a glacier terrace, we went on hugging the upper edge under low ice cliffs. This line took us above the rounded snow spur, where I'd anticipated taking a break, and onto steepening snow slopes.

Boston Steve led up direct, but I continued traversing on a line that I'd memorised which should have taken us around the crevasse barring the way. When I got to the point of a safe crossing, however, I stuck my head over the upper edge to find a steep-sided bowl with ice cliffs looming in its upper reaches. I traversed back right, along the lip of the crevasse towards the line Steve had taken, until I reached the point where a vertical crevasse split down from the horizontal one. Pam came up to contemplate the three doubtful options for crossing it.

Suddenly a voice floated up from below: 'Does your route "go" up there?' We were noncommittal and they reported that 'a meagre snow bridge' had halted them. Pam and I finally decided to make a rapid crossing of a cracked ice bridge and it held. Just as we were about to shout down that our route did indeed "go", a whoop from below announced that they had made it across their snow bridge. Now only one crevasse crossing lay ahead and we chopped out the cable of a deeply iced-in "deadman" (anchor) to protect the moves; someone had been that way before! That was reassuring but took nothing away from the adventure of working out our own route through the features of the mountain.

The slopes above steepened and we pitched them with ice axe and snow stake belays but no time for intermediate runners. Boston Steve was keeping a close eye on Canadian Steve who was suffering badly from AMS. He'd never been to this altitude before. We stayed roped in separate pairs. As the edges of the face narrowed, Boston Steve commented, 'We'll soon run out of mountain to climb!' But he needn't have worried: what we had thought was the summit proved to be only the start of a ridge consisting of a succession of false summits that sapped our physical and psychological strength.

One false summit too many and we just slumped down with one accord and rested. When we went on it was with only ski poles and cameras. It was still a head-down slog but suddenly the snow before us fell away and the vast panorama of those glorious northern peaks of the Cordillera Blanca filled our sight: the Huandoy group, Artesonraju, Pyramide, Santa Cruz, Chacraraju, glittered below. I turned to shake hands with Boston Steve and soon Canadian Steve and Pam were joining us with more handshakes and hugs. It was strange to be looking down on Pisco whose summit had

Climbing the upper slopes of Huascaran Norte with our North American friends.

felt so high to us just ten days before. We were at 6650m. We took pictures, then the cloud swirled in and it was time to go.

The descent of the ridge was so easy, no longer fighting altitude, that it was embarrassing to think how hard we had found it on the way up. Only Canadian Steve was still in bad shape, complaining of a "black hole" in the vision of one eye as his mate shepherded him carefully towards the steeper down-climbing ahead. This was a reversal of the more commonly known tunnel vision sometimes brought on by altitude sickness. It's a sign of incipient HACE but we weren't carrying Dexamethasone so the only treatment was to get him down as fast as possible. Pam and I kept just ahead as a kind of safety net as Boston Steve kept a tight rope on his friend all the way down.

After recrossing the "deadman" crevasse, the slope eased and we followed the Americans' tracks to their 'meagre snow bridge', easily jumping the crevasse in descent. Towards the spur we spotted an easier lower line to traverse the glacier shelf but as we approached the ramp a hidden crevasse sucked my leg in to the hip: I threw myself sideways, rolled, and slid out of trouble onto the other side of the break. Pam appreciated the belay but cleared the crevasse easily with a mighty leap, landing on the roll. For the Americans, forewarned was forearmed.

Down the sometimes soft, snow chute with huge strides was easy going but soft snow in the Garganta built up between crampon points causing balling. We removed our crampons and descended more easily until bare ice lower down threatened to slide us off down the ice fall without them.

Back at camp we quickly got a brew on as dehydration was bound to be contributing to Canadian Steve's condition. He arrived looking rough but cheerful just as we ran out of fuel. Our dismay soon turned to delight when they passed over a plastic bottle of *bencina blanca* (white benzene) that they'd found cached in a corner of their tent platform. When the snowmelt had boiled for a few minutes, we all drank thirstily. At such a well-used campsite there isn't going to be any unpolluted snow and bacteria can live in snow well below freezing so water had to be thoroughly boiled and might need sterilisation tablets as well. Steve's black holes were still with him but there was no way he was going to a lower camp now and a dose of Dexamethasone would help him through the night.

Settled in the tent, Pam and I dozed off to the comforting roar of the stove, waking amid clouds of steam! Next morning Canadian Steve's vision problems had become intermittent although he was very tired: another dose of medication would hopefully sort him out on the way down to base camp. Guides arrived to sort out the snow bridge; ladders were on the way! They were very interested in our ascent. Few attempts were then made on the Huascarán Norte route pioneered by the American schoolmistress Annie Peck in 1908. The previous day, Camp 1 had been crowded and our four figures had become the focus of attention when spotted on the summit slopes.

We were all back in base camp by mid-afternoon but the Americans needed to make the roadhead to stand any chance of catching their plane. Before they rushed off, Boston Steve commented, 'Thanks! It's not often things turn out better on account of a problem! Good call!'

Back in Huaraz Pam C had little free time before catching her bus to Lima. She had to get back to work earlier than the remaining three of us for whom Alpamayo was waiting.

After seeing her off, Pam, Clive and I arranged a taxi to Cashapampa where we hired an arriero and mules. The use of mules had encouraged Pam H to plan a diet of fresh vegetables for the walk in to base camp. Camping near Llamac Corral at dusk, it was only after the carrots and potatoes had been boiling for over an hour with little effect that we realised we might have a problem. At 3800m water boils at a significantly lower temperature and the stove could not generate enough heat to actually cook the vegetables. We were all hungry and became quite fractious as hours went by with no sign of food being ready. Eventually, with the arriero's help, we made do with a crunchy mixture and got our heads down for the night.

Next day we continued past Lagunas Jatunacocha Chico and Grande to reach Quebrada Arhayacocha, branching off to the left and leading to Alpamayo base camp at 4200m. There were stone wall windbreaks tucked up against boulders and we set up our tents in a couple of these, leaving the arriero to his own devices. There was a Spanish expedition next to us that he could chat to; they were waiting for some of their number who were still up at the Col Camp (5300m). Attempting Quitaraju as well as Alpamayo made sense when you'd worked so hard to get up to the high camp.

The route up to Col Camp used to be an easy glacier plod but had suffered enough from glacial recession by then to have acquired some steep ice steps and threatening seracs. More recently groups have been avalanched by unstable snow and ice. Undeterred, we planned to climb the 1100m in one push; after all, we had surely taken enough time to be acclimatised.

The following morning we loaded up and set out up the faint track through moraine debris above base camp. That track was faint enough to be guesswork at several stages; anxious about the time, I pressed on, route-finding while Pam and Clive came on at their own pace. So, I was some way ahead when Pam's shouts reached me. It wasn't possible to discern exactly what the problem might be but it was clear that she wanted me back there to help with something. I left my rucksack and quickly descended.

The scene that greeted me as I arrived was very odd. Clive was curled up on a large flat rock with Pam hovering over him. She quickly explained what had happened. She had stopped for a pee and asked Clive to turn his back while she relieved herself. He had sat quietly on a rock to wait for her but as she caught up, he made no effort to get going again, or even to register her presence. She began to chivvy him along but with no response. He just gazed at her blankly, then curled up on the rock and appeared to go to sleep. She couldn't wake him. This sounded bad.

I shook Clive into consciousness and got a few words out of him but he wasn't making any sense. I suspected HACE, but he'd been higher than this with no ill effects on Pisco so why was it affecting him now? Leaving him resting with Pam talking to him, I went back for my rucksack and the Dexamethasone it contained. When I returned he was still conscious but still not making sense. We had to get him down to base camp. Fortunately, he remained conscious and retained his swallowing reflex so I could give him a Dexamethasone tablet. Then I relieved him of his rucksack. With me in front carrying his sack as well as my own I was a hefty obstacle to prevent him falling over if he kept his hands on my shoulders for support. Pam came behind holding on to his shoulders to keep him on track and fortunately he was able to put one foot in front of the other down the path to the camp. It wasn't easy though.

Back at camp we sat Clive down and made him some tea. He still wasn't with it. At one point he seemed troubled and hesitantly asked a question: 'Shouldn't I have something? Something more than I've got?'

'What do you mean, Clive? What's missing?'

'It's something I should have.'

'Yes, but what? Hat? Walking pole?'

'Something to carry … didn't I have a rucksack?'

'Yes, it's here just by your tent.'

'Oh, is that mine?'

If it hadn't been so serious, I'd have laughed, but in fact it was progress.

The Spanish expedition next to us had a qualified paramedic on the team and he came over to have a look at Clive. He thought it was HACE too. One of his team had been on Diamox then run out of tablets; he had exhibited similar symptoms. They had plenty of Dexamethasone, injectable ampoules as well as tablets. We would just have to dose Clive up and see how he was in the morning.

Morning came and he was more coherent. That was promising but he wasn't going anywhere. The paramedic confirmed the improvement, then offered to monitor and treat Clive if Pam and I wanted to have a go at Alpamayo. It was a generous offer but we still agonised over whether we should just pack up and head back to Cashapampa. The paramedic thought that Clive probably shouldn't be subjected to the effort of trekking out for a day or two so that tipped the balance and within an hour Pam and I were heading up the path again.

Reaching the glacier, we roped up and followed tracks into a trough through a jumble of broken ice next to a rock wall that appeared to skirt a serac barrier. It did skirt the ice walls but there was a 5m vertical step that I climbed with ice hammer and axe and a certain amount of disbelief when I reached the top, still carrying my heavily loaded rucksack. Pam came up on a tight rope and we scrambled on trying to ignore the precariously overhanging ice pillars that bounded the trough on the glacier side.

Eventually we gained the col between Alpamayo and Quitaraju and dropped down the other side a little way to the campsite. It was a spectacular location with Alpamayo lifting its fluted face just across the glacier bay and the ragged snow ridge of Quitaraju rising from the col above. Turning, a wide panorama opened up in the direction of Huascarán past Artesonraju's dramatic ridges. We pitched our tent and sorted ourselves out for Alpamayo in the morning.

About midnight, Pam started retching. For the rest of the night she would wake up groaning, crawl out of the inner tent, throw up in the porch area then scrape most of the soiled snow out from under the flysheet to form a little pile out in the open. We were not going to climb Alpamayo that morning. She didn't seem to have a headache and

Climbing up to the top camp on Alpamayo.

should not have been having problems with altitude after the Inca Trail and climbing to more than 5000m on two occasions. My first thought was a stomach bug, which she agreed was more likely, so she starved herself for a day and took some Cyproxin. It didn't seem to make much difference; still spasmodic retching.

The plan had been to take a day's rest and climb the route the following day, but this wasn't resting and climbing the following day looked increasingly unlikely. There were no signs of HACE or the crackly chest sounds of pulmonary oedema but she continued nauseous and was getting weaker. I decided to give her Diamox that night and get down in the morning. She didn't sleep well but the retching stopped.

In the morning she felt better: in fact, she felt well enough to argue that we should climb the route and descend on the same day since we were going to be out of food. There was a wild-eyed determination about her that I didn't like. What if she relapsed halfway up the route? In the end it's about respect; respect for the mountain and respect for yourselves. We went down. I never have climbed Alpamayo but I still think it was the right decision.

Back at base camp, Clive was looking better and the Spanish paramedic confirmed his progress. A night's rest and then we walked out to Cashapampa.

That season in Peru gave me a healthy respect for altitude illness and its unpredictability, from person to person and situation to situation. In retrospect I wondered if we had been successful climbing high and sleeping low on Pisco but unsuccessful climbing high to camp high on Huascarán and Alpamayo, but Pam C and I had not been badly affected by that approach and it was difficult to see what else would have worked on Huascarán. Perhaps polluted water had played a part; it's difficult to be patient when the pan is boiling and you're thirsty. Even after these experiences I was caught out on another occasion. You never stop learning.

3. Politics: Classic Himalaya during a civil war

'If anyone asks you where you're from, don't say Britain! Say Australia or New Zealand, not Britain!' That was the warning our sirdar gave us on the first day of our trek in to the Damodar Himal of Nepal, a country which has supplied Gurkha troops for the British Army! His reasons? The support the British government was giving the Americans in their invasions of Iraq and Afghanistan had created a lot of ill-feeling towards the British among local Nepalis, particularly since the "war on terror" had included supplying arms to the Nepali royal family to keep them in power. It was 2002 and Tony Blair's foreign policy was unpopular enough at home. My old Mum had reminded me after one of his speeches was televised: 'The Americans didn't stand "shoulder to shoulder" with us in 1939! It took them two years and an attack by Japan to make up their minds.' More seriously, British foreign policy marked the end of any pretensions the UK might have retained about acting as "honest broker" in international disputes whether in the Middle East or elsewhere.

It wasn't as if Nepal didn't have troubles enough of its own. The last decades of the 20th century had seen growing demands for a more democratic government alternately suppressed or accommodated by a monarchy that enjoyed considerable political power. In 1995 the king had dissolved the democratically elected communist government, which resulted in the Maoist insurrection that lasted the next ten years. In 2001 Crown Prince Dipendra massacred most of his immediate family, including King Birendra, before shooting himself. Maoist rebels stepped up their campaign for a republic and the government collapsed in the face of the increased violence. A truce was declared for peace talks to commence but in November that collapsed after the rebels pulled out complaining of inadequate progress. The government responded by declaring a state of emergency and the new king, Gyanendra, ordered the army to crush the rebels. Government and rebel operations resulted in thousands of deaths during subsequent months. As the civil war continued, parliament was dissolved again with fresh elections leading to a renewal of the state of emergency but then the king dismissed the government and indefinitely postponed the elections which were scheduled for November. November was when our Alpine Club team was planning to start our expedition.

To be fair, the Maoists had declared that tourists were not a target and government forces were equally keen on tourist revenues coming into the country. That hadn't stopped tourist numbers declining by seventy per cent, however, and in response the Nepali Mountaineering Association (NMA) had released 103 new peaks from the restricted list. Our original idea had been to climb a "trekking peak" or two but the opportunity for a Himalayan first ascent was not to be ignored. David volunteered to track terrorist incidents as they were reported in an attempt to verify which areas were safe. When the NMA recommended Pokharkan, lying north of the Annapurnas and west of Manaslu, we kept our options open until David confirmed that the area seemed to be one of the "safe" ones. Game on!

Numerous teams had explored the Peri Himal, which lies to the east and includes Himlung, Gjanj Kang and Kang Guru. Similarly the Chulu trekking peaks to the south are frequently climbed but research showed that very little had been climbed in the Damodar. Apart from Pokharkan, there were at least five other unclimbed peaks including Amotsang, Jomsang, Chhib and Saribung, all around 6300m. Of course, Tilman had done some exploration hereabouts, in 1950 attempting to circumnavigate the Damodar, but he was forced to retreat and eventually made his way west via Pukhung to the Kali Gandaki (in *Nepal Himalaya*, 1952). Our best efforts turned up neither photographs nor any other western traveller who had visited the area since.

The approach would follow the Annapurna Circuit from the Besisahar roadhead to Koto, then strike north towards the Tibetan border. The drive to Besisahar was delayed by army checkpoints searching vehicles, but they had little interest in a busload of climbers and their kit. Besisahar itself was prosperous enough with well-stocked

Setting up top camp on Pokharkan.

shops and busy workshops, while in the surrounding farmlands Dick Isherwood was surprised by the diversity of crops and the proliferation of hydro-electric schemes since his time there, years earlier, working for Save the Children.

We trekked in through harvest time where bunches of marigolds had been twisted into the topknots of haystacks. A citrus-sharp scent rose from half-ripe oranges piled in pyramids on squares of cloth, for sale by the path-side. More marigolds shone orange, and poinsettia blazed scarlet from gardens where children played beneath prayer flags fluttering from bamboo poles. The rickety wooden suspension bridges that Dick remembered had largely been replaced by new constructions of concrete and steel cables. There was plenty of traffic with porters, trekking groups and pony trains, the beasts resplendent in tasselled headdresses.

Distant views of Lamjung and later Himalchuli gave way to occasional glimpses of Manaslu, haloed in shining clouds, as we climbed up the Tal gorge where the Marsyandi river disappeared into a massive boulder-choke below. Perhaps it's the altitude that makes Nepali cicadas seem to chirp their alarms at a higher pitch but we were only ambushed by the seductive scent of Luculia *gratissima* drifting down from little pink flowers above the path. Stone gateways to villages were unbarred, bearing red, white and blue mini chortens on the lintels. Beyond them the path was often divided by a central wall of prayer wheels which had to be passed to the left and turned clockwise by every passing pilgrim. At Bagarchhap, a small square building, its interior lined with Buddhist wall paintings, contained a prayer wheel two metres high that tolled a bell on every turn. A little further on, a stupa complete with the painted eyes of Buddha was surrounded by prayer flags on poles.

It was cloudy reaching Koto after three days on the trail but next morning we woke to astonishingly clear views of Annapurna 2. At the checkpoint there, the police were particularly thorough, scrutinising the porters' IDs and questioning them closely. A sandbagged machine gun emplacement overlooked the approaches to the Naur Gorge and a large bunker had been built next to the village gompa, which was locked. The windows were barred by wrought iron work including a design in which the swastika was framed by two interlocking triangles that formed the Star of David; an unexpected but potent combination of symbols.

At Koto we received some bad news. A descending Sherpa told us that he had climbed Pokharkan from the north two weeks earlier with an elderly Japanese client. His report of waist-deep snow-plodding was no encouragement to repeat their route, but a first British ascent from the south might provide more interesting climbing and would certainly be a new route on the mountain. On the other hand, perhaps we could divert to one of the other peaks. We carried on, undeterred.

Once off the Annapurna Circuit, the Naur Gorge was a wild place with soaring rock walls into which galleries had been quarried to take the path, high above shadowy depths where the river twisted and tumbled among huge boulders. A gang of labourers working on a new bridge offered us tea but otherwise we only encountered one pony train and one trekking group in the three days it took to reach Phugaon. In marked contrast to the thriving villages below, Meta and Kayang, where we camped, were

Glacier approach to the South Face of Pokharkan.

deserted, their complex irrigation schemes broken or silted up. Among the ruins were some buildings in better repair with padlocked or walled-up doors indicating possible seasonal occupation, but even those families would be but a fraction of the community that had once lived there. Chortens were crumbling although some mani walls showed signs of care and even new paintwork.

These long treks to the mountains are classic features of Himalayan expeditions and part of their appeal is the sheer variety of the landscape through which they pass. On the forested shelves of the lower Phu Khola, fir and spruce had been interspersed with stands of bamboo, arching like fishing rods, with raspberries and wild strawberry, rustling with furtive finches, tits and the cackling, jay-like nutcracker. Higher up these gave way to juniper and flame-red berberis, while lammergeier, griffon vultures and golden eagles circled on widespread wings among the shining peaks. A rock-cut passage took us behind a waterfall, hung with icicles and frost-rimed with spray. We were trekking from harvest time into winter.

Following the riverbed we came upon a huge pillar of rock, splitting the narrowing gorge and forcing a steep ascent of the flank of a tributary valley. A little further on, a ruined fort on a spur across the gorge confronted us with a commanding field of fire along the length of our precarious path accessing the valley above. There a ruined gompa guarded a bridge over the torrent and the surrounding giant chortens and mani walls staked a clear claim to the territory, emphasising its strategic significance. Dick was later to tell me that Na to the south and Phu to the north had both been part of the same kingdom so these fortifications which effectively divided them were puzzling. Tilman received a story of Rajah rivalry and warfare which may explain them.

Phugaon itself shared this appearance of fortification, its narrow twisting "streets" climbing up to a massive walled structure bristling with prayer flags cresting the hilltop high above the river. At first sight it seemed thriving enough but again there was evidence of abandoned buildings and fields left untended on the periphery. On the wooden doors of many dusty buildings crude red hammer and sickle symbols were scrawled; perhaps just the modern expression of a tradition of conflict. A moraine hill opposite was home to some kind of processional way winding up through serried ranks of mani walls, chortens and prayer flag poles to a ceremonial platform at the top, but again the gompa was locked and empty. Pottering about in the grounds, we came upon an area where bone fragments and clay figurines suggested that traditions of sky burial were still being followed.

Here we were only a few miles from the Tibetan border. Great snowy mountains, one doing a passable imitation of the Matterhorn, seemed always to be looking over our shoulders. High, cold and arid, scrub and sparse grassland supported yak and goat grazing as well as the wild bharal (blue sheep). The team spent a day, walking off in different directions to gain vantage points from which to work out an approach to Pokharkan. It was a much more complex mountain than the inadequate maps had suggested. This reconnaissance impressed us with the mountain's size and the uncertainty of finding the best route. We would have to base our decisions on the balance of probability and be prepared to adapt in the light of new knowledge of the route as we climbed it. I went west, finding little encouragement but those who went east had more luck. The east face seemed to have a feasible snow and ice route winding up around serac barriers towards a summit – perhaps *the* summit. After much debate, we determined to set up a base camp below that east face.

Pushing on up the valley above Phugaon, we were suddenly surprised by vulture after vulture sweeping in low over our heads to land among the rocks above. I crept up, using those rocks for cover, to count 16 of them squabbling over the carcass of a big bharal, their heads and necks red with blood. A Sherpa confirmed our suspicions: 'Snow leopard kill. Leaves sign but not seen.' We had probably disturbed it with the noise of our passage so the elusive cat left the kill to the ever-vigilant vultures.

We camped below an apparently deserted village on the way to the east face but the campsite quickly lost the sun. Dick and I decided to walk up to the village to enjoy the last of the sunshine and were surprised to encounter a lone yak herdsman, muffled against the cold. With a face the colour and texture of old leather, he seemed as tough as old boots and of equally indeterminate age. He chatted away in Nepali to Dick, who established that he was the only surviving inhabitant of the village. The rest had headed south, hoping for work on the Annapurna trail. Despite his obvious poverty he invited us home to share a meal of potatoes but we declined as there would be a meal waiting for us at camp. As we walked down into the shadows of camp Dick muttered as much to himself as to me, 'He's the real thing that guy, the real thing!'

Finding a base camp with a spring was an unexpected bonus on the arid hillside, but the cold was intensifying as November drew on and two of the team decided to bail out in favour of lower level trekking. A rock and moraine ridge gave access to a

Kaji struggling with the ice pitch on Pokharkan.

deep col on the south ridge, as we'd hoped, and on our first visit Toto and I climbed a subsidiary peak of 5700m in the process of reconnoitring the traverse line onto the east face. By the time we obtained a clear view the temptation to summit nearby Pokharkan SE was irresistible. Snowflakes drifted past as we descended and next morning base camp lay under 15cm of snow, putting paid to any further load carrying to advanced base camp. After much dossing around we turned out for tea to find the cook team had built a snow stupa outside the mess tent!

There was no more snow but we all knew the lateness of the season was increasing the chances of that every day so we broke trail with heavy loads up to ABC and settled in. The Sherpas went on to scout the huge glacier bay between the south-west and south-east ridges of the mountain and returned bubbling with enthusiasm for an attempt on the south face rather than the original plan for the east face. They were so keen that they had cached a rope at their high point so that we felt duty bound to give it a go, keeping the east face in reserve. Unfortunately, two of the team had to go down to base camp, suffering from the altitude, so we decided to place another camp at 5600m in the glacier bay; lightweight assault tents for just six of us.

On summit day as I left high camp in the biting before-dawn air, I called, 'See you' to John and Dick in the next tent, but when John caught up at the crampon fixing stop, he was alone. Dick had been having difficulty breathing and kept John awake most of the night with his coughing so had wisely decided to descend.

The route climbed out of the glacier bay on a broad snow ramp leading to the right from the lower left edge of the face where it abutted the rock buttresses of the south-west ridge. The ramp steepened to reach a shelf with serac barriers above. Climbing up through the seracs at about 5900m, I came upon Kaji backing off an ice cliff that barred the way above. The enthusiasm of the Sherpas had clearly affected their judgement about the difficulties presented by the ice; Kaji had described it as a gentle slope from where they'd left the rope. Now he climbed gingerly down and handed his ice axe and hammer plus a few ice screws to young Ngima then prepared to belay him. It was clear from the way Ngima handled the tools that he wasn't familiar with the techniques of climbing steep ice. It was Ngima's first trip and I suppose some kind of rite of passage was going on, but it made no sense to me so I stepped in and took the tools myself. Kaji belayed me instead. The 10m pitch was about grade 3/4 and proved to be the crux of the route. As Kaji put it later at the party in Koto, 'If you not climb that, then we not climb the mountain', and laughed uproariously.

Ngima came up on a tight rope with two snow stakes to substitute for the crossed ice tools that was my belay in the snow. Then he and Darma took the route on down into an enormous crevasse well filled with snow and the debris of collapsed ice. The exit was via a crack in the upper ice wall that provided some bridging moves, unusual in crampons, to emerge on another glacier ramp. This upper glacier led right up some steeper steps to reach the south-east ridge at about its mid-point.

It was interesting climbing with the Sherpas. The two youngest broke trail up the glacier, roped together, and the rest of us were expected to follow, unroped, in their tracks. If one of them fell into a crevasse, well, he would be pulled out and another

Help arriving during a crevasse incident on Pokharkan.

route found; it was a crude technique but at least it was fast. The only problem was when Bill put a leg into a crevasse and had to hold himself on the brink with his axe while Kaji got the spare rope to him. Bill had been directly on the track, and I'm not suggesting that he was porky but there wasn't a lot of weight in those young Sherpas.

Buffeted by strong winds on the narrow south-east ridge, the situation suddenly seemed more serious. Ngima's glove was blown away and he was heading down to save his hand from frostbite until the resourceful John dug a spare out of his rucksack. The nearer summit was close but I had a nasty suspicion that it was lower than another about a kilometre further across a windswept saddle. There was only one way to be sure; I climbed the ridge. The summit of what we christened Pokharkan 2 was definitely lower at 6250m. There was nothing for it but to go on.

I broke trail across the saddle while the rest of the team ascended Pokharkan 2. From the base of the summit ridge I watched with some disbelief as they then turned to descend, the young Sherpas in the lead; my scrape of shelter suddenly seemed a very lonely place. Then Martin and Kaji began following my trail. 'They've had enough', Martin shouted above the wind in answer to my unspoken question.

The three of us swung onto the final ridge and bent into the slope, fighting gravity and altitude; even Kaji was gasping and he'd summited Everest five times. Heads down against the wind, eyes focused on crampons biting into ice or crunching snow, there was a sense of surprise when the angle eased and, looking up, I found myself surrounded by a panorama of magnificent snowy peaks. There was another summit slightly lower than ours to the north, but we were there, on the summit (6350m). The view south-west was dominated by the Annapurna range, dazzling in the sun, while to the north shining peaks stretched away into Tibet.

116

After some unreserved handshaking, backslapping and photography, we turned to the descent. By ploughing straight across the saddle, we could avoid reclimbing Pokharkan 2, instead traversing its flank to meet the line of ascent lower down the ridge. Kaji got out the rope and I led with him as backstop and Martin in the middle. A fixed rope set by those ahead of us solved the problem of the ice wall. Retracing our steps all the way back to high camp took only two hours now we were no longer fighting altitude, although at one point Martin insisted on taking a break, saying simply, 'I'm buggered!' Despite our speed, this was 17 November and fading light meant another night at high camp was inevitable. It had been a long day.

Next morning, we descended to ABC for a large late breakfast before continuing to base camp where consensus graded the route at AD+, reflecting the difficulty of the ice wall and objective dangers. That night a Himalayan bear must have prowled around the camp, leaving tracks in the snow; three claws trailing between the deep palm prints among criss-crossings of bhural and yaks. We had intended to reconnoitre some of the other peaks but Martin reported a frostbitten toe and the weather could only get colder so we put him on antibiotics and went down to Phugaon.

There John sketched the local children and sang Scottish folksongs to them while their faces registered complete incomprehension. There too news came that our planned exit via the Kang La, a high pass leading to Manang, was impassable owing to snowfall. Concerned that there might be more snow we retreated to Koto with Kaji warning us to stay together in case of bandits. This was no euphemism for Maoists. Maoists would ask for a donation to the cause and leave trekkers with a receipt to be produced to avoid being taxed with further claims for donations. Their tactics had been to bomb government buildings and shoot the relatively poorly organised and armed police, thereby creating an administrative vacuum into which they could step. But with the police gone, criminal elements might take advantage of the opportunity to fleece tourists under threat of violence despite Maoist assurances of tourist safety.

Stream crossings were verglased and birch woodland hung with snow now, but spectacular gorges, deserted villages and the towering mountains were still achingly beautiful in the low winter sunlight. Luckily, we reached Koto without incident whereupon the tea house did us proud with a celebratory bonfire, spitting sparks into the night, and pitchers of chang. Climbers, Sherpas, cook team and porters danced in the moonlight under fluttering prayer flags.

John and I had worked out that we just had time to complete the Annapurna Circuit before flying home and Ngima had never done it so was keen to join us. The rest of the team headed back down to Besisahar to find heavily armed government forces holding the town. Maoist insurgents had given notice of their intention to attack so the party left quickly for Kathmandu.

Back in the prosperity belt, the Annapurna Circuit lived up to its reputation, perhaps because there were none of crowds of more peaceful times. From Koto to Muktinath, we trekked past water-driven prayer wheels and watermills lining the banks of streams. Ancient gompas clung to cliffs, with views like the Gangapurna Icefall or the distant spire of Tilicho striking the eye at each new turn. A cold lonely crossing of the Thorung La, at 5416m, was a high point of the trek: a dark wind lifted and dropped the mass of prayer flags heaving at the crest of the pass, like the swell of a wave. Down into Muktinath we sought out the Temple of the Eternal Flame but it was locked up. No matter, Ngima knew of another shrine where we could see the flame dancing out of the rock. At yet another shrine water poured from a semicircle of ornamented spouts which Ngima rapidly utilised for a shower. Into the valley of the Kali Gandaki we found ourselves moving back through the season into early autumn and a more Hindu culture; prayer flags gave way to shrines to Shiva and Ganesh.

At Jomosom a large army post surrounded by razor wire picked off passers-by at random for questioning at its gates. Despite paperwork that had satisfied all the checkpoints so far, a soldier suddenly demanded sirdar's identity papers from Ngima which he simply could not be expected to have. We were reasonable, calm, patient, but to no avail. The army response was to encourage us to carry on and leave Ngima to them. This we were not going to do. I decided to make a fuss and demanded to see the squaddie's commanding officer. When it was clear that we were not going to move without compliance, a ranking officer was found. His English was better and he cross-examined us on how we had come to "employ" Ngima: it seemed they were worried that we had just picked him up on the trail and he could be a Maoist using us to get

Martin climbing up to the summit ridge on Pokharkan.

himself into Kathmandu! Some forceful reassurances convinced the CO that that was not the case and we were all allowed to continue. It was clear that the more remote areas were tacitly recognised to be beyond army control.

Further down-river I encountered an army patrol out of uniform but well armed. They weren't keen to be photographed but allowed me to spectate when they covered a building while the officer crashed in for a shouted interrogation of its occupants. It was only when I saw how those on the flanks were getting ready to shoot anyone running from the house that it occurred to me there could be an exchange of fire and it wasn't a good place to hang about. Police quarters at the next checkpoint had new stone walls fortifying the doorways. After returning to Kathmandu, the two members of our party who had opted to trek in the Langtang area confirmed our impressions of the conflict with tales of burnt-out police posts and rebel slogans on banners stretched across the trail.

The civil war dragged on until April 2008 when the Maoists secured a simple majority in the country's general election with a mandate to create a republic. In May 2008 the 240-year-old monarchy was abolished with 560 of the 564 members of the Constituent Assembly voting for the change. Despite considerable political disagreement and jockeying for position the peace has held and Nepali tourism has increased accordingly.

In retrospect we took quite a risk in making this expedition, particularly since most travel insurance policies will invoke an exemption clause if there are costs incurred related to civil disturbance or war. The war on terror, which is clearly unwinnable by any side, continues and the 21st century has continued to generate more danger for travellers in a world in which religious and political disputes have grown more bitter and violent. In June 2013 ten climbers and their guide were massacred by militants who attacked a Nanga Parbat base camp. This dimension of expedition research and planning was virtually unknown to early explorers of the Himalaya but now it is an essential consideration.

4. Protocols in China: Kawarani and Haizi Shan

In 2003 Tamotsu Nakamura had produced *East of the Himalayas – To the Alps of Tibet* in a Special Edition of the *Japanese Alpine News*. It was a summary history of exploration in the Eastern mountains of Tibet coupled with more detail about his own exploratory visits and a wealth of photographs and maps. I remember it caused quite a stir: suddenly there was an area, little known to many, that seemed to have immense potential for exploratory mountaineering and challenging first ascents. Dick Isherwood had been quick off the mark and assembled a team to attempt Haizi Shan in 2004. He and Geoff Cohen got to within six pitches of the summit, but ran out of time and, without bivouac kit, decided to head back down.

I had rather lost touch with Dick as my interest had focused on ski-mountaineering expeditions since 2002, notably achieving six first ascents in Kyrgyzstan and my height record of 7546m on Mustagh Ata, then regarded as the highest ski peak in the world. So I was pleasantly surprised when, in 2005, Toto, an Alpine Club friend, and I received an invitation from Dick to join his expedition to climb Kawaranis I and II in the Gongkala Shan. He had spotted these peaks while sightseeing near Garze after having to give up on Haizi Shan, and very attractive they looked too. Dick was putting together an entirely new team with Peter who was drafted in to take Geoff Cohen's place, and including Peter's wife, Nona, who would act as trip doctor but wouldn't be climbing.

Toto and I travelled via Beijing, visiting the Forbidden City and trekking along a section of the Great Wall; the sheer scale of both structures was simply awe-inspiring. Then we flew on to Chengdu where we met the team, including Yuen Yuen, aka Vanessa, our interpreter, and the cook, Chung. That evening, on the banks of the Brocade River, people queued to float paper lotus blossom boats containing candles and the name of their beloved off downriver in moonlight. This was part of the moon festival but the sky was too cloudy for it to be seen. The ritual seemed to be something that a lot of couples did together.

Two days' driving took us to Garze via Kangding and the deep gorges of the Dardu and Yala rivers, although a new tunnel bypassed Luding and its chain bridge, which had been the focus of one of the most heroic battles of Mao's Long March (Dick was really disappointed.) The landscape became progressively Tibetan with lots of chortens and gompas, and a new stupa being erected on the highest pass. The typical flat-roofed, three-storey houses were all brightly painted in beautiful designs; animals were housed on the ground floor providing a kind of underfloor heating in winter, while the upper floors were occupied by an extended family. Mountain barley was drying on the roofs with open corners where people could sit out in the sunshine, in many cases next to satellite dishes. Some of the wealthier-looking buildings had Chinese style roofs and there were triangular "plantations" of prayer flags on nearby slopes which we had not seen in Nepal.

It was very different to be driving through this landscape rather than trekking as we had done in the classic Himalayan expedition in Nepal. Chinese policy seemed to be to invest in infrastructure and let the people make use of it: 'Build a road; people will come.' In a park in Garze there were the same sort of exercise equipment stations I'd seen in France: here whole families were having a go amid much laughter.

After arriving in Garze, we spent three days scouting routes on the mountains from viewpoints on the hills around the range. We walked up from 3300m to over 4000m every day and on the last reached 4800m gaining some useful acclimatisation, and finding a mani wall of ancient engraved stones, several metres long and more than a metre high, literally in the middle of nowhere. From the north I was attracted by a long spur leading to a steep but climbable face directly below the main summit. There was the option of the east ridge if that didn't 'go' but the rest of the team was keen on an approach to the col between the two summits via broken glaciers from the south.

We drove to the monastery village of Khur Chong but there was no one to talk to at the monastery. At the village the people were very friendly; one young man spoke Mandarin and claimed to be the nephew of the Rinpoche. Yuen explained our plans and negotiated horses to carry our kit up the trail from the village to a hanging valley below the southern glaciers where we hoped to site our base camp. Back at the hotel we packed up ready for the walk in next day.

The hotel plumbing combined ornate fixtures and fittings with inadequate drains; a shower could leave you paddling in sewage. Whether it was that or something I ate, I don't know, but I was sick as a dog that night. Too weak to walk, I slept until 3 p.m. after the team had departed early. Then I tried a few biscuits with the immediate effect of projectile diarrhoea. I took Ciproxin and went back to sleep. Next morning our driver found me some breakfast and I felt well enough for him to drive me to Khur Chong where he arranged a local guide to shoulder my pack and lead me up to base camp.

When I got there Toto, Dick and Peter were away scouting for an advanced base camp, returning later pleased with what they had found. They told me that the monastery had given its blessing in the very tangible sense by providing a monk with a large white yak to lead the way to base camp. As Dick said later, 'It could hardly have been a more auspicious start.' The feeling of well-being continued as we carried loads to ABC and reconnoitred the route above, then giving ourselves a rest day to acclimatise. On the last evening there were views of the summit at sunset. Venus appeared in a sky filling with stars that was then streaked by shooting stars and seared by quiet, dry sheet lightning while we stood around telling stories until it was too cold to stay out of the tents any longer. Later that night thunderstorms rolled in.

Next morning we packed our rucksacks to move up to ABC. As we reached a moraine ridge, we heard shouts, whistles and whoops and caught sight of about eight monks climbing up towards us. They were still some way off and we had no reason to think there was a problem so carried on to reach ABC and were sorting out kit when they arrived about 15 minutes later. Through sign language we were peremptorily instructed to go down. We queried, argued, then refused as best we could in sign language. They replied with threats. Knives came out of the ornate scabbards tucked down the back of their waist sashes and belts. Reinforcements arrived. We radioed base camp where Nona, Yuen and the cook were being similarly threatened. We reckoned we had no alternative but to return to base camp to try to sort this out. To our dismay, they insisted on taking all our kit down with us, undoing the work of days, although that involved them in carrying most of it.

At base camp we found about 40 monks and villagers; the monks from the same monastery that had blessed the expedition just four days earlier. When this was pointed out they simply stated that they had changed their minds as a result of two thunderstorms that they regarded as warnings from the Buddhas who lived on the mountain tops that the foreigners should not climb the mountain. Most of the monks appeared to be teenagers and the senior monks refused to give their names. When one seemed inclined to negotiate a younger one pushed him aside and asserted that he was in control.

Base Camp, Kawarani in the background.

At one point, Yuen appealed to a senior monk in Mandarin since he had already admitted having been to university in Beijing: 'You know that these people are not responsible for the thunderstorms. You know that there are often thunderstorms at this time of year.'

'Of course, but that is not the point.'

The point would emerge later, but for now the monks showed no respect for the permit that we produced from the Sichuan Mountaineering Association and when we told them we would make a complaint there was a display of aggression that left us in no doubt that whoever had whipped up this hysteria was no longer really in control. Literally, the knives were out for us and I realised that we could disappear up here and no one would ever know what had become of us.

There was no choice but to go down although we extracted the concession that Dick and I could stay in camp to supervise an orderly packing up of the supplies and equipment that could not be taken down immediately on horses that arrived just before nightfall. There was going to be a lot of it and Chung, the cook, deserved some support or his kitchen would have been dismantled piecemeal around him. There was some flexibility there because the more senior monks were all on the portly side and clearly going to find the walk down in darkness challenging so had by then planned to stay the night themselves. Six of them and four horses stayed with Chung cooking a meal for all of us while they rifled our stores for goodies.

After breakfast next morning Dick and I packed up our personal stuff and tent, leaving Chung and the monks to pack up the rest of the kit. We limited our own involvement in that to a few strategic interventions when it looked like damage would be done. Despite one of them claiming to have handled horses in a previous existence, the monks all exhibited a spectacular incompetence that supported the idea that they'd never done a day's work in their lives. It took them hours to load the horses only to find that when they set off the loads fell off within minutes. The journey back down the mountain was punctuated with frequent rest stops while the baggage straps were reattached.

Eventually we reached the village where we met Yuen on her way to the monastery to plead for the family of the young man who had organised the horses for us. They were going to be banished from the village by the monks, effectively making them homeless, and, once banished, it was   unlikely they would be taken in by another village. The monks were also demanding money for injured horses, producing one with a scratch to justify the claim, which, if it had any substance, was entirely their own fault for not allowing us all to leave in the morning. If she did not pay, we would not get our baggage back; that was their position.

While she was negotiating, the rest of the team was reunited at the scratch bivouac site by the roadside which was all the accommodation available by the time they arrived in the middle of the night. They had had a horrendous descent being spat at, jostled and tripped by aggressive young monks who thought it a great joke when they fell. Arriving at the village the mother of the young man whose family were being banished attacked Yuen and Nona, scratching their faces and spitting.

Kawarani.

Yuen had managed to organise a truck for the kit and Chung took it up to the monastery. Peter and I decided to walk up to see if there was anything we could do to help. Yuen paid out $250 and the bags appeared. I checked them as they were loaded onto the truck and all seemed to be there. After hours of talk with the most senior monks Yuen had only been able to extract the concession that they would have another think before confirming banishment on the family. We drove to Garze, where a complaint from our agent to the Garze Tibetan Ethnic Group Autonomous Prefecture, which governs this region, only secured the response that 'these monasteries can be difficult to deal with.' The official who delivered that response himself claimed to be a reincarnate lama. It was Friday and the following week was a national holiday so we gave up on any further official protest, which would, in all likelihood, have been similarly unsuccessful.

Dick did some research later for his report in the *Alpine Journal* ('*A Cautionary Tale*') and found from the American *Alpine Journal*s of 2001 and 2003 that we were not the only climbers to have suffered similar problems with monasteries, although the 2003 report referred to Yunnan. Undoubtedly the Chinese government has granted a considerable autonomy to the area probably in return for the local Khampas not causing any trouble about the situation in Tibet itself. Jonathan Neale in *Tigers of the Snow* (a history of the Sherpas' involvement in climbing) throws some light on the background of Tibetan Monastic Buddhism:

The popular image in the West now is of Tibetans as a calm, nonviolent people. This reflects the personality and values of the current Dalai Lama. Some Tibetans have always been like him. Most have not. Traditional Tibet was a lightly governed and sparsely populated country. Many people were herders, and all over the world pastoralists steal each other's animals. Bandits were common. The great monasteries made war on each other, and each had its own regiment of warrior monks.

Tilman, in *Nepal Himalaya*, considering the type of religion practised, is more dismissive:

> No doubt it was never a very exalted kind – by no means pure Buddhism, but a superstitious animism mainly concerned with the propitiation of a hierarchy of malign and terrible demons, over which, nevertheless, from wall, altar, and banner, the placid eye of the Master presides.

Perhaps if we had made a significant donation to the monastery when we first made contact with the village that might have made a difference but it's debatable. The most likely scenario is that we unwittingly instigated some kind of power struggle between the monks and the villagers; one that the monks comprehensively won to our cost. That appeared to have been the point referred to earlier in the Mandarin exchange with Yuen at base camp. Somehow, we missed out on whatever protocols would have avoided the events described.

We managed to get our permit switched very quickly to Haizi Shan in hopes of completing the route that Dick and Geoff had pioneered in 2004. Yuen secured a mixture of vehicles for transport and we were soon ensconced in another base camp. It seemed that the laughing thrushes that had called 'Peter, Peter' at our previous base camp had followed us to this one, but perhaps the birds just took their cue from Nona.

Making our first load carry, we stumbled onto a couple of tents pitched next to an almost circular jade-green lake that had rock gardens and a neglected Buddhist shrine on its shores. Snatches of conversation proved the occupants to be British but they were very nervous and cagey about what they were doing when we asked. Later they admitted that they were from Hong Kong and had got up to the north summit the previous year. They were hoping to do better this year but it was obvious that they were ignoring protocol by not having a permit.

In changeable weather and plagued by stomach upsets, we struggled up to establish a high camp at the foot of the glacier below the north summit. The Hong Kong team camped nearby.

Part of the problem with the stomach upsets was that Nona seemed not have taken on board the different circumstances involved at an expedition base camp compared to an urban situation in the first world. In the US, where she practised, there was an understandable reluctance to prescribe antibiotics before the patient had had a chance to go home, rest and let their own immune system tackle the problem. On expedition, however, there is never going to be the time, in this case particularly after our wasted efforts on Kawarani. Lower standards of hygiene at base camp meant that if someone

ABC on Haizi Shan.

picked up a bug and it was not killed off quickly, it would be likely to go through the whole team, which is exactly what happened. Basically, different protocols applied.

It probably made little difference. Once in position we suffered a succession of bad weather days. On one night of continuous snowfall much of it came in great surging gusts roaring down the mountain followed by intervals of total stillness before the distant rumble of the next gust. Toto worried that they were spindrift avalanches but in daylight we could see these gusts spinning down like mini–tornadoes to dissipate at lower levels. Another night, a thunderstorm seemed to go on forever, hurling hail and snow at the tent walls, bellying in under the pressure of the wind. Finally, we held a council of war and decided, with no signs of improving weather, to beat a retreat. The Hong Kong team had already descended.

Back at base camp Yuen, Nona and Chung were pleased to see that we were safely down after such bad weather. The weather promptly relented, although the spindrift plume flying from the summit of Haizi Shan testified to the strength of the wind up there. There was some fine walking that Nona had begun to explore while we had been away and that remained an option for us during the last few days. Dick seemed to be really disappointed with the trip and escaped into solitary birding in the valley. He'd had a row with Nona and back at Chengdu was to have another with Yuen. Peter, Toto and I walked up a 4000m peak to get a good view of the opportunities to access

Haizi Shan's north-west face but it was a fine mountain scramble in its own right. Peter's Scottish background led him to christen a neighbouring peak An Teallach II; it certainly looked more challenging but still appeared to be no more than an attractive scramble.

We were all rather chafing at the loss of opportunities to climb, yet it was only Peter and I that set out for An Teallach II next morning. Expecting to make a fast, lightweight ascent, we took no technical climbing gear. We followed intermittent animal tracks steeply up to a boulder-filled amphitheatre where wild bharal (blue sheep) roamed, then had to work out a traverse line onto the south ridge. Once on the ridge, we turned a big gendarme on the left and continued along the crest until we reached a deep chasm containing snow in its shadowy depths. It was too wide to bridge, very steep, and both loose and vegetated: climbing down then up the other side was way too risky. A platform on the other side was lower than the lip on our side so that jumping might be the only way forward; but would that trap us on a precipitous section of the ridge?

I made a leap of faith, having to believe that there must be a safe way off further up the mountain. It felt like I was in the air for longer than expected but at least I landed

Retreating from ABC after the storm on Haizi Shan.

safely. Peter stayed on the other side so that he could go for help if necessary while I scrambled along the further ridge far enough to find a saddle with scree slopes that we could descend if we had to. When I returned it was Peter's turn as I stood poised to field him if he landed short but he landed easily: 'Nay bother!'

Beyond the saddle was a difficult rock step but I found a line to the left, warily handling a precariously wedged flake. Above that we scrambled carefully along the ridge more or less keeping to the crest for the most solid rock. The summit ridge had snow on one side and loose rock on the other; it could have been described as knife-edged if it hadn't been for dense tufts of grass growing out of the very top in places. Finally, we reached its highest point and could take in the expansive views. Minya Konka loomed in the distant south while away across the plains snowy mountains defined the horizon. Haizi Shan was pre-eminent among the snow-draped mountains nearby although to the south-east was a big rocky pyramid that would be a real technical challenge for some teams. Our summit was higher than Mont Blanc so I suppose it represented a kind of consolation prize.

On the descent of the ridge we took a break and Peter said, 'I love this you know.'

'What? The place?'

'The mountain. The climbing. All of it.'

'Yeah,' I agreed. 'Mind you we'd have got a lot more climbing done if we'd gone to the Alps.' Our laughter echoed about the crags.

Then we ran off down the screes back into the boulder-filled cirque, where a solitary blue poppy bloomed between rocks.

Haizi Shan at sunset.

As far as protocols were concerned that was not the end of the story. From both of those final day trips it had been possible to work out that there might be access to the north-west face of Haizi Shan involving steeper climbing but avoiding the length and cornices of the north ridge. I wondered if Dick was going to organise another expedition attempt. So far, he and Geoff had got further than anyone else. In subsequent months we corresponded sporadically about ideas for 2006 and I was able to ask him directly if he wanted to go back to Haizi Shan. His answer was indirect: no, he didn't want the hassle of organising another expedition, but yes, he would go back. When I offered to do the organising, he was keen to come along.

Had Dick wanted to organise another expedition to the mountain I would have deferred to his prior claim and accepted any decision he made about including me in the team. I considered that a civilised protocol but perhaps I was naïve. Perhaps also I hadn't realised that Haizi Shan was considered quite such a prize. Dick told me later that Fred Beckey had warned him off making another attempt. In 2006, pre-monsoon, an American team, including Beckey, did make an attempted ascent but got no further than Dick's high point. Dick's response had been 'good luck to them', but we wouldn't be giving up our own plans for the mountain; even if they made the first ascent, we had the option of making a new British route.

Our proposed attempt was going to be post-monsoon, in October, when we hoped for better weather. I'd been through the process of making grant applications to the Mount Everest Foundation among other bodies and had negotiated a logistics package from the same agent who had supported our previous expedition. The grants had been awarded and we were all looking forward to returning to the fray that autumn when, near the end of the summer, I received an email from Malcolm, a fellow Alpine Club member, asking if we would like to share base camp costs with him and Pat, a New Zealander, who were also intending to make an attempt at exactly the same time. By way of encouragement, Pat said how much she had enjoyed sharing base camp with a British team on Xiashe.

I confess to being doubtful and did a little research about the Xiashe ascents which revealed that as soon as the British team turned up Pat and her partner abandoned their attempts at a harder line to rush around to an easier aspect of Xiashe in order to secure the first ascent. I had some misgivings about getting involved in a race to the summit but put the proposal to the team to see what they thought.

Several points emerged: they were happy with the service provided by our agent and would not be happy about cancelling the arrangements that we had already made in order to take up with another agent; any race for the summit would increase the danger level of the trip; were we only being invited to make the competing expedition safer in that we would be morally bound to act as back-up if the others got into difficulties? The consensus that emerged was that we didn't want to get into that situation. Our agent was happy to organise a permit for another mountain but at such short notice it just wasn't possible to research another expedition in enough detail to make a proper MEF application so we all felt that we were left no option but to cancel.

Malcolm and Pat did make the first ascent of the north-west face 'in good style', although when I spoke to him, back in London, he said it hadn't been good climbing.

Peter and Toto enjoying a consolation prize; a 4800m satellite peak.

Perhaps he was being kind. I did ask how he came to reach the decision to compete with our expedition, knowing that we had secured funding and all that that involved. His reply was interesting. The objective had been suggested to him by one of the MEF team. When I asked that person why he had done so it appeared that he had held a grudge about not being included in the Kawarani expedition. Wheels within wheels!

5. Good style and the difficulties of maintaining it: Yangmolong, China

In October 2007 I had followed up on the suggestion by our Chinese agent to research Yangmolong, at 6066m one of the three remaining unclimbed 6000m peaks of the region. It had attracted the attention of two Japanese expeditions. One, approaching from the south, recorded rockfall and threatening seracs but had gained the western saddle. They had climbed the west summit, Dangchezengla, (5830m) after deciding that the traverse of Makara, the central summit, to the main summit looked too difficult. Another had approached from the north but appeared to have been put off by the steep north faces and avalanche-prone slopes. A Chinese expedition had attempted Makara but one of their rising stars, Liu Xinan, had been killed on the climb, prompting a retreat. I opted to approach from the north with hopes of avoiding the instability of the south faces.

Dick and Peter were keen to come again, although I vetoed Peter's wife coming along; I knew this climb was going to be a tough one and was concerned that Peter might lose the required focus if he was balancing the demands of climbing with those of keeping his non-climbing wife happy. I liked Nona and it was understandably not a popular decision with her or Peter; a difficult decision to make but I had to think about how the team would work together. Making difficult decisions is what leadership is about. Toto wasn't interested so Steve who had been with me on Mount Logan was drafted in.

We all flew in to Chengdu, met with our agent, Jiyue, his brother and business partner, Shaohong, and the interpreter/liaison person he had assigned to us, Gary. We had time for some last shopping before driving to Batang via Yajang and Litang in two long days. En route we crossed passes of up to 4700m, with a long section of very high road affording views of Haizi Shan from the south-west, Xiashe, and probably Genyen and Yangmolong, all distinguished by their snowy raiment. Dick spotted three lammergeiers, and a small hawk flew straight into the windscreen. Newly built tunnels confused Gary's route-finding and provided one heart-stopping moment when the headlights picked out a cyclist at the last moment, right in front of us with no lights and dressed entirely in black. Fortunately, our brakes worked!

After a night at a Batang hotel, we drove up to the correct valley where a score of motorcycles was waiting. Gary was expecting tractors with trailers but the bags were all loaded onto the bikes and made it to the village in one piece, more or less. We walked for three hours from 3200m to 3800m up a nicely graded track through gorges to more open valley slopes where Tibetan style farmsteads were drying crops for winter foodstuffs in the sunshine. The leaves were turning with berberis flaming red and birch yellow in patches of woodland. Some of the farm buildings were of stone but most were timber-framed with massive baulks of crudely shaped wood and non-weight-bearing walls of mud brick or rammed earth between.

We stayed at the village of Sanglong Xi in one such farmhouse with cattle living below and huge airy rooms up the steps to the first floor. There was a big stone and concrete fireplace or range with water constantly on the boil and stored in vacuum flasks. Wood-panelled walls, shelves and cupboards were carved and painted with symbols and flowers. Pride of place was shared between the TV/video and framed photos of the Panchen lama. After a tasty meal Dick and Steve got very drunk on rice wine with the locals before we unrolled our sleeping bags on hard mattresses in the store-room next door.

Next morning, despite Steve looking rather the worse for wear he and Peter set off up the branch valley below the north faces of Yangmolong to find a site for base camp. Meanwhile, Dick and I climbed high up the opposite side of the main valley with binoculars to scope out possible routes.

What began as a decent path soon deteriorated into criss-crossing animal tracks and the going became more difficult the higher we went. At 4300m we gave up just below a saddle having sighted a few possibilities for climbing lines on the mountain. Down earlier than expected, I walked on further up the main valley, finding a large mani stone platform scattered with bones including a yak skull and what seemed to be clay figurines that must have been votive offerings. Dick reckoned it was probably a sky burial site.

Peter and Steve had found a good site for base camp so horses were arranged to take the baggage up next day. They should have arrived at 8 a.m. but it was 8.30 before the first dribbled in. Then there was a lot of standing around and shaking of heads while three generations of villagers surveyed the baggage and tried to make off with the lightest bags for their horses. Suddenly a flurry of activity saw all the horses loaded and we were off, barring a few stragglers, to the accompaniment of much laughter. We tucked in behind, trying to keep up on foot.

We climbed up the branch valley past a logging site with open air sawmill and planing machine powered by "farms" of small hydro-electric power (HEP) units, about half the size of a spin-dryer, placed in nearby streams. Continuing through steep forest, the undergrowth glowing with rich autumn colours, we reached high summer yak pasture with rough stone shelters where we planned to set up our base camp. When Dick and I arrived, the locals were having to lug the bags down to the stream-side campsite having been rather too quick to unload the horses, which were frisking and rolling in the dust, delighted to be free of their burdens. As we settled into base camp and the villagers departed it became clear that we had acquired a "camp follower". A sturdy young woman, bursting with self-confidence and habitually wearing a pink

ABC 2007 with Yangmolong summit and the spur falling from it by which it was finally climbed.

"cowboy hat", had decided that she was going to keep us company for a while.

Over the next few days we surveyed the head of the valley, finding an eastern glacier bay at about 5100m with a saddle to the east of it. However, attempts to climb up to that were limited by the shattered loose rock which would make load carrying difficult. There looked like only one route on the face above where a snow spur fell from just left of the summit to terminate at a rock buttress flanking the cirque on the right. It looked feasible to outflank the rock buttress on steep snow slopes to the left of it and gain the spur above. Unfortunately, there didn't seem to be any obvious places for an intermediate camp: above 5000m, 1000m of steep ground to climb and descend in a day was a tall order. The western glacier bay looked more amenable with some attractive snow ridge lines on the satellite Peak 5480 and on Dangchezhengla itself; these could provide some enjoyable acclimatisation. There was also a good site for an advanced base camp on level gravel near a stream not far from the glacier snout.

The scouting for routes and establishing ABC was good acclimatisation in itself before we moved up to climb in earnest, but Dick was having some problems with his breathing which meant I was in no hurry. Dick had had a hip replacement and his recovery from the surgery had been complicated by a mass of tiny blood clots in his lungs. He'd acted on the medical advice and the condition had seemed to have cleared up but now at altitude he was finding himself in difficulties again.

The morning light was golden with blood pheasants slinking out from the woods, flashing scarlet heads and breasts, to pick about the bushes in the yak pasture as we breakfasted before carrying loads up to advanced base camp. With a substantial rucksack Dick began to fall behind, sometimes as much as 30 minutes behind, but we waited, chatted and generally took it easy on the way up and while settling in to ABC. There was no tension and the team seemed to be getting along well. The hanging stove was in its element in Steve's spacious Hyperspace tent and out through the tent flaps we had panoramic views looking north to distant snowy spikes and pinnacles of other ranges. We planned for two acclimatisation climbs with a rest day between them.

It was 6.30 before we left the tents, with a lightening of the sky hinting at dawn behind the ridge to the east; no sunrise pyrotechnics, just a greying of the darkness as we climbed the glacier but enough for us to soon dispense with head torches. Steve and I paused at the entrance to a big scree bowl obscuring the tributary glacier beneath that only revealed itself in the icy walls of crevasses filled with rubble at the confluence of ice streams. Peter was coming up on his own. Steve and I waited for him to catch up. Dick's breathing problems had been getting worse and he had told Peter to go on alone. He would get as high as he could but saw no reason for Peter to forfeit his chance to summit the mountain. The three of us then climbed unstable screes to reach a snow tongue that stretched down in the shadow of a rock buttress to the left.

We followed neat cloven hoofprints on the edge of the snow tongue to reach steepening snow slopes between the rock and the ice snout of the glacier hanging above the scree bowl. I zigzagged up to reach the base of the long summit ridge. This rose steeply from buttressing rocks, falling away even more steeply to another glacier that fed the one we had been climbing. The ridge continued in a lovely sinuous snow crest leading over several foresummits to the distant summit itself. We climbed that crest relishing the exposed positions and the wild surroundings glimpsed through gaps in wind-driven clouds. We all hung around on the summit at 5600m hoping for an improvement in visibility and eventually it came, giving us good views of Makara and Dangchezhengla, although the true summit of the latter turned out to be a good way beyond what we had thought was the summit seen from ABC. Makara's west ridge didn't look quite so intimidating from this angle but Peak 5850m to the north-west looked particularly challenging; the only possibility was a very steep couloir that might lead close to the summit from the glacier beneath. It reminded Steve and me of ice pitches at Cogne.

We'd seen enough and a rapid descent took us back to ABC where Dick was waiting with welcome tea.

We stuck by our decision to take a rest day despite the near perfect conditions for climbing; cold, clear and almost windless. A bright blue sky lent a glamour to the texture of the highlighted rock and snow, but there was no water until around midday. Cold had called a halt to the glacier-fed streams, freezing the surface solid while the water beneath had flowed away not to be replaced. I broke a pane of ice to find only air and residual frosty confections left underneath. Going over to the shallow moraine lakes I found water had stayed pooled under the icy surface which, once broken, provided enough for brews. Once the sun got to work on the glacier the flow returned. Dick decided he was not going well enough to contemplate climbing Dangchezhengla so would return to the comforts of base camp and birding while we were on the mountain.

At 4.30 next morning we were stumbling across the dark moraine to reach the glacier snout where crampons went on for the steady crunch up the dry glacier by head torch light. Steve led up right until level with the scree bowl of our earlier climb then swung left and worked up between a crevasse field to the left and a pronounced serac band to the right. All this was glimpsed vaguely in the gloom while treading our passage over crusty ice and snow, illuminated in all its detail in the pools of light cast by head torch beams. Reaching a rock buttress, we worked out that we were to the right of the spur that we wanted to climb so made our way up steeper snow between the buttress and ghostly white serac cliffs.

Dawn broke as we climbed close to the rocks, then through them, linking bands of snow, to gain the crest of the buttress in the thin grey light. We packed head torches away and followed the crest of a snow ridge up towards what we now knew was only the foresummit of the mountain. About halfway up the ridge I took the lead and worked left towards a saddle, crossing snow bridges over huge, but thankfully well-filled crevasses. Hopes of gaining the summit ridge directly from the saddle without going over the foresummit were soon dashed, so I climbed direct on good but steep snow, crossing a tiny cornice to reach the "shoulder" as the Japanese had described it, approaching from the south. At least we had avoided the Japanese "shark's mouth", which must have been a fearsome crevasse, but now we had to descend from the foresummit to another saddle before taking the summit ridge direct.

Gaining that ridge necessitated tackling some very steep snow. Above a crevasse in the ridge was a step of poorly consolidated snow leading steeply up to a rock shoulder. It was exhausting work for about 70m, like climbing vertical porridge, with Steve twice moving up carefully to another belay as I neared the end of the rope; I was reduced to burrowing at times.

From that rock shoulder the angle eased and a corniced ridge led to the summit. This looked straightforward but proved anything but. Delicate, with several short icy steps, the ridge itself was nevertheless preferable to the north face that seemed to consist of an inch or two of frozen crust with unconsolidated "Styrofoam", or simply an airgap beneath that crust where the Styrofoam had shrunk back or trickled away. There was a mercifully short horizontal section where we had to side-step along the lip of the opening cornice break-line while gently plunging axes into the cornice itself for support. It felt as though at any moment the cornice could collapse into the depths taking us with it or leaving us teetering on the brink.

Finally, we gained the summit, taking care to stop on the safe side of the huge summit cornice hanging menacingly over the precipitous north face. The early sunshine had given way to cloud and occasional gusts of wind with scatterings of spindrift or hailstones so we didn't hang around for the views even if we'd been relaxed enough to take them in. No, it was job done and now we just had to focus on reversing the ridge, very carefully.

Pitching that ridge had taken hours and it was only when we got back to the little saddle that we could take some time out to unwind, eat and drink, though

Front-pointing up to the summit ridge of Snow Snake 5600m.

our water was so cold none of us could manage much. The sun returned and we took pictures of the ridge to Makara, the central summit. It looked climbable but we would need to place another camp at the saddle below it if we were to get to Yangmolong and back in a day. Much would depend on the connecting ridge from Makara to Yangmolong and, if it was anything like the one we had just climbed, it could be very time-consuming.

Steve surprised himself with the depth of his tiredness as he struggled with the short slope up from the saddle to the foresummit, but from there it was all downhill, taking a diversion or two from our tracks whenever one of us spotted an easier variation. Back at the tents Peter joined us for a serious rehydration session on pints of tea, although we then had to persuade each other to eat, such was our tiredness.

After sleeping in we found the sky overcast and Peter set off for base camp quickly, predicting snow. Sure enough, Steve and I followed him through flurries of snowflakes to reach a cold grey base camp where Dick was very pleased to see us. A rest day in BC luxury and then we headed back up to ABC with six days' food, finding all the streams frozen.

The weather continued changeable so Peter explored the eastern glacier bay, forcing a tricky track up to the eastern saddle. From there he had a chance to take photos of the north spur which we'd looked at before. The angle seemed more amenable than it had previously so now we had another possible route. Dick had a look at those photos on a trip back to BC to replenish supplies and he agreed that it could well be doable. Another day of cold though and Peter joined us in the Hyperspace to have a brew:

A view of the summit ridge of Dangchezhengla from the foresummit on the first ascent of the north ridge.

'I don't want to let you down but I'm not going for the summit. This cold weather is more than I'm used to. Can't say I've ever had to operate in such cold conditions. My clothing is barely coping with the conditions and climbing as a three will slow the team down so we'll get colder.'

'Well that's disappointing, but fair enough. San Diego doesn't give you much opportunity to cope with this kind of cold.'

'It is getting to the edge of what we'd accept but Dave and I had some practice at Cogne when it was bitterly cold. No hotel to retreat to here though,' Steve said and laughed ruefully.

'Yeah, it was minus 20˚. Good training for cold conditions although I'll never get used to hot aches; just pure pain.'

Steve and I were far from enthusiastic but an improvement in the weather encouraged us to pack up an assault tent and three days of food to camp in the eastern bay. Peter gave us a hand with the loads but didn't intend to camp with us. We'd been undecided about taking a tent on the route but it looked too steep for us to carry such weight and now that we were camping at 5140m it would be only 920m of ascent. The problem would be that we might need to dig a snowhole on the descent.

Up at 3.30 a.m. we found a sky full of stars and continuous light snowfall! During the morning preparations the snow eventually stopped, so we left just after 6; an unfortunate delay. We threaded our way up the glacier between snow-covered piles of moraine debris, taking to steeper slopes to outflank the rock buttress. Despite the steepness Steve came upon a complex crevasse barrier, a half buried, enormous, Y-shaped crack. He asked me to have a look at it so I climbed across but then found I had to keep on going up steep snow-ice until the angle laid back and the snow deepened enough to make a snowstake belay possible. When Steve climbed up to join me, I nearly bailed out because my feet were frozen from toes to heel. Steve was also suffering but we decided to go on to the rock corner ahead and see if our feet warmed up with the activity.

In fact, we rounded the corner and traversed right across a steeply sloping snow ledge above the rocky buttress. My feet had thawed a little but the day wasn't getting any warmer and snow conditions were alarming: an inch or two of frozen crust was overlying deep, unconsolidated and very cold snow. Hard ice probably lay beneath that but we never touched it and the time taken to excavate ice-screw placements would mean that we'd never come close to reaching the summit. We were moving together with at least one snow stake placed between us until the leader ran out of stakes, at which point the second took over the lead, but there was precious little security afforded by this. It was lucky that the angle was no more than 60˚ most of the time.

We pushed on into the couloir cutting through the upper rock buttress but it all seemed to be more of the same cold and dangerous snow. Moving too slowly to keep warm or have any realistic prospect of summitting, we weren't even enjoying the climbing as our feet and hands became colder and colder. There was a real chance of frostbite. Having made only 300–400m above camp there wasn't much debate before we bailed out, reversing our route while we still had the strength to do so.

Back at the tent we warmed up with a succession of hot drinks before packing up and heading back down the glacier to ABC. Peter must have been psychic because he couldn't see us from ABC, yet there he was coming up to help us carry the kit down. Among other items, he relieved me of my supermarket "bag for life" that Steve had remarked made me look like I'd just been shopping. We arrived back at ABC around 3 p.m. just as a full-blown snowstorm hit us, which went on until after dark. If we had continued with the route, the change in the weather would probably have killed us.

To put a camp on the western saddle and attempt Makara was the only chance left of climbing the mountain but in this changeable weather it could all be a wasted effort. I wrote in my journal, 'Expeditions are a lot about attrition. The cold and hardship wear you down until you begin to focus on going home instead of the summit. There is such a lot of time spent sitting in tents waiting for the weather to come good. And then there's the altitude: you arrive keen but unacclimatised then by the time you're fully acclimatised the enthusiasm has ebbed away.'

A clear dawn was quickly obscured by clouds and drifting snowflakes occasionally driven into flurries by gusts of icy wind. We went down to base camp. There we all had a chance to talk and I was very conscious that Dick was not getting much out of this trip. We still had a few days left and could go for the Makara traverse or circumnavigate the peak on yak trails that the villagers had told us about. In about two days, we could be in Dangba without having to cross passes above 5000m. As we watched the cloud caps settling themselves on surrounding peaks, it seemed an attractive option. We took a couple of days to dismantle ABC and ordered horses to take all the kit down to the main valley where Gary and Chung, the cook, would supervise its transfer to Dangba by road.

The last night at BC was cold and moonlit, full of stars, and gave way to a morning without a cloud in the sky and just the lightest of breezes. The gamble on Makara could have worked but there was nothing for it but to live with the decision. We'd all had our say and all agreed the plan; this was no time for regrets. The horses arrived with Pink Hat in charge and we all converged on her house in the village where we were to spend the night. It was very beautiful walking through the quiet forest with birches and tamarisks glowing yellow and red among the copper leaf-fall. As we crossed the line of prayer flags leaving base camp there was a farewell view of Dangchezhengla against a very blue sky.

There was some anxiety among the villagers that we would not get to Dangba in two days but Pink Hat suggested we hitch a ride on motor bikes to the highest village in this valley, Chojunwa Batang, probably leaving only 12 kilometres to Lake Yamou where we planned to camp. From there we should complete the trip easily in another day. As it turned out, the tracks and narrow wooden bridges over the river were coated with verglas at the time of our early departure next morning; there were moments when it threatened to pitch bikes and riders into the icy river. Whether we would have survived in those fast, cold waters was a moot point: that motorcycle ride was one of the most dangerous things we did on the trip.

Camp below the dangerous spur leading to the summit of Yangmolong in the background.

At the roadhead we shouldered our packs and walked steadily up to Yangmolong Pasture, through trees and scrub alive with birds, more or less following the river. Black and brown dippers threaded its rushing waters, while new views of the mountains opened up to our right. Above the tree line we surprised a lad who must have been checking out the herds that crowded a broad, damp, but very sheltered yak pasture, but he quickly recovered himself. It was strange that the other yak herds had been brought down in the valley we were leaving to the north; here they looked settled for a while longer.

Crossing a pass at 4900m, we strode on into the valley of the "Heavenly Lake". Lake Yamou was surrounded by rock walls plunging straight into its waters with little in the way of pebble beaches, reminding me of crater lakes I had seen in South America. The faint trail to the west of it ran well above the waterline. Steve and I raced on to find a campsite at the far end where outwash gravels had formed a level spit but Dick and Peter settled for a scratch tent placement near a trickle of fresh water. Steve and I cooked under a huge full moon with a sense of utter peace brooding over the lake's still waters.

Next day lammergeiers wheeled above us as we plunged down a good trail through forest, past deserted logging camps, to the village of Upper Zhongba. We met no one but suspected the population had been marshalled into the Lamasery Sandens opposite the village, perhaps for a festival of the full moon; some kind of sermon was being delivered in hectoring style over a PA system. In contrast to the northern valley there was a remarkable dearth of birdlife: Dick thought that this valley had been settled longer, and people had probably hunted the birds almost to extinction in the course of various famines. We descended steadily through a desiccated landscape seamed with gullies to find Lower Zhongba also deserted, then on to Dangba where Gary was waiting with cold beers and a hotel reservation in Batang.

We were told we were the first western visitors to make the trek around the range and it was fascinating to see the eastern and southern aspects of these mountains. The bird life, the sacred lake and the ever-changing landscape brought the expedition to a successful and enjoyable conclusion even though we hadn't climbed Yangmolong. At Dangba we knew it was just a matter of driving back to Chengdu but Dick was kind enough to thank me for organising the expedition and said, 'You know this has been one of the best expeditions I've been on because I haven't heard a cross word between any of us the whole time we've been here. Not once.' Praise indeed from someone with his depth of experience in expeditioning!

The year 2008 had been the year of the Beijing Olympics which was not an advisable year to go climbing in China, but by September 2009 I had put together a team to investigate the eastern approaches to Yangmolong that we had sighted on our motorcycle ride up to Chojunwa Batang in 2007. Dick and Peter were still interested in the mountain and this time Derek joined us. Derek had a crowded climbing programme hence our decision to go in September rather than October although we also hoped that might make it a warmer experience.

The valleys were mistier on the drive but the air cleared as we gained height. At around 6 p.m., approaching Yajang, the blocky farmsteads, chortens and temples were bathed in a golden light revealing that leaves were on the turn and picking out the bright fluttering of prayer flags. As the sun sank and the valleys moved into shadow it seemed the very air was full of sifted motes of light so that even those shadows had a subdued glow to them. The following evening was a hot one in Batang and I noticed that lots of first floor windows were now fitted with shiny new bars.

Back at the roadhead Gau-je, our liaison interpreter, had arranged a tractor with trailer to take the luggage up to Sanglong Xi. I was surprised to see a gaggle of child-nuns who had hired motorcycles to take their bags up to the village and casually added a few items to our trailer with a supreme sense of entitlement: there had been no sign of organised religion in the valley in 2007. Our enjoyment of the trek up to Sanglong Xi was marred by the presence of machinery in the process of bulldozing the old horse trail to form a driveable road. Alongside the road marched brand-new pylons bearing electricity cables up the valley.

At Sanglong Xi there was a new headman so Pink Hat was not to be our "fixer". It seemed she no longer spent much time in the valley, but it was interesting that only her house and the headman's had followed the new fashion for barred windows. There were very few people we recognised from our previous visit. They appeared to make us welcome but there was an edginess in their behaviour bordering on rudeness and Gau-je told us they were demanding much higher prices for the use of motorcycles to take our gear up to Chojunwa Batang. In the morning they seemed to want us to hire extra bikes despite the higher cost and there was simply no need. It was almost as if all the motorcyclists of the village wanted a share in profiteering from us. The tension only subsided after we set off, with Gau-je and I riding pillion in order to make sure that they reached the correct campsite.

After setting up camp near a bridge crossing the river, which provided access to a forest track leading up to the eastern approaches of Yangmolong, suddenly the motorcyclists began suggesting reasons to move camp. These ranged from the possibility of theft to the location of better campsites upriver, which we knew to be untrue. We resisted these suggestions and Derek and I lost no time in heading up the forest track to reconnoitre an approach to an advanced base camp, crucial because base camp was so low.

We returned to find that Dick's binoculars had been stolen when a motorcyclist roared off with them and items including spare batteries had been removed from Peter's rucksack en route. All were returned eventually, but only after payment of a significant ransom. That night Gau–je and Chung decided to sleep in the main tent containing the stores. Despite this, the sound of the nearby river must have masked the noise of thieves who stole a tent, hill food, large base camp stove and pans, and a trekking pole from under the tent flaps. Gau–je was disheartened and unwilling to do anything about it but I sent him down to Sanglong Xi with Dick (who did anger much better than me!) to lodge a complaint.

The police took statements but tacitly admitted they did not expect to get anywhere with an investigation. Gau-je told us that their view was that everyone

A view of Yangmolong from the north-east in 2009 with our proposed route up the ridge in the foreground.

knew who had done it but no one would say anything because they had to live in the village afterwards. The police advice was to go elsewhere, although when we suggested the next valley, which could access some other peaks that we had noted, they told us the people there had burnt down the local police station! Their other suggestion was to hire local guards and Gau-je took that option, setting up a father and daughter, recommended by the headman, in protective residence. Our cook had to make do with only a single-burner stove for the rest of the expedition and did a fantastic job.

The team then concentrated on exploring the area, both to get an idea of routes on the mountain and to establish ABC in the hanging valley above. In the course of this, the value of the base camp site was confirmed but we were shocked by the devastation caused by illegal logging of virgin forest. Not only had vast swathes of forest been wastefully clear-cut, with early signs of soil erosion, but also one huge abandoned logging camp was a wasteland of trash. They seem to have thought they could float logs down the twisting river but this had clearly not worked as massive blockages of smashed timber dammed the river in many places. It seemed as if they had gone mad with greed and abandoned the more sustainable practices we had witnessed on our earlier visit to the valley. Inevitably the government must have stepped in to shut them down under the terms of its obligations to international treaties to conserve virgin forest. That probably explained the new road and power cables to the village, which must have been some attempt at compensation.

Exploring the NE flank of Yangmolong.

At least some of the cut timber was going towards providing more substantial dwellings, perhaps to support transhumance in the valley, so it wasn't entirely wasted. On one of our occasional forays up valley trails to try to acquire some acclimatisation Derek and I stumbled upon one cluster of new buildings hidden in the forest, although it was not at all clear what the community composed entirely of young men with motorcycles was doing there. They seemed to have acquired two or three rifles, which we assumed were for hunting, but they were nervous and aggressive, leaving us in no doubt that we weren't welcome. It was another indication of how much had changed in two years.

ABC was located on glacial moraine below the east ridge of Yangmolong and there was nothing for it but to repeatedly make the arduous 1000m ascent with loads of equipment and food to stock it. Once we had established ABC the weather promptly broke and we retreated to base camp to fester for days listening to the remorseless hammering of rain on the flysheets.

Pink Hat and her daughter surprised us with a visit en route to see relatives still on the high yak pastures but now her hat was white and she gave us presents of fresh apples and sweets. She was taking a break from her job in construction in Batang and was pleased to have caught us in the valley rather than away on the mountain. She thanked Peter for the pictures of her and her family in traditional costume that he had emailed to her in 2007, but overall she seemed very subdued.

The weather must have encouraged the yak herders to come down from the high pastures. One day, during and after breakfast, we were treated to the sight of cavalcades of yaks, dzo (a hybrid of a cow and a yak), horses, even a couple of long-haired goats, and, of course, the families; men on horseback or motorcycle, women on horses with the smallest children up behind them, others just walking, hurling stones at recalcitrant beasts or carefully herding those heavily laden with all the paraphernalia of the family camp. Tashi Dorje walked by with a bolt-action rifle slung over his shoulder, barrel down. He no longer had the motorcycle he was so proud of when joking and learning English words with Steve in 2007. There was something of a hunted look about him and he barely raised a hand in greeting.

The rain eased off so Derek and I took a walk down to a sacred lake, its shores festooned with prayer flags. Nearby the crude stupa seemed neglected; the central shrine had been glazed with blue glass that was now cracked and broken while rough plaster was peeling from a pillar bearing the "moonboat". A chainsaw snarled from the woods where felled timber was being turned into firewood, but soon the rain returned and everyone sought shelter. Only the bawling of yaks broke the rhythm of raindrops on the tent skin.

Running out of time, on the first clear morning for days, we headed up to ABC loaded with food, to begin probing Yangmolong's eastern defences. In changeable weather several forays onto the flanks of that east ridge provided some entertaining climbing but no safe line and views from the slopes opposite gave the impression the ridge itself was going to be hard enough. Finally, we were left with only one option: to camp on "Peter's Col" at the head of the cirque and attempt the shallow ridge that rose from it to the steep face above. That should have put us at least a third of the way along the east ridge when we reached it. Dick decided it would be too much for him and Peter was again unhappy about climbing as a three, but they both helped carry kit up to the col to establish the tiny assault tent where Derek and I spent the first night.

The alarm went off at midnight: heavy cloud swagged across the moon and banked up on the mountain; there was just one star out. I reset the alarm for 4 a.m.: thick clag! At 6 a.m. it was no better so we resigned ourselves to a day waiting it out and another attempt on the morrow. The weather remained unstable all day.

Midnight arrived again with strong winds and snow showers: we had no confidence in setting out. At 6 a.m. the weather was no better so we packed up Camp1 and stumbled down to ABC. Dick and Peter had been standing by in case of trouble but now felt that for them the climbing was over. They packed up loads and set off back to base camp for the night. Derek and I stayed up in hopes of climbing the 5700m satellite peak to the north-west as a consolation prize.

Up at first light, we found a little fine snow but not enough to deter us from climbing snowy screes then through a rock band via a thin mixed couloir to gain the upper section leading to a snow col on the skyline. The weather had been steadily deteriorating and we reached the col to find wind–blown snow curling over it. The continuation ridge to the summit looked serious: a difficult mixture of rock and ice climbing. Buffeted by a fierce squall there was no question of us going on. We reversed the route from our high point of 5550m. At least the climbing had been interesting.

Exploring the north-east ridge of Yangmolong.

Bad weather overnight eased by morning and by the time we had packed up the camp Gau-je and Chung had arrived to give us a hand carrying all the kit back to base. This was much appreciated as Derek had resembled nothing so much as a Christmas tree with all the bits and baubles dangling from his rucksack and his person before they arrived. At base camp packing became the priority amid tension about transport out of the valley. The lawless motorcyclists were demanding even more money and Gau–je later revealed that they had threatened to steal everything and that no one would even find our bodies if we didn't pay. We didn't bother to stop at Sanglong Xi where people called and gestured various rudeness as we passed on to the roadhead with heavy sacks.

When the motorcyclists arrived, there was more threatening behaviour during a tense wait for the bus. This included slitting my Gore-tex® jacket with some razor-like blade in an attempt to persuade me to part with it to one or other of them. 'It's no use to you now!' Ironically, or perhaps not, they were all keen to flash photos of the Dalai Lama on their mobile phones.

When the bus arrived, they stole money from the driver's cab while he was helping us load the bus, but our watchfulness and refusal to be intimidated managed a more or less orderly, if rather expensive retreat. When we returned to Chengdu, Jiyue, our agent, was convinced he had made a loss on the trip!

By 2009 something had changed in that valley where the people had been so friendly and welcoming in 2007. Clearly there was a lawless element that worried the older local people but it seemed there was little they could do about it: they had to live there after we'd gone. We coped by hiring one of the local headmen and his daughter as camp guards/helpers after the night of major theft but this was yet more expense on top of the extortionate rates charged for transport, including the hire of unnecessary motorbikes. Base camp was an area of tension rather than relaxation, and the Chinese staff slept inside the main tent with one of them sleeping inside a small tent in that tent and containing the most important kit to try to foil any further thefts.

The only significant event in the intervening period that could have had a bearing on such a change in that valley was the 2008 Olympics and the subsequent unrest: there had been reports of Tibetans burning the shops of Han Chinese in Lhasa, sometimes with the owners still in them, or beating up Chinese settlers. It was a nasty business. Nearer to Sanglong Xi there had been the burning down of the police house in the next valley.

Objectively there were two main changes that we noticed: the logging had been closed down and there were Buddhist monks and nuns in the valley where there had been none before. Had the Buddhist clergy moved in to take advantage of the understandable resentment against the government closing down the logging business? If so, they may have lent legitimacy to a lawless element in an attempt to make political capital out of local disaffection with the government. Perhaps they had encouraged

Camp on Peter's Col with the route up the snow ridge rising from it on the left.

groups of young men to hide out in camps like the one Derek and I discovered like some kind of guerrilla army, and absolved them of any respect for the law or non-Tibetans.

Jon Otto led an American–Chinese team into the same valley later in October 2009 and recorded, 'We were told to leave the valley that day or the villagers could not guarantee our safety. Climbing the mountain brings about ominous events such as bad weather, sickness, and natural disasters. Reasoning with superstitions is impossible.' This was beginning to sound familiar to me and confirmed my suspicions that much of the monastic organisation of Tibetan Buddhism is about political control through the manipulation of superstition as we had experienced on Kawarani. In *Tigers of the Snow* Jonathan Neale also records a Sherpa joke about the Tibetan fondness for carrying two knives and it seemed that here in these ethnically Tibetan valleys the knives were out for visitors like us again.

Jon Otto's team switched to an approach from the south and made the third ascent of Dangchezhengla via a new variation on the north-east ridge. Then, in 2011, with another American–Chinese team, they succeeded in making the first ascent of Yangmolong. They approached the northern side of the range by a complex route from the south to avoid the valley of Sanglong Xi, but the route they climbed was essentially the one that Steve and I attempted in 2007 with an additional camp on the spur. It was a fine achievement and his report acknowledged our pioneering efforts on the mountain. I was pleased to see that Yangmolong had been climbed at last, particularly since none of my 2009 team had any inclination to go back. It was remarkable how such a positive experience had been completely reversed after the passage of just two years; circumstances beyond our control!

6. Coping with adverse conditions: the Kagbhusandi Valley, Garhwal, India

'How quickly can I get home from here?' The thought popped into my head as the sub-surface gave way beneath my feet and I sank from knee-deep to thigh-deep in wet snow. I was at 3900m in the Garhwal and the first flurries of the next snowfall were gathering up-valley where clouds swagged around obscured summits. Climbing prospects looked bleak.

Stumping back to camp I thought back over our considerable efforts to reach this point. The night train from Delhi to Haridwar-Rishikesh had been crowded and the team was still jet-lagged enough to appreciate being woken at each stop in case it was ours. Getting off the train was a frantic scramble that didn't prevent it departing with Chris's brolly and Mark's iPod. The station was littered with people sleeping on the floor but largely due to the good offices of Harish and Atul, the Indian contingent of our expedition, we managed to find our onward transport for the death-defyinging, horn-blasting drive to Joshimath. En route we passed a monument recording Jim Corbett's shooting of the man-eating leopard of Rudra Paryag in 1926. No self-respecting leopard would be seen dead in the area now; the jungle has been completely cleared for farming.

Then there were the days spent acquiring a little acclimatisation at the out of season ski station of Auli, taking advantage of the ski lifts to discover elaborate shrines and a family of wild boar in the woods, while Parvan, the agency's Mr Fixit, explored the labyrinth of bureaucracy surrounding our permits. Another drive took us along the Badrinath road to Govindghat (starting point for the Valley of Flowers trek) where the walk in began; and all the way the "monsoon" rainfall and the regular stomach upsets took their toll.

It had not all been negative: on the first day's trek from Govindghat, we had a timely reminder of the Alpine and Himalayan clubs' links with tradition by a chance meeting with Nanda Sinh Chauhan. Ninety-four years old, he was a local guide who accompanied Frank Smythe in 1931 and 1937 when Smythe explored the Valley of Flowers. This was, after all, a joint club expedition that Harish Kapadia had organised to celebrate the AC's 150th anniversary: I told myself I should be made of sterner stuff.

151

Harish had first entered the Kagbhusandi valley in early May 2006. Hathi Parvat and Otika Danda had been climbed from the north but the other peaks around the valley had not been touched. With so much left to do, Harish's interest in the climbing potential of the area was soon shared by Atul Rawal and AC members Chris, Mick, Mark and myself. By returning in late May 2007 we had hoped to avoid the unexpectedly deep snow that had thwarted Harish's attempt to cross the Kankul Khal pass in 2006.

Leaving the Valley of Flowers trail at Bhuidhar, we had trekked up the Kagbhusandi valley in three days to a base camp at Chhaiyan Kharak (3815m) with Hathi Parvat (6727m) towering to the north. It was just above BC that I had recognised that this year conditions were no better and was tempted to cut and run.

Doubts persisted as an attempt to get higher on the glacier foundered among the snowed-up rocks of a moraine ridge after we'd taken hours to reach 4127m. Then a fine morning prompted an exploration of the approaches to the Kankul Khal. Mick heroically broke trail in deep soft snow all the way to the pass at 4665m despite the deteriorating weather, while I reeled along in his wake nursing a stomach upset and wondering why I hadn't brought skis. There was a good view of cloud at the pass and we descended the last slopes in a thunderstorm. However, by evening back at camp the weather had cleared and the moon came up like a lamp from behind a ridge of Otika Danda, setting the whole cirque glimmering.

Climbing up to camp before making the first ascent of AC 150, 5030m.

With improving weather the team then made several forays up the steep flanks of the valley in hopes of spotting likely lines. Plenty of ridges and couloirs attracted attention but looked to be tough propositions in the prevailing conditions. Ridges were plastered with snow and the couloirs avalanching. Mick pointed out a possible line on the peak immediately west of the Kankul Khal and early on a clear morning we headed up the ablation valley on the true left bank of the glacier, going on to kick steps in our old tracks back towards the pass. We probably wouldn't have been able to carry our camping and climbing gear without the consolidation of the snow in our earlier tracks. We camped on a broad snow terrace at 4350m enjoying spectacular views northwards to Gori and Hathi Parvat.

The expected low temperatures overnight meant we were away at 6 a.m. next morning across the crisp snow to scramble up a wide jumble of boulders that fanned down from the first snowfield. Mick and Chris made for a weakness in the rock band ahead near a large avalanche cone while I headed right, up a snow slope towards a saddle that looked to access the upper snowfield more easily. It didn't. I emerged at a breche on a very narrow and technical ridge that did indeed lead to the upper snowfield but nothing like safely enough for me. There was nothing for it but to go back and traverse over to the other line, by then about half an hour behind the others. Route-finding on virgin peaks is always a challenge!

The line of weakness was as scrappy as I'd imagined, a mixture of unstable snow, loose rock and wet earth, though we soon emerged on the upper snowfield looking forward to using the steps kicked by the earlier pair. Unfortunately, that half hour had made a significant difference. Although only 8 a.m. the temperature had risen to a point where the steps regularly collapsed and, as the snowfield rose into a broad ridge that then narrowed into a steeper continuation spur, Mark and I found it hot, hard going. Mick and Chris took the couloir flanking the spur on the left but Mark and I were concerned about it avalanching so instead climbed the spur direct in four pitches of about Scottish 3, largely unprotected.

At the top of the spur our routes converged as a narrow ridge swung west to merge into the east face. We climbed four more pitches of mixed ground to gain a massive granite block that we had originally thought to be the summit. The true summit, complete with blade-like rock pinnacle, was another 60m along the narrow snow ridge beyond and gave a GPS reading of 5030m. Consensus later graded the route at AD. The weather deteriorated as Mark and I descended to camp in a snowstorm as Mike returned to BC. We remained at the 4350m camp with Chris, gaining a little more acclimatisation and later having to rescue the detachable tent porch of my Bibler assault tent that was ripped off by a ferocious wind during the night.

Next morning the weather had improved and I dawdled down alone, enjoying it. A weasel popped out on the snow from under a boulder, took a look at me then slipped back under. Lower still, birds were singing and a carpet of tiny purple flowers had sprung up in the waterlogged meadows exposed by the melting snow. Back at BC, the team was unanimous in its recommendation of a name for the mountain – Peak AC 150. There was a common recognition that it might be the only peak we would climb!

Mark climbing the
north ridge of AC150.

Much debate ensued about our next route. The poor weather led to speculation that the monsoon had arrived a month early. High temperatures meant poor snow conditions with enhanced avalanche danger. Mixed routes threatened to be unstable as the ice that cemented rocks together melted and any exposed earth rapidly turned to mud. On one occasion, at a stream crossing, the rocks had collapsed and closed around my leg, trapping it; alone, I would have been in serious trouble but the others soon helped me out. We needed to get higher where temperatures would hopefully be lower, but that would mean an uncertain number of intermediate camps since in these conditions the weight of our loads would slow our climbing; we didn't know by how much. Ever since the 19th century when Whymper had observed that alpinists could make better time on snow than on rock, couloirs had been the preferred means of rapid ascent but here they were avalanching by mid-morning.

Chris was no enthusiast for snow camping and wanted to solo a couloir route from base camp overnight. That would be a perfectly reasonable approach from a hut in the Alps in summer when the avalanche risk would be minimal for the descent. Here though it was not summer but more like early spring and at that season in the Alps mountaineering would be on ski, making early starts but also rapid descents to huts by around midday. We didn't have skis and slower descents would be much more likely to trigger avalanches. We could only agree that we needed more reconnaissance.

Despite being on an Immodium tablet each day, Chris succumbed to another stomach upset so Mick, Mark and I geared up for a night out to reconnoitre the upper Barmal Glacier while Harish's team made an attempt to traverse the Kankul Khal. In the end they had to settle for a "picnic in the snow' as conditions were far too dangerous for porters to carry loads over the pass.

From our glacier camp the reconnaissance yielded good views of the peaks at its head and the discovery of Barmal Khal, a previously unknown pass at over 5000m. Unfortunately, the north face of Barmal proved to be uniformly threatened by serac fall, although the southern glacier approach to the unclimbed rock tower of 5490m Dhanesh Parvat looked objectively safe. Next day the team decided to head north to cache camping gear at the foot of that glacier; we needed an objectively safe route and this looked like the only one available! From the cache we descended the ablation valley on the right bank of the Barmal Glacier, which proved less than straightforward with a long tricky traverse of a crumbling moraine ridge before we could gain that ablation valley and boot-ski down the soft snow. Back at base camp yellow azaleas were opening their delicate pale flowers among the blowsier purple blooms of dwarf rhododendrons. Harish and Atul had given up on the idea of traversing the Kankul Khal but stayed to have lunch with us before heading back down the valley in search of trekking alternatives.

Chris turned out to be unhappy with the glacier route while neither Mick nor I were convinced of the merits of Chris's chosen couloir as we couldn't see how to safeguard the descent. In the end Chris decided he wanted his tent, which Mark and Mick had used, to be brought down for him to plan an alternative. He seemed reluctant to climb with Mark and confided that he thought Mark was 'out of his depth'. Perhaps for that

*Mick, seeing the funny side of the
atrocious snow conditions.*

Scouting the upper Barmal glacier with the glacier approach to Dhanesh Parvat in the background.

reason, Chris still favoured night soloing although it was clear that Parvan and Harish were extremely anxious about that idea. This was not the Alps and the infrastructure was nothing like that of Europe, so if anything went wrong the agency support team would be in the front line for sorting it out. We all spent a stressful evening while Chris prepared to set off overnight, but by morning it was clear he had thought better of it, somewhat to the relief of us all. Mark was suffering badly from sunburn so it was just Mick and I who set out next day, with a couple of porters to bring down Chris's tent, to attempt Danesh Parbat.

I really appreciated Parvan's generosity with the porters since I'd had diarrhoea overnight and felt very rough but determined to give the route a go; I'd just have to continue taking Ciproxin! The porters did very well in the snow, getting up to within 150m vertical of the cache despite their lack of crampons or ice axes. I waited with them while Mick soloed up to collect the tent and spare gear. Unfortunately, it later transpired that he'd thought a lot of Mark's cached kit was mine so it was a light load the porters shouldered as they chased off back to BC, sliding on their bums and whooping, while Mick and I went on to make camp.

Next morning we climbed on up the right side of the tributary glacier where avalanche debris from the couloirs of Otika Danda had filled in the crevasses and well away from the seracs piled to the left. At about 5000m we found a reasonably flat site for Camp 2, a safe distance from the nearest couloirs, and settled in for a day of dozing before a night of climbing. The couloirs had other ideas and from 2 pm until 4 pm unloaded an impressive tonnage of ice blocks, snow and rocks. It was like listening to a truck delivering hardcore followed by a freight train thundering through a tunnel. Just as we had convinced ourselves that the campsite was safe the nearest couloir would unleash a particularly loud roar that had us ducking our heads out of the tent door to check through the clouds of ice crystals that we really were sufficiently far away from it. By 4 pm the cloud that had been building up all afternoon was sufficient to take temperatures down and switch off the avalanche machines. Relieved, we had dinner and snoozed on through the evening.

The moon was casting shadow profiles of the ridges of Otika Danda onto the snow as we left at 1 a.m., but somehow it didn't seem to be cold enough and we still found ourselves post-holing at 5200m. The glacier headwall was little better, although a narrow snow ridge running north to a broader saddle eventually led us to firmer snow below the west ridge of Dhanesh Parvat. The darkness was deceptive, making a snow dome seem steeper than it was and rocks larger. We took a rest, snacking and gazing over mountains slowly redefining themselves as more than a bulking darkness. To the north lay the shadowplay of Tibet while the pre-dawn glow built steadily in the east, silhouetting peaks a deep black against the orange sky.

The ridge climbed steeply to a narrow crest of snow and rock running into the sheer south face of the granite summit block. It looked hard. Several lines might be possible: a steep crack to the left, a wider chimney crack with a couple of wedged chockstones, a zigzag chimney closed at the top with overhanging blocks, a traverse onto the south-west face to gain a snowy gully filled with precariously balanced blocks.

All proved too difficult, loose, cold or unstable to commit to, though we spent two hours taking turns to establish this.

Conceding defeat, we retreated down the ridge. Fortunately, Mick still had his wits about him and was looking for route alternatives. From below he spotted a narrow snow ramp rising under the overhanging north face of the summit monolith. High above the glacier the doubtful snow seemed on the verge of sliding off into the void, but we were able to fix good nut runners in the rock wall above the ramp and two pitches led to the east face of the summit block.

Sun-warmed rock, just, but only just, the right side of vertical, rose in cracks and spaced narrow ledges above us. Mick led the first pitch, finding it harder and looser than expected. Above I found it harder still. A good nut unlocked a difficult sequence that Mick reckoned was at least British 4c. Now I don't normally lead 4c in plastic boots with a rucksack but the moves just seemed to be coming together so I went with it. No one really conquers a mountain; the mountain whispers the way, but you have to be listening. A poor runner provided dubious protection for a precarious traverse along a narrowing boot ledge. As I moved further and further from the gear, I became more and more aware of the weight of the rucksack and the inappropriateness of the high-altitude plastic boots for the delicacy of the climbing. I did a lot of talking to myself and God before a crack offered another nut placement and I breathed a sigh of relief. More cracks and broken ledges led to easier ground. Then with unexpected suddenness I was there, pulling over the top block to see the glittering ridges of Hathi Parvat beyond and shouting a great 'Yes!' of delight.

I belayed an impressed Mick up to the summit where we took some photos. It was 8.30. A bite to eat, and then we were abseiling down the icy cracks of the west face before carefully reversing the west ridge. By daylight it was possible to avoid the unconsolidated snow that had slowed our ascent and was actually the remnants of avalanche cones on the glacier so we made better time back to Camp 2. 10.30 am – time enough to break camp and get back to BC, although after we collected Mark's stuff from the original cache the extra weight meant that I found the final stages of the descent pretty gruelling. Mick waited for me and we walked into camp together to receive the congratulations of Parwan and Raj. We graded the route Alpine D.

Chris and Mark were away, making the first ascent of a peak lying to the East of the Kankul Khal. Next day they told us how, from a camp below the pass, very early, they first ascended a couloir falling west from the north ridge of the main summit. Gaining the ridge, wet snow obliged them to traverse into a rocky couloir on the east face that led to the summit. The peak was showing 5080m on the map though the GPS reading was lower than AC 150 and they graded the route at about AD. Kankul Peak was recommended for its name.

Running out of realistic objectives and time, the team retraced its steps to Bhuidhar where we celebrated the 150th anniversary of the Alpine Club and its fraternal relationship with the Himalayan Club with a memorable party, complete with birthday cake! However, our descent had been rather faster than expected, which left a day for an excursion to Hemkund Sahib, the highest *gurdwara* (Sikh temple) in the

159

Mick leading pitch 4 of the east face of the summit block of Dhanesh Parvat.

Dave on the airy summit of Dhanesh Parvat, 5490m. Otika Danda in the background.

world. Each day 5000 Sikhs were passing Bhuidhar on pilgrimage. While the numbers were something of a culture shock after our remote valley there was no denying the determination of whole families, motivated simply by faith, to leave Birmingham or the plains of the Punjab and climb to more than 4000m. I was glad that I hadn't failed my own test of faith all those days ago, thigh-deep in wet snow.

The weather and snow conditions had resulted in far greater difficulties than any of us had imagined. The backstop objective had been the traverse of the Kankul Khal but because of its lower altitude snow conditions would be worse and it was still well snow-covered; there was no chance of porters carrying loads over the pass so the trekking circuit was never on. The bigger peaks like Barmal were simply too dangerous to climb on this occasion. One might consider traversing under hanging seracs in much colder conditions but not in the temperatures we experienced. We tried to overcome the problems by camping as high as possible and leaving such camps very early. Perhaps we should have started climbing soon after dark and made night ascents as I once did traversing from the Aiguille du Midi over Mont Blanc, but the evenings never became cold enough to encourage that and we reckoned the coldest it got was during a window of opportunity from around midnight to dawn. Even then it was a long way from ideal conditions.

The conditions put a strain on the team as the objective dangers dented our confidence. None of us had climbed together before and we could all see how each of us was suffering at one time or another from stomach problems that sapped energy and morale. Acclimatisation was not really possible on training climbs so we never developed really confident climbing partnerships although I think Mick and I got close to that in the end. The overnight solo tactic, fast and light, caused a lot of controversy. It might have worked, but if it didn't the results could have been disastrous and the whole team would have been at risk attempting a rescue; there were no mountain rescue teams to call on!

Through a lot of debate, some of it heated, we did succeed in coming up with objectives which were justifiable although some of the climbing wasn't exactly enjoyable and, as climbing objectives, they were quite limited. What made it all worthwhile for me was the ascent of Danesh Parvat, an unclimbed peak that provided hard high-altitude rock climbing: a new experience!

7. Equipment failure and team issues: Mongolia

I had already organised several expeditions for the Eagle Ski Club (ESC) to Kyrgyzstan when I proposed to go to Mongolia in 2011. I stumbled upon a report of the North Face team of women who in 2002 skied the Five Holy Peaks in the north-west corner of Mongolia where Russia, China and Mongolia meet. This included Khuiten, at 4374m the highest peak in Mongolia. It had taken the North Face team around two months, with full marks for persistence in the face of the weather, but I thought we could do it in three weeks. David Hamilton had guided a mountaineering group to the area in summer and was kind enough to provide a very useful briefing on what to expect; strong winds and brief interludes of good weather! This led to me deciding to dispense with the usual catered base camp on the glacial moraine and instead set up a self-sufficient snow camp much higher up the Potanina Glacier at 3600m. That would put us in a good position to ski the 4000m peaks of the range in the short weather windows that typified the climate in those mountains.

The ESC has an established application procedure for its expeditions which must be open to all members. Two experienced expeditioners, Derek and John, signed on quite quickly. Martin applied with positive references including one which said he showed 'sound mountaineering judgement', but Howard had no referees from ESC sources and Iona had no experience of snow camping. A number of phone calls to the applicants and to people who could vouch for them led to me accepting both onto the expedition although Iona had to confirm that she had acquired experience of snow camping before departure. I reckoned that I could team up each of the less-experienced with one of the experienced members in two-person tent teams. Who exactly would be matched with whom was left undecided until the pre-expedition weekend when we all met at my house to talk through issues and get to know each other.

As it turned out, the problem solved itself. Howard opted to join John in one tent while Derek and Martin were both so tall that they could share Derek's Quasar, allowing me to take my Crux which, although significantly smaller (and lighter!) would be just adequate for me and Iona. As possibly the most experienced member I also felt a responsibility for Iona, at 23 the youngest member, although as events turned out there was a grim irony in that. Howard had only ever skied with friends before and later told me that he had opted to join John because he thought they had least in common so that he would make more of an effort to get on with him: 'If I can get on with John I'll be able to get on with the rest of the team.' It was a risky strategy but had a certain logic to it.

In Batbayar I found a very capable agent who quickly tuned in to what we were trying to do, anticipated problems and provided solutions so that the logistical package provided by Mongolian Expeditions ran very smoothly and economically. The only hitch was on the drive into the mountains when the guide lost his bearings in the admittedly rather featureless steppe. But when we dropped in to a local farmstead to ask for directions they turned out to be eagle hunters and offered us the opportunity to get up close and personal with one of their trained eagles: a bonus!

The equipment failure on our first morning on the glacier was not down to the agency but to me.

I woke with the relentless wind rattling the flysheet to see Martin looming over my sleeping bag and thought, *I don't share a tent with Martin. What's he doing here?* The last thing I remembered was spooning breakfast cereal out of my mug between attempts to sort out kit for departure. *And where's Iona?*

I tried to ask but the words wouldn't come, then tried to sit up but a wave of nausea slapped me back down.

'Just lie back and take it easy.' Martin's voice betrayed his anxiety.

'What happened?' I managed to slur through the barrier of rubberised lips and tongue.

Skinning up the glacier to base camp beneath the outcrop right of centre, with Khuiten 4374m left of centre.

'You passed out. Carbon monoxide we think.'

'Iona?'

'She's OK. Derek is looking after her. Just rest.'

Over the next few hours, I gradually regained coherence and co-ordination, retained the contents of my stomach and even managed to eat and drink a little. Iona was less lucky, repeatedly vomiting, but on the other hand she'd never stopped breathing. In a sense I owed my life to her. If the team had not come to investigate the noise of her fits they might never have dragged us from the fume-filled tent until it was too late. But it was a close thing. They went for the noisy one first, as you might with someone blue and foaming at the mouth, but consequently had no idea of how long I had not been breathing when they turned their attention to me. It was about 20 minutes before Howard managed to get me breathing on my own.

Fortunately, my pulse was strong because my heart was hunting for the oxygen it needed, but my heart would have stopped if the hunt had failed. Without the artificial respiration I would never have recovered consciousness. They later told me there had been some discussion about adding chest compressions but a year or so later a doctor friend confided that had they done so it was likely my heart would have stopped. Thankfully Howard and Derek didn't see any point in heart massage for a heart that was beating!

Base camp was at 3600m in the Tavn Bogd range of the Mongolian Altai and medical help was three days away at Olgii, yet after Iona and I had stabilised, advice

Base camp on the Potanina glacier, Mongolia.

was literally at hand when Derek rang through to a medic on the satellite phone: without oxygen cylinders there was nothing more to be done beyond making sure we had plenty of fresh air, but there was every chance of recovery in 24 hours.

It's not often that you have a disaster on the first day on a glacier, so how had it happened? Well, like most of us, I've read all the warnings about cooking in tents but frankly the conditions on many expeditions can leave you with no alternative and after a decade of experience there is a certain confidence about doing so, well-ventilated of course. The constant gusting winds of Mongolia were a case in point; they could blow out a stove set up outside the inner tent. This time, however, there was a difference; the tried and tested hanging stove system had been modified by the addition of a pan fitted with an integral heat exchanger. That had worked perfectly well on a recent expedition to Antarctica (always below 1000m) and on this expedition at 2500m at the roadhead and 3000m at a camp on the moraine of the Potanina Glacier. This reinforced confidence, yet at 3600m we were at the highest altitude at which I'd ever used the system.

That difference was crucial: the cooling effect of the snow in the pot, coupled with the lack of oxygen, reinforced the tendency for the increased surface area of the heat exchanger to quench the flame to the point where carbon monoxide generated by combustion was simply not being burnt off as it would have been at sea level. Unfortunately, I didn't know all this at the time. None of the stove manufacturers highlight the dangers of heat exchangers. The usual ventilation was just not enough in those circumstances. It had been too easy to put a headache down to altitude and we nearly died.

The following morning, 7 May, we set off for Tavn Bogd peak (4104m), Iona and I gaining confidence as the exertion took no great toll, though I caught a few searching glances from the others.

As we moved into more crevassed territory, I stopped for the team to rope up. Martin waved me over and asked, 'Could you just remind me how to tie a figure of eight knot?'

It was a moment when I wondered if I was still suffering from the after-effects of the carbon monoxide poisoning. Was this "sound mountaineering judgement?" I tied him on and then warned Derek to keep a close eye on him.

Cloud gathered on the summits and we climbed into it from an icy saddle on the south ridge of Tavan Bogd. It was icy enough for half the team to leave their skis but Iona and I were going well enough to join Howard in carrying ours to attempt a ski descent from the summit. The borders of Russia and China meet with that of Mongolia on this summit and we wandered about sufficiently in the snowstorm that greeted us there that we must all have put a foot into each country, with or without permits. In descent some edgy skiing down the icy ridge in increasing snowfall was succeeded by much pleasanter conditions as we popped out under the cloud ceiling, losing the snowflakes and gaining sunshine as we cruised back to camp. Once the adrenalin subsided there was a tendency for Iona and I to drop off to sleep mid-sentence and we kept a wary eye on each other while managing the stove, but it was definitely "game on" again.

Climbing the broad north ridge of Khuiten, carrying skis because of the steepness and underlying ice, with peaks of Russia and China in the background.

This was confirmed when a worryingly stormy night gave way to a morning of glorious light and we set our sights on Khuiten, the highest mountain in Mongolia. The team skinned north towards Tavn Bogd peak then bore north-west up a crevassed ice valley under Khuiten's north-east face. Crossing a bergschrund we gained the broad but steep north ridge that forms the border with China. When this reared up, becoming too steep and icy for safe skinning, all but Martin carried our skis, booting up to the summit. There we relaxed in the sunshine, taking in the vast panorama of the Altai mountains stretching away into China and Russia.

Then it was skis on for a high traverse above ice cliffs before plunging back down the ridge. Ice lurking under the new snow provided a surprise or two but we all coped, leaving some impressively neat tracks. A quick swing around an ice boss on the ridge and we were able to sneak over the bergschrund to the base of the exposed and sinuous south ridge of Nairamdal (4192m): on this thin blade of snow there was no ski descent; we climbed up and down on foot. The long run back to base was less demanding although Martin did manage to find a crevasse slot into which he briefly dangled a ski before lurching back onto solid snow. Back at the tents we basked in the late sunshine, congratulating ourselves on what had been a magical day.

The next day was stormbound and we had a chance to take stock. It was clear that the winter had been very cold and windy but without as much precipitation as usual: instead of presenting the expected steep but skiable snow faces, some of the mountains were clad in hard ice with a high potential fall factor. Our objective to make ski descents of all five of the holy peaks did not look feasible in the case of Naran and Chinggis, so we decided to make the best of the situation by exploring the ski-mountaineering potential of other 4000m peaks in the area.

The team, however, was having problems. Howard's snoring was testing John's patience and his cries of 'Turn over! Turn over!' could be heard above the wind on the dark glacier. Derek too was becoming impatient with Martin's lack of confidence in mountaineering matters and supreme faith in God regarding everything else. Perhaps that faith had led to him ignore my advice on test-driving and adjusting his new boots before setting off on an expedition; his blisters were horrific and did nothing for his confidence in skiing or climbing. Unknown to me a plot was hatched for swapping tent partners, and it was with sheer disbelief that I found Martin tapping on my tent flaps with the announcement that he was swapping with Iona. That disbelief gave way to laughter as I pointed out that he would be sleeping with his feet or head sticking out of the tent's zipped doorway; he was just too tall to fit in. In the end he and Howard swapped so John had some relief from the snoring and Derek some relief from religious debate and responsibility for Martin.

Skiing the north ridge of Khuiten.

Howard descending the summit ridge of Pik 4152m., south of Khuiten.

Over the next few days the weather held and we made very satisfying ascents of Peak 4117, aka Russian Tent, to the north of Tavn Bogd peak, and Peak 4152 on the border ridge south of Khuiten. This last meant crossing the south-east ridge of Khuiten quite low down where we found to our surprise that we were not alone in the range. Another party was working its way up the glacier beyond. They turned out to be largely Swiss, led by two French guides based in Chamonix, and had designs on Khuiten's summit via that south-east ridge. We continued onto the airy summit ridge of Peak 4152m and from there watched with some disbelief as the guided team skinned halfway up an approach couloir then carried their skis up the rest of the couloir and for at least a couple of kilometres along the ridge.

We were back at camp by the time they had made the summit and skied the border ridge of our ascent that I recommended to the guides, although I gathered that the less confident had carried their skis at least some of the way down. They dropped in to our camp for a break and as it was going to be a 12-hour day for them we, shared a brew while they invited us to return the visit at their catered camp 600m below on the moraine where we might share a beer.

But we had more mountains to climb before that. We saw fresh wolf tracks on the approach to Malchin (4051m), before cramponing up its north-west ridge. On returning to our skis we found its neighbour across the pass, Peak 3926, too much of a temptation so we climbed that as well with four of us carrying skis, just in case there was a good descent possible. Despite a doubtful scratchy approach off the north-west ridge, the ski descent of a very steep south-facing couloir provided the most exciting skiing of the expedition, carving deep curves into great spring snow.

We then decided to explore the Alexandrov Glacier from a new camp at its junction with the Potanina at 3100m, and spent Friday 13th relocating. Unexpectedly, Iona kept getting left behind on the long schusses down the glacier. The only factor that seemed to explain it was the textured surface of her haul bag which had been sourced from a different supplier. Undoubtedly it provided a tougher material but also increased the drag that was holding her back. However, this was an equipment problem that was not life-threatening; we could put up with it. The new camp was more sheltered and, at a lower altitude, less subject to frosting of the inner tent overnight. The weather too was noticeably warmer if no less windy. Across the glacier was the Swiss base camp and we went over to socialise and drink the promised beers.

On 14th May we set off to explore the right-hand branch of the Alexandrov glacier, following it all the way to a high and very crevassed pass east of Naran from which we could see the guided party following our route on Peak 4152. We booted up a short steep ridge to the border summit of Peak 3962 with light snow falling and peered into the Chinese Altai: as with the Russian Altai, there was lots of potential there if only the permits were obtainable. We were tempted to take a chance as Batbayar had told us only the Russians patrolled the border, on ski, of course, but decided not to risk a diplomatic incident. On the way back to camp we diverted from our line of ascent to take a much steeper slope direct. It was great skiing but so steep that I came upon the bergschrund break in the snow with a suddenness that meant making a split-second decision on the safest line over it. Relaxed turns and steady schussing then took us back down the glacier in fine sunshine.

Next day, fine weather was accompanied by an even stronger wind that swept clouds across the peaks like ships before a storm. The guided party passed our camp on their way to boot up a rubbly couloir on to Naran, but we were intent upon exploring the left branch of the Alexandrov. Later we saw them bunched in the rocky narrows near the foot of the face as we passed.

On the glacier we had our own problems. The fierce wind was bodied forth in whirling dervishes of spindrift that could hurl past or hit you head on and knock you back on your heels. We dug deep into our reserves and slogged on with views of the elegant snow spire of Snow Church (4073m) offering some compensation. Eventually a break in the east ridge of Chinggis turned out to be an easy pass. We took it, gaining a little more shelter on the other side. In better conditions this pass could have opened up the prospect of exploring the glaciers south of Chinggis but at that time we could not safely get across a steep-sided valley of gleaming, wind-polished ice. Instead we made an attempt on the westerly point above the pass. Derek was leading, with John second, and I appreciated the good deep steps they were kicking into the snow, but I began to be worried about its stability. My ice axe, plunged into the slope at right angles, encountered little or no resistance to the full depth of the shaft. Below we would be swept over a cliff if the slope avalanched. I called up my concerns to the others who then confessed that they, too, were having misgivings. We retreated. Carefully. The wind hustled us all back to camp like an aggressive usher as we skied down the glacier.

With time running out we lost a second day to bad weather, but on the final day on the glacier Derek and Howard opted for an ascent of Naran on foot following the couloir used by the French/Swiss team. Without the incentive of a ski descent and tired of the wind, the rest of us packed up and headed across the glacier although ironically Derek and Howard found dead calm on the summit. Gaining the moraine camp, we found our camel drivers had turned up early. When the climbers joined us, the camels were rapidly loaded and we marched the 15 kilometres back to the roadhead where the minibuses were lined up, waiting. The head camel driver's wife prepared a delicious meal for the whole team of skiers and support staff that was all the more welcome in that it was not dehydrated, then we turned in for the night.

An early start meant that we travelled the 200 kilometres to Olgi in a day where a call to head office confirmed that the support team had picked us up a day early, or rather we had put two days into one on our exit from the range. An extra day's gentle R & R in Olgi was no problem, although it was not until we reached Ulan Bataar that we found a shower that really worked. Progress indeed for a city which had been nothing more than a Ger camp a few kilometres away from the present site until just over a hundred years ago. Now it is a small but modern city and the food proved to be excellent. The Mongolians we met were friendly and helpful with an integrity born of a strong sense of self-reliance, although some felt that independence and globalisation had sponsored an explosion of corruption fostered by the mining companies vying for Mongolia's mineral wealth.

Batbayar believed that we were the first self-sufficient ski team to go into the Tavn Bogd and it certainly opened up possibilities with that level of flexibility in such a fine remote mountain area.

In both cases the equipment failures had been the result of small changes to previously effective systems. In the case of the textured haul bag the inconvenience was minor, although in a blizzard it might have resulted in losing track of a member of the team as the others erected psychological barriers against the attrition of the storm. In the case of the heat exchanger the results could have been lethal.

I was later to research the stove issue and discovered Paul Ramsden's excellent research which was summarised in his article "The Silent Killer", in the *Alpine Journal* of 2012. I have tried to publicise the problem with heat exchangers on stoves, but still encounter people who are unaware of the increased danger. Let's hope that can be remedied.

For me there were consequences. On my return to the UK I found that when typing I was making many more typos than had been the case before and when under pressure might make some inconsistent decisions. This did not improve with time and eventually psychological tests demonstrated a processing time that was at variance with that which would be expected of someone with my level of problem-solving ability. The psychologist told me that would be consistent with CO brain damage and offered some very helpful coping strategies that have enabled me to function normally, whatever that may mean. I still make an excessive number of typos!

Iona giving the descent some angulation on account of its steepness in the south couloir of Pik 3926m.

Camels transporting our kit out to the roadhead from the Potanina glacier.

The team had some interpersonal problems at times and the weather meant that we spent too much time in our separate tents which explains the lack of discussion before attempting to swap tent partners. I think I may have contributed to that. After the CO poisoning incident at the start of the trip I think I may have become wary about taking on too much and inclined to retreat into myself. It had been a damaging experience in more than one way and I'm sure I was less pro-active than I would normally have been as leader.

Even though half the team had never skied with any of the other members before, the combination of an experienced expeditioner and a less-experienced tent mate proved to work. When there were problems with those combinations they were sorted out more or less amicably and unforeseen team weaknesses were compensated for in the field once we were aware of them. We were all supportive and dealt with a potential disaster effectively in difficult circumstances.

My thanks will always be due to the team for their excellent work in keeping us all alive.

8. Incident creep and team problems: Oman

To be honest I was uncertain about including this case study because although the objectives were challenging, it really just scrapes into my remoteness criterion for an expedition. However, for me, it illuminated issues about personal interaction and team composition, navigation and incident creep.

Paul and I had met informally through the Alpine Club, and climbed and walked together in the Lake and Peak Districts. We didn't know each other well but respected what we had done and made a couple of plans for expeditions. I recall one idea for climbing in the Kongur range but I ended up skiing Mustagh Ata instead with an international team. Paul moved from the UK, first to Morocco and then to New Zealand, so opportunities to climb together diminished with distance. Then, on a visit to the UK for an academic conference, Paul stayed over at my house and floated the idea of climbing in Oman that winter. Another prospective partner had failed to commit and Paul had been to the country on four previous occasions so had worked out the logistics in some detail. It was an interesting idea. I'd led a team to Mount Kenya in winter to climb Alpine rock routes on the satellite peaks of the mountain and thoroughly enjoyed the challenge despite being unlucky with the weather. When Paul confirmed details a month or so later, I thought it was an opportunity too good to miss.

The Gulf state of Oman had benefitted from oil production revenues so that there was urban development along the coast and a modern, if limited, road network. However, maps were totally inadequate for exploration of outlying areas and Paul's navigation often relied on waypoints extracted from Google Earth. An off-road vehicle was essential to access many villages along dirt tracks that could become watercourses in the event of flash flooding from sudden storms in which vehicles could be washed away. Bedouin had warned us about camping in some wadis when I visited Jordan because storms in the mountains could drown campers in the dry desert valleys that could suddenly be transformed into raging torrents. Drowning is an unexpected hazard of desert mountains!

In Wadi Rum there had been springs overgrown with mint at the foot of many of the sandstone cliffs, and pools in shady canyons. A web search on Oman produced stories about swimming in wadi pools and deep-water soloing on the coast so I thought it would be similar. I should probably have done more research, but with Paul having organised four previous climbing trips it was a relief to be able to hand over such organisation to someone else for a change.

The Western Hajar consists of mesa-like limestone mountains of over 2000m pushed up from the seabed by geological processes which are still not fully understood. Cliffs of up to 900m offer Alpine rock routes with a lot of scope for new-routing in winter when temperatures would be low enough for climbing to be possible. Winter days can still be hot but the diurnal range in a desert environment can be dramatic with temperatures falling below −10°C at night on the summits. This means that there is some practice of transhumance with herds of sheep and goats going up to high pastures on the mesas in the summer but being brought down to valley villages in the winter. The longer rock routes or potential routes tended to finish on these high summits.

I flew out to meet Paul in Muscat on 28 December, and should probably have taken more notice of the fact that in the depths of winter it was going to be a lot colder than my experiences in the deserts of Jordan and Morocco at Easter. Paul had briefed me by email on the need for lightweight kit so no walking boots, just lightweight approach shoes but tough enough to take the very rough ground. I'd acquired a collapsible carbon

Camp in the desert before a climb.

fibre ski pole to help with that and a very lightweight rucksack but Paul was dismissive. 'We'll only have one rucksack, mine. For technical climbing it's essential that the leader climbs without a sack so you'll be carrying the ropes while I carry the rack, a couple of energy bars and some water in the sack: that way there won't be much in it for the second to carry.' That meant no medical kit, no spare clothing; it went against my principles of alpinism that included each member of a climbing partnership being largely self-sufficient in terms of basics like food and water just in case the unexpected happened and a rucksack or even a person was lost in a fall.

I hazarded a question but Paul was adamant that he'd used this approach successfully before and that's what we needed to do now. It was after 10 pm and all climbers can be a bit OCD about equipment, so I deferred to his experience and let it go. Four trips without mishap were a recommendation after all and he was talking about our first route as a warm-up route so in theory it would allow me time to evaluate his approach.

Next day, after picking up supplies, we drove into the interior, grinding up a recently bulldozed dirt road to reach a deserted village below the north face of Jebel Kawr where we camped for the night. At 6.30, an unexpectedly chilly morning found each of us wearing microfleece pullovers as we picked out a trail across scree-scattered slopes towards a distinctive, shallow, cave-like feature at the base of a gully, with the intention of climbing the pillar to its left. This route had been scouted by Paul on a previous visit. On the north face, it was intended to keep us out of the sun but the morning had been cold enough for even Paul to allow the inclusion of microfleece tops which I took as an encouraging sign.

A debris-littered traverse ledge took us to the edge of the gully where a broken diedre led onto its bounding rib. That rib continued easily pitch after pitch with some linking ledge-walking and a few harder moves to the top of a pinnacle from which we could see that we'd been climbing the right edge of a pyramidal feature semi-detached from the main cliff. An unusually cold wind had reinforced the chill of climbing on the shadowed, northern side of the mountain but we doubted that adding a windshirt was going make much difference, so it was good to keep moving. By now it was clear that the climb was bigger than it had seemed from below. Much bigger.

I scrambled down to the col that separated the pyramid from the cliff and Paul led a wandering line up a testing slab on the main face. Further tricky pitches followed, trying first one line then another. A crack would run out in the middle of a blank wall or a likely line founder among crumbling rock and detachable holds.

One long pitch involved a steep slab that gradually became very smooth. Having climbed myself into an impasse, I retreated, traversing beneath a shattered chimney to climb the wall to the right on small incut solution pockets and very spaced protection from only a thread and a tied-off "chickenhead". The "neck" of the chickenhead was such thin, sharp-edged rock that I couldn't make my mind up whether it would be more likely to snap off or cut the sling if I fell on the runner. Only rope-stretch enabled me to find a belay. Paul was generous enough to describe it as 'a fine lead'. We were getting on well, absorbed in the routines of effective climbing but time was running on.

Paul seconding a pitch on the Dark Side.

A later chimney crack proved equally challenging, involving precarious bridging and laying away, facing first in one direction then the other. It was tight enough for Paul to have to swing the sack up separately on one of the ropes when he followed. Such pitches would be hard to reverse and we had not planned for an abseil descent. We shared an awareness that we were committed to something much bigger than expected but both felt that we had no option but to go on. Paul was convinced that we would be able to walk off easily across the summit plateau on the virtual route he had plotted on Google Earth until we reached his GPS waypoint in territory he would recognise from a previous visit.

After 17 pitches we gained the broad shelf at the top of the face. From there a walk and a short, tough scramble through an upper cliff led to the summit plateau. It was 6 p.m. As we sorted our kit, our euphoria was tempered by the recognition that we were at 2400m and night was falling. Paul shouldered the rucksack while I tied both ropes on "rucksack fashion" and thus loaded we hiked across the summit plateau as the night reddened into darkness.

With the benefit of a full moon Paul was confident we'd be back at camp soon after midnight and keeping moving would keep us warm. That confidence was soon revealed to be misplaced: he was shocked by the unexpected complexity of the topography and, despite the moon, we kept finding ourselves on the brink of cliffs with no clear way down in the darkness. Google Earth appeared to be very short on detail in this area.

It had been cold all day and at the setting of the sun a bitter little breeze began to leach away our warmth as uncertainty regarding the route slowed us down. With temperatures that could drop to −10°C overnight there was a real danger of hypothermia. We back-tracked to a deserted Bedouin shepherds' camp to look for shelter and found a small, stone-built hut with a stout, earthed-over timber roof. The cold stone floor meant there was no chance of lying down comfortably but Paul sat on the ropes while I perched on a rickety stool, which meant that if ever I drifted off it was only to be awoken with a start as I tilted off my perch.

We made one further attempt at finding a way off when we thought the moon might be high enough to make a difference. It wasn't, and we were driven back to shelter by uncontrollable shivering. There was nothing to be done but resign ourselves to eight hours of sitting bivouac, enlivened by occasional fits of shivering as body core temperatures dropped with inactivity.

In the merciless dawn light Paul looked as rough as I felt. A blue, plastic bag hung from a roof beam and we could see the dates pressing stickily to its interior, presumably

Dave posing in the sunset having completed the 17 pitches of The Dark Side.

emergency rations. But neither of us thought of ourselves as being in enough of an emergency to justify taking any: we'd be back in camp by lunchtime with any luck, although the remaining water might need rationing. It seemed somehow churlish to steal the dates after the shelter had probably saved our lives during the night. We finished the crumbs of our last energy bar and swallowed a couple of mouthfuls of water before setting stiffly off.

Crossing a small dam, we skirted the cliffs that fell away to our left, heading more or less in a south-easterly direction. Sooner or later we hoped to strike back north to reach Paul's col and the waypoint. Scrambling down a rake circumvented the first cliff band leaving us on a broad bench above a second band with a valley lying below that ran north and seemed a good bet. It was as we tried to find a way down to that valley that we became separated.

We had been moving on parallel courses, somewhat on autopilot, with Paul nearer the cliffs, scouting for a break, while I plodded dully along, hoping my well-trodden path would lead to an obvious descent: it had to lead somewhere. I caught sight of a big cairn that the path was leading to and turned to shout the news to Paul, but he was nowhere to be seen.

I back-tracked to where I believed I'd seen him last and shouted. No reply. He must have found a way down so I started descending in hopes of catching him up, repeatedly stopping to shout. Nothing. There was a lot of steep rock below me so I tried traversing further right, shouting again as I did so. The sound echoed from the cliffs above and opposite but with no answering shouts. I came upon a black hosepipe, dry and coming from who knows where, but didn't like the look of the terrain below it, so descended further on what I thought was a safer line. I shouted again and again. Still nothing.

Paul later told me he pursued a similar course of action; both of us encountered the black pipe. Neither of us can understand how we managed to miss each other despite our best efforts to reconnect. Perhaps it was the emptiness of the landscape; perhaps it was our poor physical state after the night out. We shall never know for certain.

There was no option but to climb back up to where I'd last seen Paul and wait, hoping that he would do the same. I probably didn't wait long enough. At 9.30 the heat was intensifying and Paul had all the water. There was also an anxiety that he might have had a fall and be unable to reply. I decided to take the cairned route I'd found which, sure enough, led to a straightforward gully. There was one section of uncomfortably smooth slabs, but that was the only difficulty before reaching another valley just to the south of the col I'd seen below the cliffs. Climbing up to that col, I found no sign of Paul so decided to descend the valley to the north: it had seemed to be in the right general direction and perhaps that was the way to the col with the waypoint that Paul had described. Not having any way of confirming that was my first inkling of the seriousness of my position.

Persuading myself that I was on a path became increasingly difficult as the trail unravelled into what looked more like animal tracks. These finally ran out among a jumble of boulders above a precipitous water-worn drop-off. My continuing shouts had elicited no response. I realised I had no real idea if this was the way out and could be getting myself into trouble if I tried to force a route down the rock, so toiled back up to the col to try the valley to the south. That seemed more promising as I descended past discarded blue plastic kegs and rusty tins, but this valley also narrowed to a drop-off.

I retreated to the shade of a huge boulder and took stock, leaning against the cool rock. I had the clothes I wore, two ropes, a helmet, a lighter, and no real idea of how to get out of these mountains. It was gone noon and my last drink of water had been six hours earlier. Given that I'd probably drunk less than a litre of water the day before, I might live for 48 hours, but this was a desert environment and I'd been sweating uphill in full sun more than once that morning. Then it struck me that there were at best only another six hours of daylight. There was little chance of finding my way out in that time and I was still at around 2000m. Without shelter it was unlikely that I'd survive the night. That meant there were two ways I could be dead by morning.

I considered casting about for alternative descents but there had never been any plan to walk out to the south. If Paul had reached safety, a search party would focus on the area to the north. If he hadn't, I'd have to find my own way out or I was dead. Either way, north made sense.

Looking back up the slope in the hard light, I knew I had to climb back up to the col. But now I could see that there seemed to be two cols separated by a broad ridge. Perhaps there would be a path over the col I hadn't yet reached. It was a struggle to reason out the options and remain calm in the face of odds stacked against my survival.

I discarded my own rope, knowing that Paul had a spare back at camp. Recoiling his rope in a loop that I could sling over my shoulder rather than lash to my back, I clipped the chin-strap of my helmet around it. Windshirt and microfleece were tied about my waist and my long-sleeved base layer turned into protection from the sun by tying it into a sort of turban about my head. I was ready to leave the shade of the boulder.

The slope was in full sun. Slowly I struggled upward linking islands of shadow created by bush, rock, or stunted tree, and leaning my forehead against any cool stone as I paused at each "island" to regain my breath. I tried not to breathe through my mouth to avoid exhaling too much water vapour, and tried not to swallow, for my throat was literally sticking to itself.

Nearing the cols I stumbled across a faint path and, following it, I glimpsed a splash of colour beside a tree and called out, thinking it might be a person resting in the shade. There was no reaction and, closer, I could see that it was just blankets draped over a branch to dry in the sun after any downpour. Blankets! I could survive the night!

I was on the edge of another deserted shepherds' camp and the heavy blankets had been left for future use. They literally saved my life, although during the night the temperature dropped so low that I found myself shivering uncontrollably and had to unearth another blanket from among the camp debris in order to survive.

During that evening I discovered that drinking one's own urine only leads to instant gut evacuation: a doctor friend later explained that the toxins in my urine were

Blanket bivouac that saved Dave's life on the second night out.

probably so concentrated that my gut just expelled them immediately. I managed to preserve my trousers but had to throw my pants away.

Then I pursued the sound of voices only to fail to locate the camp I'd seen, or thought I'd seen, down in the southern valley. Dismayed, I had to toil back up to my blankets if I was going to last the night. Finally, as darkness fell, my hopes rose with the sight of head-torch lights up near the col but again my shouts were unanswered. Perhaps I was hallucinating.

An orange dawn found me rested but, as I sat up, I began to choke on the build-up of solidified mucus at the back of my throat. I had to hook it out with a finger, fighting down the reflex to retch, before I could breathe easily. Looking down-valley there was no sign of anyone. Still, I was now sure that there had to be a way out over the pass above: no one would have gone over it by torchlight unless the destination was close enough and the route easy enough to be completed in the dark.

After a bit of a false start, I struck a good trail under the overhanging cliffs down the valley beyond the col where brushwood lean-to shelters and stone circles showed evidence of intermediate campsites.

By then I was very slow and even more unsteady. If I slipped on unstable rocks I was less and less likely to recover myself and I took several tumbles. With each it was more difficult to get up. Mercifully, the valley faced north so remained in shadow but

I still had to stop, rest, and cool my forehead and wrists against the cold rock with increasing frequency. My temperature was rising in response to the decreasing volume of blood plasma. I had time to think about how I might die. Would it be heart attack or stroke as my blood thickened? Or would my kidneys just pack up? I was glad not to know the details.

By late morning I was on the sunny side of the valley, forced to link shadow to shadow to keep going. I reached another campsite where the valley opened out briefly before descending steeply into a dry but complex gorge. No trail went that way. Instead, a mesh of tracks led up a bare rocky slope to the north. It was in full sun. Above could be the col Paul had talked about with a village beyond. I sat in the shade of a big rock, looking at the slope, and knew I wouldn't make it. There wasn't a trace of shade on it. The only chance was to try it in the cool of evening, but would I last till then?

I sat on the bare earth with my head in my hands: it was so desperately unfair. Then I got angry: surely there was some patch of shade, no matter how small, that could be used to get me up it! I scanned the slope and there was a flash of colour, movement ... people.

I rocked to my feet, took a step forward into the light with my arms widespread and called, 'Help! I need help! I've been lost on the mountain and have no water.'

And a voice called back, 'We have water. We have everything.'

My arms dropped and I stepped back into the shade, slumping into a sitting position again, watching them picking their different ways down through the rock and scrub towards me. There was something familiar about the one coming fast, ahead of the rest. It was Paul. As he arrived, I reached out to shake his hand but he hugged me, then produced a water bottle. No drink has ever tasted better.

I met the rest of the search party, a team of Rob's trek leaders from Muscat Diving and Adventure, in the process of being plied with oral rehydration solution, banana, apple, dates, chocolate, biscuits and water, water, water; slowly, so that I could manage it.

'Happy New Year! This is a plus for us you know. We normally bring out bodies.' They were cheerful enough after spending most of New Year's Eve getting in position for the search. I had completely forgotten the date.

'Didn't you hear our shouts and whistle-blowing from the col up there?'

'Not a sound. The desert must have just swallowed it up in all that space.'

As I rehydrated, I chilled down and had to move out of the shade and into the sunshine. After a couple of hours I was able to walk up the slope in one push, always with one person ahead and one behind me in case I collapsed. Then it was a rest before the steady slow descent of a loose gully to the village beyond.

There was a police presence at the roadhead: a squad of them in dark blue overalls and big boots, waiting for word to carry out the body. Two officers drove me in a Landcruiser down to the tarmac road where the ambulance was waiting to take me to A & E.

When the hospital discharged me, Paul and I spent the night in camp before returning to Muscat for a couple of days' rest. Then a gentle reconnaissance of Wadi

Serious talk between Dave and Rob who led the rescue party with Paul

Sawyga revealed some interesting rock but no obvious ways down, so we camped by the wadi pools and managed a swim next morning before driving to the south side of Jebel Kawr and camping in the desert. A wild road up to the remote village of Nadan allowed us to scout approaches to the impressive cirque that surrounded it. A line looked feasible for the following day but we had to put it off after I spent a night interrupted by bouts of vomiting and diarrhoea. Clearly, more time was needed for recovery. A couple more days were spent visiting spectacular forts and canyons.

Then it was back to Nadan to try the rock pillar we'd scoped out earlier. The first third of the route was mostly scrambling linked by harder steps that provided some nice problems. The route then reared up and we linked rakes, ledges and cracks to find a way through steep territory. The final third fell back to easier scrambling up to the summit. Triassic Superbowl was ten pitches plus a bit of scrambling. Paul was very methodical about noting down the features and estimated the length of each pitch in a little notebook. We graded this 430m route as TD−, VI−. The 800m descent was to the south via an AD+ route that Paul had put up with Richard Simpson in 2007. One abseil was necessary near the summit but the rest was just exposed scrambling with the occasional tricky move and some loose rock. It was very hot. Despite Paul's previous acquaintance with the route, it was me who found the old abseil slings and one of the rock shoes that Richard had lost on their way down in 2007. The heat and sharp rock left my hands raw by the end of the day.

Threatening weather hung over us as we packed up camp, but just as we were leaving a local Omani turned up to invite us for a second breakfast of dates, spiced chicken, coffee and tea at his home: a generous offer that we felt would be impolite to refuse. We then drove over to Sidaq village where shorter routes might be possible in the uncertain weather. I scrambled up to some crudely fortified caves above the village and on my return found Paul in conversation with locals who then invited us to their village hall for tea. There was a little awkwardness about the ensuing conversation, perhaps because of differing levels of expertise in English, although it turned out one of the villagers had been to college in Newcastle! I'm not sure that helped the others.

We drove over the pass to make camp. However, during the evening meal my stomach felt like there was some animal moving around inside to make room for the food, but it settled down overnight so that we were able to put up Giant Slab 193m, V– on the long grey slab above Sidaq next morning. Four pitches on good sound rock with reasonable protection ended at a long arête that we traversed to reach a col down which we could scramble back to the foot of the face. We had time to drive to near Jebel Murri for the night.

Away at first light, we walked over a couple of cols then followed goat tracks around the shattered bulk of the main peak to reach the more resistant rock of a satellite cone. Paul had climbed an easy route to the right of the south face but wanted to check out the possibilities further left. We scouted around before deciding on a shallow gully line left of the centre of the face. Easy pitches led to a walk on to a steepening slab. Paul led up cracks in an increasingly exposed position with some quite technical moves and not much protection before belaying on a narrow ledge under the headwall. Again, I had to scramble up a few metres to give him enough rope to make the belay. Reaching the belay block I immediately checked to see if it moved; it was that sort of block. It didn't move but equally there didn't seem to be any reason why it wouldn't.

More testing pitches led to a big flat shelf with a steep crack in the wall above. Thin unprotected moves led up to a dubious runner behind a loose flake, then better gear in the crack as it steepened. Tough moves to the right of the crack using small solution pockets took the skin off my fingertips, bloodying the rock as I climbed. There was nothing much of a belay above so Paul had to move across the shelf to give me enough rope to climb the shallow diedre to the left. This was delicate with no gear until its upper half, then two good cams before hauling out on a decent ledge with solid belay blocks. Paul climbed on up the easy connecting ridge to the summit and that was it: a good route, Arabian Knights 311m, D+, VI–.

Over the days, we had returned to the circumstances of our losing track of each other on the first climb but without reaching any conclusions. On the descent from

Arabian Knights we became separated again and gained further insights. I'd lagged behind on the rough ground. The unstable rock jolted my knees, damaged by decades of alpinism, and the pain increased with distance covered. I thought Paul was just ahead of me although out of sight and I was some way down before I recognised that he wasn't. As the trail unfolded, I realised that the broken nature of the land meant that we could have been quite invisible to each other despite being only a hundred metres apart. Shouting again made no difference; sound seemed to be deadened by the terrain. I couldn't face climbing back up to look for him but could see the nearest col and worked out that it had to be visible from anywhere in the bowl we were descending. I made for it.

From the col I could see Paul casting about the upper slopes looking for me. I laid out my kit as conspicuously as possible and hollered until he noticed and made his way down. He was pretty grumpy and I could appreciate why. We had an exchange of views; nothing unpleasant. It highlighted our differences in that he hadn't really appreciated the knee pain I was experiencing on the descents: the problem of 20 years age difference! When climbing, there hadn't been a problem, which hadn't helped his perception of the situation. I was an unusual element in this scenario and it required an adaptation that he wasn't expecting to have to deal with. We were also learning that this was unforgiving terrain. I led the rest of the descent so we kept more closely in touch. Back at camp, my hips and knees were aching badly; dehydration didn't help.

There was time for a final route on Jabal Nakhus where Paul had climbed Hand-grater in 2010. We camped in the pleasant Chains Wadi where a series of pools were separated by huge boulders. A group of Omani young men offered us chicken and rice from their picnic after we'd walked up to the cliffs to scout a route. They left a formidable amount of rubbish in their wake which we dutifully gathered and burnt, leaving the organic material to passing animals. Then we could camp for the night.

At first light, we walked up to the base of the cliff then scrambled up ramp lines to reach the foot of a long corner on the right of a pyramid of rock. The corner more or less gave the line of the route with deviations onto the cracked slab on the right or up the arête and face to the left: Karst Corner 242m, V. We unroped at a ledge where the angle fell back but there remained some interesting scrambling up chimneys to get over the top and onto the descent traverse.

There we found Paul's abseil sling of five years ago, looking pretty weathered, but he was set on finding the descent line of the first ascentionists on this crag so we worked back right and down towards a brown spur. At a steep step I found their first abseil point which sounded worryingly hollow when struck. I voiced some misgivings but to Paul it was simple: 'If we want to get off we have to use it.' As I slid down the ropes, the thought crossed my mind that after surviving being lost in the desert it would be truly ironic to die in an abseiling accident. Untangling the ropes as I went, I made for the next abseil point on a ledge below and rigged a new sling on the good rock anchor the other team had used while Paul hauled down the ropes.

Another long abseil meant much rope-untangling as the ropes bound to the rough rock and would not fall free. They hooked up on tiny flakes and solution features, then

*Paul leading a typical Oman pitch on
Triassic Superbowl TD- VI-.*

tangled about themselves to tax our patience. Down on the easy ramp below I found another abseil point, but it was really simpler just to scramble on down to the neck of rock that linked the main face to a shattered brown spur. Paul reminded me that the earlier team had been descending by moonlight so would probably have felt safer on the rope. Down a gully then back onto the spur, loose scree slopes finally allowed us to walk out onto the gravel plains below. Back at camp a visiting herd of goats had eaten every sign of the picnic debris, including silver paper that we had failed to separate from the rice.

The goats arrived as I was frying eggs next morning but were chased on to higher ground by the mother and son team of goatherds. Paul and I had time to explore the shady wadi which was claimed to have a through route; it proved to be challenging scrambling on water-worn rock polished to a fine sheen by the passage of feet. Pools between the rock had to be waded and while I stopped to remove shoes and trousers on a couple of occasions, draping them around my neck, Paul just plunged on getting thoroughly wet. This was the New Zealand norm he was used to. That was all very well until we reached the final section of very polished rock. Despite being fixed with steel cables, it was far too slippery for Paul in his wet shoes but I was fine to go on to the end of the wadi which opened out into a mini oasis. We then reversed the route with me retaining my on-off approach and Paul getting even wetter. It was a fun couple of hours to end our stay.

Back at camp Paul dried off his shoes in the sunshine while we brewed and snacked before driving off to find the hot springs at Nazl. These burst out of channels in the rock but there were cave-like sumps where it was possible to soak away one's aches and pains. Then it was back to Muscat for the night and we flew out a day later.

As it turned out, the trip had been remarkably successful: five new routes had been climbed. But it could have been very different. I'd nearly died, and for years afterwards certain triggers, a snatch of song for example, could reduce me to tears as the recollected emotions flooded back. I think both of us were aware of our particular idiosyncrasies but had underestimated what it might take to cope with them. Paul's relative youth meant that some physical aspects of the experience were a lot easier for him than for me and while he might not have realised that, I too was also reluctant to admit all of the implications.

A team of two is not unusual. One thinks of Mick Fowler and Paul Ramsden climbing as a self-sufficient pair and making it work, but it has to be said that there is much less room for manoeuvre than in a larger team. Climbing together in the UK is very different from new-routing in a country in which the infrastructure, culture and climate are nothing like the same.

Climbing as a team of three on Alpine rock routes has been preferred by some climbers. With careful ropework, two seconds can climb at the same time, rather than in turn, and the leader has a rest while belaying them before leading the next pitch. When swinging leads, climbing as a pair, it can be a daunting prospect to lead the next long hard pitch having just seconded one. As a team of three, at the belay one second can be handing over gear cleaned from the route while the other second is pulling the

Dave leading on Arabian Knights D+ VI-.

ropes through, then after a few pitches leading, each of the seconds can take over in turn for a few more. Such an approach is easier on known routes in the Alps but could work on new-routing in more remote areas by adding a little strength in numbers.

Of course, the actual process of climbing is very similar; holds might be tested more thoroughly but moves will be much the same as those practised on climbing walls and crags over the years. However, it's unlikely that there will be other people about and helicopter search and rescue may well not be an option. The inescapable conclusion is that we should therefore be more careful about what and how we climb, but in this case we both expected to climb close to our limits. This was influenced by Paul's previous experience in the area, which is fair enough, but in retrospect I was prepared to defer to his judgement more often than was really healthy. A good partner should challenge as well as support; it makes for better decision making. I should probably have done more homework on the area as well, reading up more reports of other visits.

Paul's previous experience also reinforced a certain inflexibility in his approach. As I mentioned before there's a tendency to Obsessive Compulsive Disorder in many climbers who may have to have certain gear or do things certain ways, carry certain talismans, etc. I know I do. Another climbing friend described it as "an autistic tendency". The authority supplied by previous experience in the area can lend more inflexibility to that sort of tendency. It's a kind of heuristic trap. We can overvalue experience. I remember the education adviser who told me about "Mrs A" who was dismissive of his suggestions for improving her practice:

'Mr B, I have twenty years' experience of teaching in this school, which tells me that your suggestions won't work.'

'Mrs A, you haven't had twenty years' experience, you've had one year's experience twenty times and I would recommend a more open mind.'

Small differences added up to produce a dangerous situation, which is classic incident creep. The colder than expected weather, the longer and harder than expected warm-up route, the uncertainty about the descent route and the inaccuracy of the Google Earth model, the concentration of food, water and navigation details in the hands of only one of the team, the deterioration in our condition after a cold bivouac, all added up to the tipping point when we lost contact with each other that could so easily have led to disaster. Yet we could have got away with it, and the fact that we so nearly repeated the scenario later in the trip, but with fewer factors contributing to the incident creep, shows how hard it can be to challenge underlying assumptions and assess those contributory factors.

Communicating more effectively and adopting more flexibility would probably have helped, but in the midst of action and the need for speed it is often difficult to recognise how a series of incidents, each small in itself, can combine to create the potential for tragedy. Ultimately, tragedy was averted through sheer persistence, both in my determination not to give up and in Paul's rapid organisation of a rescue party.

9. Gender issues: Denali to Pik Lenin

To me, gender issues have been a very rare problem. I enjoy the company of male and female climbers and have welcomed both onto expeditions that I have led, but a fellow climber drew my attention to the way that attitudes have changed over the years and the potential impact of gender issues on expeditions. This case study attempts to consider that by comparing one expedition with another and the influence of gender issues on both in an effort to avoid this aspect of relationships becoming a kind of blind spot in a more emancipated era.

   I first met Yvonne on an expedition to climb Denali organised by Bill through the Alpine Club. It was a mountain that she had always wanted to climb. There were four

Yvonne relaxing at camp 1, Denali.

in the team and Yvonne and I ended up sharing a tent. We were both well organised in the tent, with an "everything in its place and a place for everything" approach so the potentially messy business of melting snow, brewing and cooking went like clockwork.

As a climbing team too, we shared the same attitude to risk assessment and learnt to trust each other's judgement. This meant that when we gambled on a late in the day ascent of the headwall above the 4000m camp to avoid traffic jams on the fixed ropes and ran into trouble in the wind on the crest we still managed to cope. Yvonne's hands went dead since she suffered from Reynaud's disease but I was able to get the tent pitched and her into it with a hot drink before frostbite had time to take effect. On another occasion, load carrying on the ridge leading to top camp, my right hand completely lost all feeling so she found shelter for us and spent ten or fifteen minutes working on restoring the circulation with massage. Denali is a very cold place!

On our first attempt at the summit we probably set out a little too early. Crossing the glacier bay to the start of the traverse, we had to stop and add layers of clothing a couple of times as the cold penetrated those we were wearing. Frost sparkled in the thin new snow reflecting the slanting early light. The angle wasn't steep but the ice was bone hard and steps had been cut around seracs outcropping from the slope.

Perhaps because we hoped a fast pace would keep us warm, we made good time to Denali Pass where we took a break in the sunshine. The strategy didn't work very well; Yvonne was feeling numbness growing in her feet; the height and cold were taking their toll. It took us 90 minutes to make just 150m, climbing up through rocks on the ridge above the pass. Then she called a halt. She had lost all feeling in her feet and couldn't increase the pace any further to generate more heat.

We stopped in a sheltered spot and one by one took off her boots. Her feet were a yellow waxy colour; when pressed her toes showed no evidence of capillary refill. The dints stayed dinted and white. I massaged each foot in turn until they stopped feeling wooden and some pinkness returned after pressure was applied to the toes. The immediate danger of frostbite was over but it could return. She wanted to go back to camp.

I was prepared to go back with her but then it occurred to me that this could be my only opportunity to summit. I was going well. It would take over an hour to return to camp but by then it wouldn't make sense to set out again that day. I hesitated, then asked the obvious question: 'How do you feel about going back to camp on your own if I carry on? I mean, I'm going well and this could be my only chance to get to the summit.'

We took time to discuss the situation thoroughly, evaluating the risks. Then there was a pregnant pause. 'OK … Yes. You go on.' She'd made up her mind. 'It's not far back to camp.'

We gave each other a hug and went our separate ways.

I made good time to meet Bill and James, who had set out before us, just below the summit on their way down. Bill was kind enough to insist on climbing back up to take a summit picture of me before I roped up with them for the descent. We took a short break at Denali Pass before making the traverse on a track well trodden

Yvonne descending the ridge back to 4000m camp after load-carrying to top camp.

by those lured all the way up from Camp 4 to take a shot at the summit in the fine weather. Not many had made it. Much of the day had actually been cloudy or hazy and many times my hands and feet had suffered from the cold. For only the second time that day my feet were completely warm as we staggered up the little rise into Camp 5 where there were tears from Yvonne as well as congratulations.

We could have cut and run next day but that evening Bill and I both put it to Yvonne that she could solo the route if the weather held and we'd wait for her. Unfortunately, the day had taken too much out of the rest of us to consider going up again. She remained doubtful, but overnight the pressure rose dramatically and the weather continued fine! Over breakfast, Yvonne quizzed me on details of the route.

'It's well within your abilities and if you set out later it shouldn't be so cold. We'll wait for you and I'll go over to Denali Pass around the time you might expect to reach it in case you're tired for the traverse.'

'Right. OK. I think I'll go for it.'

Outside the tent I caught snatches of French and German from our new neighbours and it suddenly occurred to me that that might mean they were Swiss. Two months earlier I had stayed at the Hollandia Hut in the Bernese Oberland. In conversation with the guardian we had learnt that we both planned to be on Denali at about the same time in May.

I'd left the hut, joking, 'I'll see you on Denali!'

He'd replied in the same spirit, 'Right, I'll look out for you!'

Realistically, the chances of an encounter were remote, but as I stuck my head over the snow wall and called, 'Are you Swiss? Do you have a guy called Willi with you from the Hollandia Hut?' across the compound, a figure straightened from beside a tent.

'Who wants me?'

'Willi?'

'Hey … Dave? We meet again!'

I wasted no time but asked directly if his team was going up that day. They were going to have a try but weren't well acclimatised and weren't sure how far they'd get. So I asked him if he would look out for Yvonne.

'Sure, sure. We'll watch out for her; see she is Ok. Don't worry.'

I introduced Yvonne to Willi and his team and they set off together about 11.30.

Willi's team returned to camp later but without Yvonne. They had not been sufficiently acclimatised and it was too cold for them to go slowly so they had turned back near the top of the ridge. Yvonne had gone on.

'She was going very well. She should make it.'

Setting out too early on the traverse to Denali Pass.

'Thanks. Thanks a lot.' And I left him to get on with brewing up and settling back into camp. I had not expected to be as anxious as I was but now at least I had a better idea of when to go over to Denali Pass. Atmosperic pressure was still high.

At the estimated time, I put my boots on but as I clambered out of the tent, there she was, just swinging down onto the last rise up to camp. It was 8.30 p.m.

Tired but elated, Yvonne told me how she had found the traverse laced with snow stakes and ropes set by earlier guided parties. Her feet had been fine because of the later start but her fingers were frost-nipped and her nose and cheekbones were smudged with black where frostbite had killed the surface of her skin. It looked only superficial though. A strong wind had blown up mid-afternoon but two guided parties refused to let her tie on to their ropes for the exposed section of the summit ridge. Continuing alone she heard one of the clients ask, 'What's the best way to put my crampons into the snow, John?' and decided she was probably safer on her own.

In descent, blowing knee-deep spindrift had completely obscured the trail; it had been like wading through water. Without the marker wands sticking out above the spindrift surface, she would have lost the track and been in danger of straying onto ground where there have been fatal falls in the past. Down the ridge the way was obvious and despite the wind she'd made much better time than I'd expected back to camp.

Next morning the wind had dropped as we packed up camp. Descending the ridge to Camp 4 for the last time, we could relish the wide-open panorama of Alaska, blue and white in the unaccustomed calm. It was very beautiful with a blink of the Pacific away in the distance.

We made a good team.

One thing led to another and within a year we were living together. Climbing was a big part of our life together, whether it was walking and rock climbing in the Picos de Europa or tackling the high snow cones of Cotopaxi and Cayambe before failing on Chimborazo in Ecuador. While we sometimes had different priorities, we achieved a lot in a supportive partnership and if I was more interested in technical climbing, she had an insatiable appetite for Scotland: potential conflicts of interest were generally resolved by not living in each other's pockets.

Yvonne worked as an IT contractor and when a contract finished, if there was nothing else in the pipeline (and sometimes even if there was) she would take as much time off as would allow her to fulfil one of her mountaineering ambitions. Such an opportunity came up in 2002. The UN had declared 2002 the Year of the Mountains and in Kyrgyzstan the authorities decided to celebrate with a Pik Lenin Festival. Logistical packages could be purchased at a discount and the idea of meeting other climbers of many nationalities was an appealing prospect.

With Pik Lenin rising to over 7000m acclimatisation would be challenging so we decided to spend the early part of the summer climbing in the Alps. I still needed to add Piz Bernina to my tally of 4000m peaks so we camped in Pontresina and did a couple of training climbs including Piz Morteratsch, which might have been a mistake. Yvonne looked down from its summit onto the airy snow ridge of the Biancograt and

*The team of summiteers looking cheerful despite
the loads to carry back down to base camp.*

flatly stated that she wasn't doing it. I was a bit non-plussed as it was well within her
capabilities, but there was no sense in forcing the issue. We decided to traverse from
Piz Palu to Piz Zupo then stay the night in the Marco e Rosa Hut before climbing the
Spallagrat of Piz Bernina instead.

We set out confidently from the Diavolezza Hut, treading the snow crest of Piz
Palu under a clear blue sky while the valleys below were filled with cloud. However,
descending the blocky granite of the west ridge, Yvonne complained of feeling tired
and when we reached the Fuorcla Bellavista she didn't want to go on to Piz Zupo.
So we dodged around the side to the Bellavista terraces and crossed them instead,
descending some heavily crevassed glacier before we could climb up to the Fuorcla
Crast'Aguzza and the Marco e Rosa hut. The guardian's taste in rock music cheered
Yvonne up on arrival at the hut and, despite the numbers in the dorm, we had a good
night's sleep.

It was freezing when we left at 6 a.m., zigzagging up the snowfield as fast as we
could to generate some heat until we found sunshine and, co-incidentally, the wind also
dropped. Looking back a tiny moon still shone over Monte Disgrazia. A steep slope
above the bergschrund led to a breche on the ridge where we passed another party via
mixed climbing to reach the snow ridge which stretched, with one rocky outcrop, almost
level to the summit rocks. It was very narrow and late descents on soft snow had made a

mess of some of the steps kicked by earlier parties. Now it was early enough to be crisp névé, frozen hard enough to ignore the steps on the flank and crampon along the very crest of the ridge. At the summit rocks we took off our crampons and scrambled along the last hundred metres to the incised crosses, plaque and summit book in its case. It was 8 a.m. We sat for a while drinking in the view, then I noticed Yvonne was crying.

'What's wrong?'

'I never thought I'd do this sort of thing again.' Her voice broke.

I was stunned. It was only a year since our successful trip to Ecuador yet, despite her undoubted ability, she seemed to be plagued by sudden crises of confidence and I realised at that point how deep-rooted those feelings were.

I mumbled awkward reassurances, and gave her a hug and some time to get over her tears. When she was ready, we headed back, all the way down to the valley.

We drove to Courmayeur and attempted the Grandes Jorasses but more snow than expected slowed us down on the glacier above the Boccalette Hut and route-finding difficulties on the snowed-up rocks of the Rocher de Reposoir led to disagreements which undermined our confidence in each other. Tense, slow and intimidated, we turned back from the traverse to the Rochers Whymper. Back at the hut we collected our kit and went all the way back to the valley.

That didn't bode well for an attempt on Les Droites after driving through the Mont Blanc tunnel to Chamonix. We were both twitchy about the instability of the glacier margins near Montenvers where huge boulders seemed poised to tumble onto passers-by. When claps of thunder heralded a squall blowing in at the foot of the ladders leading from the Mer de Glace up to the Couvercle Hut, Yvonne had had enough. She took the keys to the campervan and returned to the valley while I continued, to arrive at the hut soaked through. I did succeed in soloing Les Droites, but returned to the valley to find Yvonne in such a bad mood that I was briefly the target of a cascade of crockery that broke about my ears.

Instead of arriving home acclimatised and confident for a week's rest before flying to Kyrgyzstan there was tension and uncertainty as we packed our kit. But we were committed and determined to make the best of it.

In Kyrgyzstan the logistic package might have been discounted but it worked. We arrived in Achik Tash base camp in massive 6WD troop carriers that drove up shallow river beds to reach it, surprising local herders who rode as if they were born in the saddle; I wondered how the children managed to mount horses more than twice their height. The women in flowing colourful robes, the men more sombre but with distinctive tall white felt hats watched the formal welcome celebrations, some from horseback. For some reason there was a parade of climbers in improvised fancy dress. I was wearing a Berber headscarf for the sun and had a blanket draped around me to join in. When I was announced as Taliban, there was much audience amusement; perhaps it was the beard. The festivities closed with some wonderful traditional music and a thunderstorm.

The locals' yurt camp had been swollen by an influx of yurts and tents supplied by different agencies to accommodate the visiting climbers. The permanent buildings

Yvonne at ABC, Pik Lenin.

of the Soviet-era climbing camp were still in good condition but had been sold into private hands and none of the agencies had been able to negotiate realistic prices for use of the facilities. That meant no hot showers, but there was water for washing and Yvonne and I had roughed it before.

The climbing had already started and one night the Iranian and Taiwanese teams celebrated the first ascents of Pik Lenin by their nationals. We all joined in, learning more about our community of climbers but trying not to overdo the vodka at 3700m. Inevitably we gravitated towards the English speakers, but Swedes, Tomas and Niklas, and Ilse the Lithuanian-Canadian were heading up to Camp 1 next day while Yvonne and I had planned to acclimatise on Pik Petrovsky.

Up at 6 a.m. we forded the river, passed the Soviet buildings, and found a horse-track to a pass on the ridge above base camp. We followed the ridge south, all the way to the summit, at first over rock and scree, then, from about 4000m, snow. There was a delicate passage on thin snow and icy slabs between two rock horns where the ridge swung west, but a fine snow foresummit led easily to the top at about 4800m; classic Alpine PD. I found myself reeling with the altitude as we descended but Yvonne strode away whistling the theme to Heidi! We deviated from the ridge line to take a scree-run of about 400m, which was great fun and meant we returned to base camp early enough for lunch. A good start!

A rest day, packing, and organising a horse to carry our bags up to Camp 1 meant lighter rucksacks for the long trek to the foot of the north face. We walked up with

Ingrid, the only other British participant in the festival. She had climbed in Kyrgyzstan with Pat Littlejohn's International School of Mountaineering (ISM) teams and got to know Vladimir who managed the International Travel & Mountaineering Centre Tien-Shan (ITMC) agency. She'd been working in the City of London but decided to take a year out and work for ITMC. Her job during the festival was to keep track of what was happening at the mountain camps. We chatted amiably through the meadows grazed by herds of horses and dotted with isolated family yurts, then climbed up through marmot country to a barren moraine pass at 4100m. From Putshestvennikov Pass a path traversed down to where glacial rivers spouted from caves and canyons of ice, skirted by a treacherous moraine track that brought us out above them on the huge Lenin glacier. It was "dry" ice, snow-free but slippery in the sunshine and a dollar per kilo for our loads didn't seem so expensive when we came across a horse wedged and dead in a crevasse.

The long trudge over, we found a tent space among the rocks and gravel surreptitiously sliding into half-buried crevasses at Camp 1 (4200m). The north face was enormous and despite its aspect had taken the sun almost all day so we were glad to be well back from any potential avalanches. Perhaps hiring the horse had not been such a good idea as the amount of kit we had was daunting, but we worked out loads and planned a schedule of rest days and double carries that we hoped would put us at Camp 3 with time to make a couple of summit bids. That evening Yvonne asked me what I thought of Ingrid and her plans, then surprised me with the accusation that I was taking too much interest in her: after all, I'd only just met the woman! I tried to put her mind at rest and the hard day meant that I didn't lose any sleep over the issue. I hoped that was also the case for Yvonne.

A very early start for our first load carry to Camp 2 was well justified. Leaving the dry glacier the north face reared up steeply at first to break into crevasses as it laid back above. A trail in the snow zigzagged through a crevassed zone towards a step where a fixed rope dangled, providing aid for a vertical pitch over the upper lip of a particularly tricky crevasse. We passed dragonflies frozen into the snow, but as the hours slipped by the heat quivered in the air around us and we knew why this section of the route was known as "the frying pan". Reaching a high point, we traversed a long way right, losing about 50m of height, before climbing up to Camp 2 at 5300m. It had been sited in the snows of the glacier bowl until 1990 when an earth tremor triggered a massive avalanche that virtually wiped out all who were in residence. 43 climbers died in what has been recognised as the most deadly climbing disaster in history. Since then, the campsite had been relocated to frozen screes below a rocky spur falling from the north ridge of Pik Razdelnaja.

Yvonne had been going well but I was dehydrated, headachy and irritable. Ali, an *in situ* Iranian, plied us with orange pop and tea while pointing out the best tent placements. The rest of his team was at Camp 3, primed for a summit bid, but he had been having problems with altitude. Ingrid was berating squatters who had occupied her tent and were cooking her food with her gas as Yvonne and I cached our loads and left.

The next couple of days were spent rehydrating, sleeping, and in my case, nursing an altitude headache, but when we next hit the slopes, I felt fine. Everything was carried up this time so that we could sit out bad weather in camp if necessary, although until then there had been nothing but fine sunny days. So fine in fact that the ascent proved to be a long hot struggle. We took several rests to catch our breath and cool off a bit but it still took a lot out of us. At one point Yvonne tried to persuade me to take some of her load, which was completely out of character. She prided herself on her load carrying capacity and had always been amused by couples out walking who only had one rucksack, carried by the male. In any case I was also suffering from the heat and in no mood for concessions: probably because I still had the dead horse on my mind, I asked her if she thought I looked like a beast of burden. Any temptation to argue the point was overcome because an earlier serac collapse had unleashed an avalanche across the trail just before the long traverse with some big ice blocks having bounced down randomly on either side. It was not a place to hang about.

We arrived at Camp 2 severely dehydrated but just in time for the snowfall, which rolled in to enforce brewing in the tent. All night I woke repeatedly to drink to find it still snowing, but next morning was bright enough for Ingrid and Ilse to set off with a load for Camp 3. By midday it was snowing again and Ilse was soon back but Ingrid had pushed on in hopes of getting the tent up at Camp 3. That night I woke periodically

Yvonne at 6100m camp with the long summit ridge of Pik Lenin in the background.

to check that we still had a flysheet as wind smacked at the nylon in crackling gusts. Weather is an issue on Pik Lenin. An entire team of elite Russian women climbers had died on the west ridge route that we were attempting. Trapped by storm they were determined not to retreat and let down the women of their country as they saw it. It's not only men who are seduced by macho stereotypes.

Ingrid arrived back by lunchtime, having camped in a blizzard halfway to Camp 3 to rescue a crazy Russian soloist who would probably have died after crawling under his tarpaulin that was no match for the conditions. He shared her tent, sleeping in her duvet jacket as his sleeping bag was saturated. That morning she'd found him padding around barefoot in the snow because his inadequate trekking boots were frozen until she loaned him socks and ordered him to get his boots on. He'd told her that his father had been a famous Russian alpinist and he was trying to live up to that reputation, but she could see that he basically had no idea and was probably driven by more self-destructive motives. It can be hard growing up with a famous father!

A girl arrived from Camp 3, short-roped between two of her companions. She struggled ineffectively with her zips and fell into a heap whenever they stopped. It looked like cerebral oedema to me, but none of them spoke English and they all looked very rough so I just let them reel off down to Camp 1 and hoped she would recover at lower altitude.

Another day of snow showers and gusting wind with nobody going up but plenty going down and then we woke to sunshine, a light breeze, and were packed up by 9.30 to carry a load to Camp 3. We had negotiated an agreement with Ingrid and Ilse that they would occupy our tent at Camp 3 to make their summit attempt while we returned to Camp 2 and occupied theirs. When they came down it would be our turn. That way we wouldn't have to carry both tents, stoves etc. to Camp 3 and would have a secure retreat at Camp 2.

Trail-breaking in the hard, white light, I found the slopes up to Pik Razdelnaja were thigh-deep with snow in places and just forged ahead on autopilot. Then I linked wand to wand across the mountain's flank to find Camp 3 at 6100m. The west ridge stretched sinuously into the distance. I walked over to the south side of camp and gazed away across Tajikistan and the peaks of the Pamirs for a minute or two before starting to dig out a good placement for the tent. It was really just a matter of clearing out an old and broken one and buttressing the snow walls, but in the process I found a titanium ice screw wound into the ice for an anchor; I still have it.

When Yvonne and Ingrid arrived they gave me a hand, although Yvonne was wasted by the altitude that dizzied me too with all the bending and straightening involved in digging out the campsite. Ilse turned up later and we left them both in our tent, wishing them luck for the morning, before plunging off with lightened sacks and heads. It was classic "climb high, sleep low" acclimatisation strategy.

On our rest day, Tomas and Niklas arrived. Avalanche danger had driven them back from the north face but now Niklas wanted to climb the west ridge to attempt a snowboard descent of the north face. Next day we set out for Camp 3, meeting Ingrid and Ilse on their way down, elated after summitting the previous day. This time there was a track to follow and we weren't carrying such heavy packs, but it didn't seem to make the ascent any easier for Yvonne and I was resigned to another rest day for acclimatisation at 6100m. However, settling into camp, Yvonne seemed more cheerful and as we brewed up she convinced me that we should go for the summit in the morning.

The stove struggled to melt water in the chill morning air so we weren't away until 7 a.m., finding the initial descent to the saddle of the ridge not just disheartening but damned cold too. It was hard work climbing the snowy zigzags in frozen scree beyond the lowest point of the saddle but generated a welcome warmth and soon golden morning light was bathing peaks stretching away south to the horizon.

We stopped at the top of a steep step for refuelling. Yvonne was feeling rough but remained determined to go on. The broad easy ridge ahead climbed gently to 6500m and, cocooned against the wind in my shell hood, I was just concentrating on putting one high-altitude boot in front of the other without realising that Yvonne had been falling further and further behind.

I stopped below the "knife blade", a steep section of ridge with a fixed rope above and an old oxygen bottle below, marking a possible campsite perhaps. It might even have been the one the Russian women used on their tragic attempt. The views were becoming hazy and wraps of cloud closed in. Yvonne was a long way back and I dragged on my duvet jacket to wait.

Beginning the long ascent out of the saddle below 6200m camp in the background.

There was a crowd of Austrians who had left two hours before us hauling in turn on the fixed rope. Some were so slow that they didn't look likely to get much further. One of those waiting turned back, nodding 'Another day,' as he passed me. I watched him down to where he met Yvonne. With a wave to me she went back with him. There was a flurry of snow and I thought it best to go on as far as possible while I still could.

I skirted the fixed rope and loose rock, preferring good névé, to gain a scrappy ridge of peaklets and rock steps steepening towards a satellite peak on the right. The trail crossed its flank to the left via a couple of indefinite snow spurs and entered a huge snow basin. I found myself passing Austrians regularly by then, although the climb up the last few hundred metres steadily eroded the number of steps I could take before stopping to hyperventilate. Cloud closed in and there were gusts of cold, then warm, air followed by rumblings of thunder, but no one was turning back; the summit was just too close.

Finally, I was there. Wind and snow blasted into my face and a Russian guide offered to take a summit shot with my camera. I pulled on extra clothing, shook hands with everyone still standing and compos mentis, then headed back down the tracks into what little shelter remained below. Recrossing the snow basin, I found the trail had been blown out and I had to wait, chewing a cereal bar, for the white-out to clear and shadows of wands to become solid reality. I caught up with the leading Austrians who had stopped to plant extra wands for summit stragglers. The slowest, still climbing upwards, turned back in the face of the deteriorating weather.

It was a long way in cloud and snow showers. At the top of the first step I had to cast about for memories of the ascent or I'd have strayed off into Tajikistan. Then in the saddle there was that final 100m climb up to Camp 3; a real sting in the tail!

At the tent I found Yvonne tearful and dejected. Not only had she been forced to turn back but had spent most of the rest of the day trying, without success, to light the stove and get a brew on. I couldn't understand it. She was normally so confident about camping, even in conditions of hardship, and had had no trouble with the stove previously. Perhaps unfortunately, I had it melting water in no more than ten minutes and she cheered up a bit after a few brews before we got off to a well-earned sleep.

Next day we descended all the way to Camp 1, greeting Niklas as he snowboarded off the north face. We were lucky to find a Kyrghiz horseman who was prepared to take a lot of our kit on the following day's trek out to base camp. Tomas joined us on the walk out and remarked on the absence of marmots near the pass where there had been so many on our walk in. A few minutes later I caught sight of a grey shadow moving along the recessed riverbank, dumped my rucksack and followed it to find a wolf at a marmot kill. As I inched closer for a picture, the animal would threaten me, ears back, teeth bared, growl rumbling in its throat, then settle again as I stopped before inching forward again, repeating the ritual, until I judged it unwise to push the issue further; I think the photos were worth it. Then I rejoined Yvonne and Tomas for that first stage of the long journey home.

Within a year Yvonne and I had split up, and my mind turned often to the wolf during that time. There was something about its bristling defence of its prey, the

Wolf at a marmot kill amongst the moraines, Pik Lenin.

kind of game we played before I was allowed to get closer, but ultimately the absolute insistence on its territorial independence that reflected aspects of Yvonne's attitude to our relationship. Differences were no longer resolved but hung on worryingly and, in the end, she found someone else whom she believed would fulfil her aspirations better.

A month or so later he had turned her out and she arrived on my doorstep 'having nowhere else to go' as she put it. She later told me that she expected me to laugh in her face and tell her to push off but was taken by surprise when I told her she was welcome to stay although there was no going back as far as our relationship was concerned. I suppose that's why we stayed friends over the years that followed, even attempting Ancohuma together during an expedition to Bolivia that I organised for the Alpine Club. Her habitual reluctance to scrap any kit until it was thoroughly worn out meant that her old water bottle leaked a puddle into the centre of our cramped assault tent, but there was no dismay; she was able to laugh at the situation as we cleared it up. So I asked her about what had gone wrong years earlier, on Lenin and subsequently.

'Oh, that,' she waved a hand dismissively. 'That was just the menopause.'

Being a good life partner can be a lot more challenging than being a good tent partner or climbing partner. It's more of a full-time job than a temporary contract for the duration of a climb or expedition. The intensity of experiences in wild situations can be what brings people together but that relationship then has to operate within the context of everyday life and work. People's priorities and ambitions can change. Their mental health may suffer under pressures that were absent when they got together. That can influence the way a team behaves in the field, whether it's a team of two or more.

As the examples above indicate, a couple in a group of singletons may respond in different ways compared to the rest of the team. I remember someone complaining about a couple's "constant bickering" which he found unsettling but they saw only as banter, displaying an unwillingness to take themselves too seriously, which was normal for the way they related to each other. They had to make a real effort to tone it down to keep him happy but he also needed to see their behaviour in a different light. If a romantic entanglement occurs during the expedition the team needs to be aware that it may affect the judgement of those involved. Gender issues can add an emotional dimension to the way a team interacts in an expedition situation; they should not be ignored.

Appendix 1. Food rations

- A minimalist approach will mean the loads are manageable though we will only be carrying a maximum of X days of supplies for any single ascent.

- We will be operating on a deficit calorie intake on those days, but should all have the reserves to cope with that.

- Below is the daily food ration I work on. One day should be about 500gm.

- The suggested ration is a <u>guideline only</u> and everyone will have his/her own favourites to substitute.

- Weigh everything in making up your rations and reweigh the total amount at the end. If it's more than you expected, chuck out all those little extras that crept in in the process.

- Pans should be used only to boil water, i.e. <u>not to be cooked in</u>.

Suggested daily food ration per person:

Breakfast: Coffee/tea. At least 2 large mugsworth.*

Muesli: Mix 3–4 spoonfuls of Readibrek with the same amount of Alpen. Add a spoonful of dried milk and another of raisins and a few chopped nuts (make up portions in small freezer bags).

Lunch: 2–3 cereal/choc bars (Nutrigrain and Bounty bars don't freeze solid) or 1 Blackfriars flapjack as they turn in a hefty 500 calories per bar.
2–3 mints/boiled sweets to suck on the march (Murray Mints really do last longer!)
Cheese sticks and pepperoni are savoury options.

Evening meal: Cup a Soup**
Hot chocolate drink **

Extras: Herbal tea bags (that can be repeatedly reused in extremis!)
Sugar (0.5kg will last 10–12 days!)

* Cappuccino sachets are easily counted (packaging helps organisation) and removes the need to carry dried milk.

** Make sure soups and chocolate drinks, for example, are high calorie and high fat (such as Cadbury's Instant Break) for maximum nutritional value for the weight. There are too many slimming drinks on the market!

*** I know a lot of dehydrated food is crap but Mountain House have shown for years that it doesn't have to be. Mountain House is harder to find in the UK, but the 'boil in the bag' meals of Expedition Foods' (www.expeditionfoods.com) are just as good and there are other websites to increase variety.

Please note that people who think they need much more than this usually end up throwing it away!

Appendix 2. Pulk construction pictures

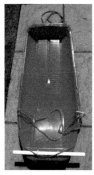

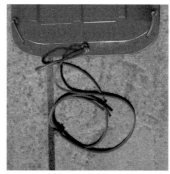

Left: Tail for attaching the rear of the pulk to a rope with a prusik loop when in crevassed territory.

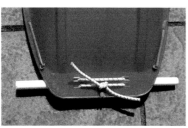

It's worth tying the bungee cord tightly then forcing the pipe through the upper loops for better stability.

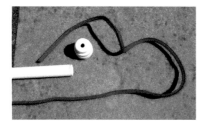

Waterproof bags to be strapped to the pulk; roll-top and zip closure both have their pros and cons and sizes vary. Roll-top dry bag (left) and a larger zipped dry bag (right).

Appendix 3. Haul bag construction pictures

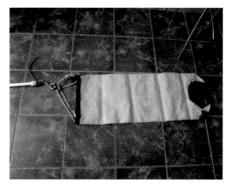

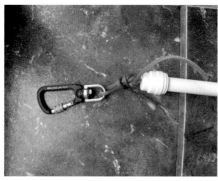

Appendix 4. Medical kits

Two examples are recorded here for comparison but both were assembled by a qualified medic which would be recommended practice. Advice is included with the Mount Logan documentation to illustrate issues to think about rather than just items for inclusion or not. Note that Greenland does not contain medication for AMS.

Note that dosage and treatment recommendations are likely to change over time so will need checking before deployment in the field.

1.Group medical kit for Greenland

Expedition medical kit – divided into 2 kits:
Base Camp (Medical) kit – A
Field kit – B
Expedition medical kit

The expedition medical kit is designed as the main medical kit for an expedition of 7 people for 3 weeks in an area such as Greenland, where medical help is available within 1–3 days.

These two kits also catered for the eventuality that the team divided to pursue different objectives on any particular day.

The total quantities break down and pack as Medical Kits A and B

	Total:	A	B
• **Dressing materials and equipment** (in a polythene bag with list of contents)			
- Medium plain wound dressing, field dressing No. 2	2	1	1
- Release non-adherent dressing 10cm × 10cm	4	3	1
- Release non-adherent dressing 5cm × 5cm	4	2	2
- Triangular bandage	2	1	1
- Crepe bandage 10cm × 4.5m	2	1	1
- Elastic adhesive plaster 2.5cm × 4.5m	1 roll	1	
- Clingfilm	2 rolls	1	1
- Antiseptic swabs	20	10	10
- Blister dressing – Compeed	3 packs	**2**	**1**
- Savlon antiseptic concentrate	100ml	1	

	Total:	A	B
- Chlorhexidine			
- Gauze swabs 10cm × 10cm, packets of 5	3 packs	2	1
- HemCon bandage 5cm × 5 cm	1	1	
- Jelonet paraffin gauze dressing 10cm × 10cm	4	3	1
- Elastoplast – waterproof and fabric dressings (plasters)	16	10	4
- Steri–strips 6mm × 100mm × 10 tapes	4 packs	3	1
- Adhesive tape 1.25cm × 5m Micropore	2 rolls	1	1
- Tubigrip elastic tubular bandage × 8	size D 1m	1	
- Disposable gloves	6 pairs	4	2
- Scissors	2 pairs	1	1
- Plastic dressing forceps, sterile	2 pairs	1	
- Safety pins	6	3	3
- Space blanket	1		

- **Medication**
  - **Painkillers**

	Total:	A	B
- Paracetamol tablets 500mg (2 × 4 daily max)	40	32	8
- Ibuprofen tablets 400mg (1 × 3 daily)	30	24	6
- Tramadol 50mg tablets (1–2 × 4 daily max)	40	30	10

  - **Allergy and asthma medicines**

	Total:	A	B
- Chlorpheniramine tablets 4mg (1 × 4 daily for allergy)	20	20	8
- Loratadine (1 daily for allergy)	10	16	4
- Salbutamol inhaler (2 puffs as needed)	1	1	
- Prednisolone tablets 5mg (1 × 6 daily for severe asthma)	50	42	8

  - **Gastrointestinal medication**

	Total:	A	B
- Buccastem 3mg (1 twice daily for vomiting)	20	15	5
- Omeprazole 20mg (1 daily for stomach acidity)	10	8	2
- Loperamide capsules 2mg (up to 8 daily for diarrhoea)	40	30	10
- Dioctyl (up to 5 daily for constipation) stimulant laxative	20	20	
- Docusate 100mg (1 × 3 daily and increase) softener	30	30	
- Glycerol suppositories	6	6	
- Xyloproct ointment (for haemorrhoids)	1 tube	1	
- Dioralyte (for rehydration following diarrhoaea)	12	10	2

  - **Antibiotics**

	Total:	A	B
- Amoxycillin 500mg (1–2 daily)	21	21	
- Ciprofloxacin tablets 500mg (1 × 2 daily for severe diarrhoea)	32	30	2
- Co-amoxiclav tablets 375mg (1 × 3 daily for chest, skin)	21	21	
- Azithromycin tablets 500mg (1 daily for 3 days)	6	6	
- Metronidazole tablets 400mg (1 × 3 times daily for 5 days)	15 tabs		

  - **Nose, ears and eyes**

	Total:	A	B
- Otosporin eardrops	1		
- Amethocaine eye drops 1%, single dose units (note 10)	2	1	1
- Chloramphenicol eye ointment	1 tube	1	
- Fluorescein eye drops	1		

  - **Skin**

	Total:	A	B
- Mupirocin (apply × 3 daily) antibacterial cream	1 tube		
- Canestan HC (apply × 3 daily for eczema or fungal infection)	2 tubes	1	
- Silver sulphadiazine cream 20g antibacterial cream for burns	2 tubes	1	1

  - **Cardiac**

	Total:	A	B
- Aspirin tablets 300mg (1 chewed for suspected heart attack)	12	10	2
- GTN spray (1 spray under tongue for suspected heart attack)	2	1	1

	Total:	A	B
• **Exhaustion**			
- Energy Gel	2	1	1

• **Suturing Kit – Base camp A**
- Sutures 3 packets (3/0 and 4/0 nylon) 2 packs
- Green needles 6
- Disposable scalpel, No. 15 blade 1
- Splinter forceps 1 pair
- Artery forceps/needle holder 1
- Paper clip 1

• **Injectable medications – Base camp A**
- Tramadol injection 100mg in 2ml (strong painkiller) 1 ampoule
- Naloxone 400mcg/ml 1 ampoule
- Diazepam 10mg/2ml 1 ampoule
- Diclofenac 75mg/3ml 1 ampoule
- Prochlorperazine ampoule 12.5g in 1ml 1 ampoule
- Metoclopramide 10mg in 2ml 1 ampoule
- Lignocaine 1% injection 5ml (local anaesthetic) 2 ampoules
- Syringes 2ml and 5ml plus 38mm × 0.8mm needles 5
- Butterfly 21 and 23 2
- Anaphylaxis medications (essential if taking injectable drugs)
- Adrenaline injection for intramuscular use 1mg in 1ml (1 in 1000) 1 ampoule
- Chlorpheniramine injection 10mg in 2m 1 ampoule
- Dexamethasone 8mg/2ml 1 vial

• **Emergency dental kit** 1

• **Paperwork**
- Insurance details, evacuation plan and emergency communication details
- Instructions on use of drugs and dressings
- List of contents of medical kits

• **Camp hygiene**
- Water disinfectant – chlorine dioxide not needed
- Alcohol gel encourage 1 bottle per tent

2. Mount Logan medical kit

Advice:

1. Exped medical kit

Injectables – these are probably not worth carrying as they're difficult in cold environments and draw you into an advanced medical care role that is not sustainable in the field. However, it may be worth you carrying a syringe needle and 2 vials of Dexamethasone 4mg/ml – this might make the difference in getting a collapsed HACE victim mobile enough to be assisted down.

Tramadol

I can't find and don't imagine there is any major restriction on taking Tramadol capsules into Canada, but I will write a formal letter explaining that you are a doctor carrying an expedition medical kit with the listed contents – in effect my prescription to you.

(For the US, however, from 18 August, 2014, travellers through the ports of entry have been required to have a US prescription to bring Tramadol purchased in Mexico across the border.)

Antibiotics

As the risk of infectious diarrhoea is lower in the high cold, I would suggest we reduce the anti-diarrhoeal antibiotics to:

– Azithromycin tablets 500mg (1 daily for 3 days) 3 tabs
– Ciprofloxacin tablets 500mg (1 × 2 daily for severe diarrhoea for 3 days) 12 tabs
– Metronidazole tablets 400mg (1 × 3 daily for 5 days) 15 tabs

Although there is some giardia (a tiny parasite that causes the diarrhoeal disease giardiasis) in Kluane National Park, it takes about three weeks from contact for the cysts to hatch and to become symptomatic i.e. on the way home!

We might also drop the Amoxycillin – if everyone carries a personal antibiotic?? (see below)

Altitude Rx

I would suggest increasing the quantities to cover treating Acute Mountain Sickness for up to 5 people for 3 days

- Acetazolamide 250mg   30   (1 × 2 daily for AMS)
   to cover treating HACE/HAPE for up to 3 people for 3 days
- Nifedipine 20mg   18   (1 × 2 daily for HAPE)
- Dexamethasone 2mg   84
   (8mg to start then 4mg every 6 hours for HACE/severe AMS)
   AMS prevention

This is contentious – sensible to some (if falling behind schedule or hit by intercurrent illness) or outright cheating in sport to the purists. I would suggest letting everyone make their own personal judgement – but rather than the group medical carrying huge quantities of Acetazolamide, I would suggest each member decides whether or not to carry it in their own personal medical kit (see below).

- Acetazolamide 250mg   30
   (1–2 × 2 daily for the prevention of AMS for 15 days)

3.Personal medical kit

I suggest posting the following to the Group:

Pre-trip medical questionnaire –

Generally, it is a good idea to check and plan for any medical situation that might arise and I attach a simple pre-trip questionnaire to facilitate confidential pre-trip risk assessments of any declared major medical conditions e.g. diabetes, cardiac conditions, asthma and epilepsy.

If there are any complex medical issues that need more intensive assessment then I will be able to advise how to proceed and/or ask for comment (with your permission) from a wide body of interested specialists.

The usual duties of medical confidentiality apply, though I may ask that you share your medical details with the team leader if appropriate and with the rest of the team if necessary. The limits to medical confidentiality are only if you are carrying on with a condition that could put others at significant risk.

Those with pre-existing medical conditions must declare them to their insurers and get explicit cover agreement otherwise the insurers will exploit any wriggle room after the event.

Personal medical kit

Each expedition member should take some personal medical equipment, including:

Elastoplast or some small dressings, Micropore if allergic
Blister kit – e.g. Compeed – multiple sizes – quantity at your discretion
Simple painkillers – Paracetamol or Ibuprofen – 20 tablets
Anti-diarrhoeal medications:
- Loperamide (Immodium) 2mg – 2 tablets to start then 1 tablet with each episode of diarrhoea up to 8 daily – 8 tablets
- Rehydration sachets (e.g. Dioralyte) – 2 sachets
- Alcohol gel – small bottle for hand hygiene
• Antihistamine
- If previous allergic reaction to insect bites for example, Chlorphenamine (Piriton) 4mg – 1 tablet, 4 times daily – 4 tablets
- If hayfever/sleeping bag, house dust allergy, bring own non-sedating antihistamine e.g. Loratadine 10mg
• Personal antibiotic, for example, for skin, chest or urinary infection
- Amoxycillin 500mg 1 tablet 3 times daily – 15 tablets – if penicillin allergic let me know.
• Acetazolamide prophylaxis – this is contentious (see above). I would suggest each member decides whether or not to carry to carry it in their own personal medical kit (see below).
- *Acetazolamide 250mg*   *30 tabs*
   (1–2 × 2 times daily for prevention of AMS for 15 days)
   Before taking Acetazolamide please familiarise yourselves with travel at high altitude http://medex.org.uk//medex_book/english_version.php
• Personal medications
Quantities are scaled down so as to carry the minimum. If necessary, top up from central kit.

4.MedEvac Plan

From my research, a request for Search and Rescue or medical evacuation would be co-ordinated through the Kluane National Park via:

Parks Canada 24 Hour Emergency Dispatch
1–877–852–3100 (toll free)
1–780–852–3100 (if calling from a satellite phone)
It might be timely to begin collecting next of kin contact details and insurance details – a spreadsheet might be useful.

5.Group medical kit

	Total
• **Dressing materials and equipment** (in a polythene bag with list of contents)	
- Israeli dressing 4in	1
- Release non-adherent dressing 10cm × 10cm	1
- Release non-adherent dressing 5cm × 5cm	2
- Triangular bandage	1
- Crepe bandage 10cm × 4.5m	1
- Cohesive bandage 5cm × 4.5m	1 roll
- Clingfilm	1 roll
- Antiseptic swabs	20
- Gauze swabs 7.5cm × 7.5cm, packets of 5	1 packet
- Jelonet paraffin gauze dressing 10cm × 10cm	1
- Elastoplast – waterproof and fabric dressings (plasters)	4
- Steri-strips 6mm x 100mm × 10 tapes	2 packs
- Adhesive tape 1.25cm × 5m Micropore	1 roll
- Tubigrip elastic tubular bandage × 8	size D 1m
- Disposable gloves	2 pairs
- Scissors	1 pair
- Plastic dressing forceps, sterile	1 pair
- Safety pins	3
- SAM Splint	1

- • **Medication**
  - • **Painkillers**
    - Paracetamol 500mg tablets (2 × 4 daily max)   16
    - Ibuprofen 400mg tablets   (1 × 3 daily)   30
    - Tramadol 50mg tablets   (1–2 x 4 daily max)   10
      Or
      Codeine 30mg/Paracetamol 500mg tablets (2 × 4 times daily)
         16

	Total

- **Allergy and asthma medicines**
  - Chlorphenamine tablets 4mg (1×4 daily for allergy)   9
  - Loratadine (1 daily for allergy)   4

- **Gastrointestinal medication**
  - Buccastem 3mg (1 twice daily for vomiting)   5
  - Lansoprazole 15mg (1–2 daily for stomach acidity)   4
  - Loperamide capsules 2mg (up to 8 daily for diarrhoea)   25
  - Docusate 100mg (1×3 daily and increase) softener   30
  - Glycerol supp   6
  - Dioralyte   6 sachets

- **Antibiotics**
  - Amoxycillin 500mg (1 tablet 3 times daily)   21
  - Azithromycin tablets 500mg (1 tablet daily for 3 days)   3 tabs
  - Ciprofloxacin tablets 500mg (1×2 daily for severe diarrhoea for 3 days)   12 tabs
  - Metronidazole tablets 400mg (1×3 daily for 5 days)   15 tabs

- **Nose, ears and eyes**
  - Tetracaine eye drops 1%, single dose units (note 10)   2
  - Chloramphenicol eye ointment   1 tube
  - Fluorescein eye drops   2

- **Skin**
  - Canestan HC (apply x 3 daily for eczema or fungal infection) 1 tube
  - Silver sulfadiazine cream 20g (antibacterial cream for burns) 1 tube
  - Aloe vera cream for frostbite   1 tube

- **Cardiac**
  - Aspirin tablets 300mg (1 chewed for suspected heart attack) 10 tabs
  - GTN spray (1 spray under the tongue for suspected heart attack)   1

- **Exhaustion**
  - Energy Gel   1

- **Altitude Medication**
  To cover treating Acute Mountain Sickness for up to 5 people for 3 days
  - Acetazolamide 250mg (1 x 2 daily for AMS)   30
  To cover treating HACE/HAPE for up to 3 people for 3 days
  - Nifedipine 20mg (1 x 2 daily for HAPE)   18
  - Dexamethasone 2mg (8mg start then 4mg every 6 hours for HACE/severe AMS)   84

- **Injectables** – probably not worth carrying as difficult in a cold environment and will draw you into an advanced medical care role that is not sustainable in the field. However, it may be worth carrying a syringe needle and **2 vials of Dexamethasone 4mg/ml on your person** – this might make the difference in getting a collapsed HACE victim mobile enough to be assisted down.

- **Steri-strips and Histoacryl medical glue**
    - Paper clip (for trephining nail haematoma)   1
    - Handwarmer

- **Paperwork**
    - Insurance details, evacuation plan and emergency communication details
    - Instructions on use of drugs and dressings
    - List of contents of medical kits
    - Injury report sheet
    - Pencil

Appendix 5. Expedition experience

The following is a list of expeditions I led or participated in during twenty years. Some may be considered relatively small adventures compared to others but I have included them to indicate both range and progression.

1994 Climbing: Tanzania: Kilimanjaro by Umbwe route through Western Breach (led)

Kenya: Mt Kenya – planned to climb Firmin-Hicks route on N.

Face of Batian but partner's AMS meant I trekked around the mountain climbing Point Lenana twice (led).

1997 Ski-touring: Morocco: Tazaghart; Lepiney hut to Neltner hut via Tizi Tadat; Jebel Toubkal; Tizi Likemat from Tacheddirt (led)

Climbing: Peru: Cordillera Central: Punta Bareita, 5000m (1st British)Nevado Padrecaca 5200m (1st ascent), Ticlla 5897m. W. Ridge (2nd British), Quepala 5300m (2nd Briton)

1998 Ski-touring: Caucasus: Pik Cheget; Chiperazau Pass; Dongusoran Pass; Pik Gumachi; reached 5000m on Elbrus before being stormed off (led).

Climbing: Peru: Inca Trail

Cordillera Blanca: Pisco 5900m; Huascarán Norte 6650m; Alpamayo (failed owing to bad weather and partner's AMS) (led).

1999 Climbing: Denali: Reached 3350m on ski then continued to summit via W Buttress route on foot

Hindu Kush: Expedition to make first British ascent of Saraghrar 7300m – failed at 5500m owing to bad weather.

2001 Climbing: Ecuador: Fuya Fuya – Cerro Negra 4200m; Imbabura 4600m; Cotacachi 4900m; Illiniza Norte 5100m; Cotapaxi 5900m. Cayambe 5800m.; Chimborazo – turned back at 6000m suffering from hypothermia (led).

2002 Ski-mountaineering: Iran: Zagros Mountains – reconnaissance Alborz Mountains; Kolom Bassk 4100m; Sarak Chal 4220m; Damavand 5600m (turned back at 4800m in bad weather)

Climbing: Kyrgyzstan: Pik Lenin 7134m (N Face and W Ridge route) (led)

Nepal: Pokharkan (6350m) First ascent of South Face.

2003 Ski-mountaineering: Kyrgyzstan: Traverse of the Ak-Shirak Range; failed to make the traverse but made first ski ascents of six 4000m peaks in the western reaches of the range.

Canada: Mount Logan; reached 5200m before we ran out of weather and time (led).

China, Xinjiang: Muztagh Ata 7546m the highest ski peak in the world. Solo (met David Hamilton on the summit).

2004 Ski-mountaineering: Russian Caucasus: Peaks and passes in the Adyrsu valley including Pik Lokomotiv(3750m), Pik Gumachi (3800m) and Mestia-Tau (4230m).

Mount Elbrus. Turned back in vicious winds at 5000m with dislocated shoulder (led).

2005 Szechuan: Gongkala – reached 4800m before being run off the mountain by aggressive monks.

Haizi Shan – reached 4800m before bad weather forced a retreat.

Pik Yuan 4750m (first ascent)

An Teallach II 4800m (first ascent)

2006 Ski-mountaineering – Kyrgyzstan: Ak-Shirak Range

First Traverse on ski S–N via Kara-Say – Petrov glaciers

First ascents of Pik Chasovoi 4764m; Pik Kyrgyzia 4954m; Pik Karga 4831m; Point Anna 4658m; Pik Koyon 4876m; Eagles Peak 4822m; Snow Cannon 4720m (led)

2007 Ski-mountaineering: **Kyrgyzstan**: 4 first ascents including Pik of the 150th Anniversary of the British Alpine Club 4836m; Pik Ak Illbirs 4887m; Pik Plavnik 4720m and Pik Solidarnost 4815m (led)

Climbing: **India**, **Garhwal**: Kagbhusandi Valley: 2 first ascents of AC 150 5030m and Dhanesh Parbat 5450m

China: W Sichuan: Yangmolong range:

First ascents of Snow Snake 5598m and the North Ridge of Dangchezhengla 5830m (led)

2008 Ski-mountaineering: Kyrgyzstan: Ak-Shirak Range: 60+km of travel in 24 days making 5 first ascents and 2 first British ascents:

Pik Stepi or Stepped Peak 4790m N 41° 47.301´ South Ridge PD

Pik Volk or Wolf peak 4980m N 41° 45.332´ North-west Ridge AD

Prospekt Pik 4767m N 41° 47.123´ E 78°15.726´ South glacier and North-west Ridge PD

Pik Volna or Wave Peak 4856m at N 41°48.086´ E 078° 16.2´ D–Pik Cirque 4966m N 41° 49.237´ E 78° 17.682´ East glacier and North Ridge PD (first British)

Pik 5004m N 41° 49.087´ E 78° 17.928´ West Ridge AD.

Pik Petrov 4837m N 41° 6.92´ E 78° 5.38´ North Face (Ramp) and North-west Ridge (First British) (led)

2009 Climbing on Mount Kenya: led AC meet: routes South Gully Midget Peak; South Ridge Point John; South-east Ridge Point Dutton; Scramble to Arthur's Seat.

Climbing in Bolivia: led AC meet; ascents of Pequeno Alpamayo 5300m; Pyramide Blanca 5300m; Illimani 6500m

Climbing in China: Szechuan: Reached 5400m on Yangmolong (6066m) before weather drove us down and time ran out (led).

2010 Climbing: Chile: AC expedition to the Tupungato area
Climbed Tupungatito 5388m
Ski-mountaineering: Georgia: Ascent of Piks Kudebi 3006m,
Sadzele 3200m and Kazbek 5042m (led)
Ski-mountaineering: India: Kullu Valley near Manali
Ascents included: Rohtang Ri 4725m; Beas Rikhi
4677m; Khrei Ra Jot 4575m; unnamed peaks adjoining the Sagu Nala and a descent of the Rohtang Chute in its entirety. (led)
Ski-mountaineering: Chile: Ascents of volcanoes Villarica and Llaima, and reconnaissance of Argentine valley of Los Cuevas.
Ski-mountaineering/Climbing: Antarctica Peninsula
First ascents of Mount Nygren 1454m; Mount Matin 2415m; Mount Cloos south 935m; Mount Inverleith 2038m. Also made ascents of Mount Banck 710m and Jabet Peak 552m.

2011 Ski-mountaineering: Mongolia: Ski ascents and descents of Tavn Bogd peak 4104m; Khuiten 4374m; Nairamdal 4192m; Peak 4117m to the north of Tavn Bogd peak; Peak 4152 on the border ridge south of Khuiten; Malchin 4051m and Peak 3926m; the border summit, Peak 3962m (led)

2012 Ski-mountaineering: April: Canada Bugaboos to Rogers Pass. Traverse attempted but had to be evacuated by helicopter owing to high avalanche risk. Transferred to the Drummond Icefield for a further tour (led).
July: Mount Elbrus Finally climbed Elbrus on ski.

2013 January Climbing: Oman First ascents of Jebel Kawr: The Dark Side, 680m, TD-, VI- Triassic Superbowl, 430m, TD-, VI– Sidaq village: Giant Slab, 193m V– Amqah Tower: Arabian Knights, 311m D+, VI–Jabal Nakhus: Karst Corner, 242m, V
April: Ski-mountaineering: Greenland: Liverpool Land
Narretfjord: 5 first ski ascents of peaks around 800m and traverse to Mariager Fjord (led)
July: Russia; Caucasus, Beizingi; led CC meet; Climbed Ukio, South Ridge 4300m (bad weather)
2014 August: Ski-mountaineering: Argentina and Chile; Climbed Challhuaco; skied numerous steep couloirs from Refugio Frey; climbed a peak on the border near the border pass; climbed Piltriquitron, Casablanca and Osorno volcanoes in Chile.

Appendix 6. – Recommended reading

Walter Bonatti – *Mountains of My Life* – Penguin Classic 2010
Rob Collister – *Days to Remember* – 2016
Andrew Greig – *Summit Fever* – 1985
Brad Johnson – *Classic Climbs of the Cordillera Blanca* – 2009
Tom Longstaff – *This My Voyage* – 1951
Don Munday – *The Unknown Mountain* – 1948
Jonathan Neale – *Tigers of the Snow* – 2002
Cathy O'Dowd – *Just for the Love of It* – 1999
Robert Roper – *Fatal Mountineer* – 2002
Eric Shipton – *Six Mountain Travel Books* – 1985
                           Nanda Devi
                           Blank on the Map
                           Upon that Mountain
                           Mountains of Tartary
                           Mount Everest Reconnaissance Expedition 1951
                           Land of Tempest
Frank Smythe – *The Six Alpine/Himalayan Climbing Books* – 2000
                           Climbs and Ski Runs
                           The Kangchenjunga Adventure
                           Kamet Conquered
                           Camp Six
                           The Valley of the Flowers
                           Mountaineering Holiday
Steve Swenson – *Karakoram* – 2017
Lionel Terray – *Conquistadores of the Useless* – 1963
Bill Tilman – The Seven Mountain Travel Books – 1983
                           Snow on the Equator
                           The Ascent of Nanda Devi
                           When Men and Mountains Meet
                           Everest 1938
                           Two Mountains and a River
                           China to Chitral
                           Nepal Himalaya
Edward Whymper – *Travels amongst the Great Andes of the Equator* – 1892
C. Clarke and A. Salkeld (editors) – *Lightweight Expeditions to the Greater Ranges* (Symposium papers published by the Alpine Club) – 1984

The *Alpine Journal* – http://www.alpinejournal.org.uk/

The *American Alpine Journal* – http://publications.americanalpineclub.org/

The *Japanese Alpine Club Journal* – the JAC has been through a few changes with regard to its publications, although relevant issues can still be found in the Alpine Club Library http://www.alpine-club.org.uk/library/library

BMC (British Mountaineering Council) https://www.thebmc.co.uk/cats/Mountaineering/International

Appendix 7. Glossary

The glossary lists items found in the book that the reader may be unfamiliar with, including others that may be found in Recommended Reading.

abseil – a means of descent by sliding down the doubled rope on a friction brake attached to the harness

abseil point – a prepared attachment to the rock from which to abseil. This can range from twin bolts and chain to a loop of rope around a rock spike.

à cheval – making progress by straddling a narrow arête, like riding a horse

arête – a narrow ridge

arriero – a muleteer

belay – a secure point of attachment to the rock or snow/ice from which the second climber pays out rope to the leader and brakes that rope in the event of a fall (hence "to belay")

bergschrund – a large crevasse that opens up at the head of a glacier where it breaks away from the mountain slope above

breakable crust – a snow crust that cannot be relied upon to bear the weight of the skier

breche – a break or low point in a ridge

to bridge, bridging – the action of bracing legs and/or arms against opposite sides of a chimney or diedre (like a bridge) in order to make progress

boot crack – a crack in the rock that seems to be the exact width of a boot

boot-pack – climbing in boots on a ski-mountaineering route

boot-ski – the action of sliding downhill in soft snow on the soles of one's boots imitating the action of skiing but without the skis. Aka standing glissade.

cam – a protection device to provide security when climbing. Opposed cams lock the device into a crack.

cascade climbing – climbing frozen waterfalls

chang – a traditional Tibetan/Nepali barley wine, similar to British beer

col – a saddle or low point on a ridge sometimes crossed to access the valley beyond

chorten – a Buddhist shrine or monument

concretised snow – snow that may be transformed to the consistency of concrete after an avalanche or even a small snowslide

balled, balling (of crampons) – when snow is trapped by the points and frame of the crampon, effectively creating a slippery platform sole for the boot

couloir – a gully in the rock or snow

crampons – metal frameworks with sharp downward points attached to climbing boots to facilitate progress in icy conditions

crevasse – a crack in the surface of a glacier created by the movement of the ice over underlying obstructions

crux – the crucial point of a climb; the most difficult section to be overcome

diedre – a corner like an open book in the rock

exposure – the precariousness of the position of a climber as in "an exposed move". The term also refers to suffering from exposure to the elements or hypothermia.

gendarme – a tall pinnacle of rock

ger camp – substantial domed tents, a collection of gers in Mongolia, aka yurts in Kyrgyzstan

gompa – a Buddhist fortified combination of temple, teaching centre and monastery

gneiss – good rough generally solid rock

heavy (snow) – snow that contains a lot of water and impedes movement

hot aches – colloquial term for the pain that accompanies the return of warm blood to freezing fingers or toes (American "screaming barfies")

jump turns – ski turns when the skier attempts to leap clear of difficult or steep snow to effect a change of direction

kick-glide – the action of moving the ski forward when ascending on skins

lamasery – a type of Buddhist monastery, usually training lamas

mani-wall – a wall made of stones inscribed with a Buddhist prayer usually '*om mani padme hūm*'

micro-traxion – self-locking pulley to aid climbing a rope

moving together – a technique of Alpine climbing when both climbers climb at the same time putting their faith in each other's skills or running belays to avoid a fall

névé – good consolidated snow that can be climbed easily

nuts – derived from the original engineering nuts that had the threads machined out of them so that they could be threaded with a short rope sling and wedged into cracks in the rock. A karabiner would link the climbing rope to the rope sling attached to the nut to protect the progress of the leader (see *runner*). Now the term is applied to any wedge that fulfils that function.

pitons (aka pegs) – metal spikes with an "eye" at the blunt end into which can be clipped a karabiner. They can be driven into cracks in the rock to provide runners or main belays.

piste – a prepared track, usually in snow, but also "abseil piste" where one abseil leads directly to the next in a long sequence of abseil descents.

pitch – a section of a climb between 2 main belays

post-holing – leaving deep holes at every step in soft snow (exhausting!)

Prusik (knot) – a loop of cord knotted, attached to a rope that can be easily slipped along the rope until it comes under tension when it locks. Also the knot itself.

pulk – a type of sledge, pulled by a person and/or dog and used to transport kit

rappelling – abseiling

rognon – a rock outcrop

ropeman – a self-locking pulley to aid climbing a rope

ropes (as in "2 ropes of 3") – teams of climbers (2 teams of 3 climbers on each rope)

runner (aka running belay) – a temporary attachment to the rock or snow/ice, placed on lead, that limits the distance travelled by the leader in the event of a fall

run-out – 1. an area at the foot of a slope that may be more easily angled and with no obstacles as in "a safe run-out"

run-out – 2. interval between runner placements as in "a long run-out"

sastrugi – wind-sculpted structures of frozen snow found on the surface of snow-slopes particularly in winter. They can be anything from a few centimetres to a metre in height.

schuss – a straight run on skis with no turns

self-arrest – using the ice axe to act as a brake and bring a sliding climber to a halt

serac – derived from the name of a crumbly white cheese this word now refers to a semi-detached block of ice usually found breaking away from steep ice cliffs

sirdar – the foreman or leader of a team of Sherpas working for an expedition

sugar snow – unconsolidated granular snow offering insecure purchase for boots or tools

skins – self-adhesive strips of fabric attached to the bases of skis that have a nap allowing the ski to slide easily forward but resisting backward movement when weighted. They enable skis to be used to ascend snow-slopes.

skinning – the action of climbing on skins

soloing – climbing without being roped to a partner

stupa – a Buddhist shrine often containing remains, usually with a short "spire"

tat (as in abseil tat) – pieces of rope or tape that can be or have been used to make a loop around an anchor through which an abseil rope can be threaded

thrutch – technical climbing term describing a strenuous awkward sequence of moves

verglas – almost invisible water-ice forming a thin coating on rock (very treacherous!)

wedels – the classic ski tracks; regular curves

white-out – a condition encountered in snowfall when all definition in the surrounding landscape is lost so that it may be very easy to drop off an unseen edge